Chantal Pontbriand
[ed.]

Parachute:
The Anthology (1975–2000)
Photography, Film,
Video, and New Media
[Vol. III]

JRP|RINGIER & LES PRESSES DU RÉEL

Table of Contents

Introduction
*Alexander Alberro and Nora M. Alter**

In 1975, a small group of enterpris-
ing, ambitious members of the
art community in Montreal posed
the following question: "What
do we know of contemporary art
outside of Quebec, in Canada
or abroad? Do we even know what
contemporary art exists in
Montreal? How does information
about art circulate?"[1] By way
of an answer, the artistically
unconventional and theoretically
cutting-edge magazine *Parachute*
was launched. Founded by Chantal
Pontbriand and France Morin,
the emergence of this Montreal-
based magazine coincided with that
of a number of other international
art journals in art world capitals,
including *October* (New York),
Art Press (Paris), *Flash Art* (Milan),
and a few years later *Parkett*
(Zurich).[2] The proliferation and
success of these print publications
is symptomatic of the unprece-
dented expansion of the art world's
discursive spheres that took
place in the 1970s. What is often

forgotten today, however, is that this expansion (for some it came to characterize "postmodernism") affected not only the production and exhibition of art, but also the sites where theoretical debate could take place. Following Conceptual art's problematization of the function of the art magazine in the late 1960s and 1970s, few would now question the important role that magazines and journals play in the operation of the art world.[3] Art periodicals today operate as vehicles for the evaluation and dissemination of artistic practices, as well as locations for the elaboration of interpretive approaches capable of addressing the extraordinary complexity and sudden tentativeness of art following the collapse of the modernist paradigm. Furthermore, they address a remarkably diverse readership comprised not only of artists and those connected with exhibiting and marketing their work, but also of academics and a general public increasingly interested in art and culture. It is within this expanded field that *Parachute* must be considered.

The new magazine, the editors hoped, would "achieve an interdisciplinary and international exchange which [would] break down the cultural barriers and find an antithesis to regionalism."[4] Just as a parachute is designed to save lives, so *Parachute* was conceived of from the outset as a necessary remedy for the shortcomings of the contemporary cultural scene in Canada and abroad.

By publishing in two languages, *Parachute* functioned paradigmatically as a hybrid entity. It combined Francophone and Anglophone voices from North America and Europe, and incresingly over time from other continents, with each contributing to an essential international dialogue. From the standpoint of the contributors, the possibility of publishing in either French or English, and to have one's work disseminated in a bilingual context, was always an attractive prospect. The dynamic effect of the placement of essays by these figures alongside each other in issue after issue of the magazine radically questioned and helped to dismantle the established national and cultural borders that had impeded intellectual exchange. Furthermore, the mix of cultural traditions was paralleled by the authoritative roster of writers from different disciplinary backgrounds:

philosophy, art history, literary criticism, cultural anthropology, sociology, and art. An inventory of contributors reveals a truly impressive international list.[5] The result is an intricate intermixing and weaving of the local with the international, Francophone with Anglo-American intellectual traditions, creating a multicultural intervention in the field of contemporary art.

From the beginning, then, the editors of *Parachute* emphasized the multi-disciplinary aspects of art and recognized these hybrid practices as major sites of creativity. The magazine's mission was thus to break down all barriers: linguistic/cultural, national/political, and disciplinary/institutional. As underscored by Pontbriand in 1999, "the traditional boundaries of art continue to explode under similar circumstances as those of territory and language; technological advances are in the process of transforming art and perception."[6] Indeed, the conviction that new media, genres, and concepts for creating and understanding both art and the world needed to be invented was central to the editors of *Parachute*. This process, also known as heuretics or the logic of invention, explains, for example, the strong link between photography and the genre of portraiture in the 19th century, or between cinema and narrative in the 20th century.[7] Pontbriand continues, "communication has engendered a blurring of artistic disciplines, which relates to the urgency of creating new languages for a new and changing world."[8]

Pontbriand's notion of hybridity is illustrated by the list of art and artists featured in *Parachute* over the years. Many of the artists given prominence in the magazine produce works that in some form or another transcend conventional media and genre boundaries. This is coupled with a list of contributors that emphasizes writers who self-reflexively question not only art, but the practice of writing as well. Indeed, the world of artists who explore new media such as video, performance, the body, installation— works that push beyond conventional parameters toward multi-media, multi-disciplinary, hybrid creations—has been a consistent point of focus for the magazine from the beginning. Furthermore, *Parachute* has also been persistent in its efforts to erase the barrier between the makers of art and the writers of art by including the voice of the artist alongside reviews and essays written by critics, art historians, and theorists.[9]

Parachute was a quarterly journal since its inception in 1975. Changes in its format over the decades have tended to reflect the increasing expansion and significance of the publication. Thus, in 1980 a "Reviews" section was added that was designed to provide coverage of current national and international exhibitions and shows in a more concise form than was previously the case. At the same time, beginning in 1984, there was a move to focus more closely on specific topical themes and developments, with at least one volume a year devoted to a "special issue." The topics of the latter are revealing, and include, among others, cinema, architecture, sculpture, installation, video, new technologies, photography, mass culture, fashion, gardens, museums, collections, the city, and the body. Some of the essays reprinted in this publication were originally published in this context. In 1985 part of the magazine was consecrated to a lively debate section, and in 1989 the column "Books and Magazines" was added to meet the growing interest and demand from readers for reviews of recent publications in French and English. Following the year 2000, the journal decided to focus one issue a year on "cities of emergence," namely cities presently coalescing cultural conditions that in turn generate novel art practices such as Mexico City and Beirut, thereby keeping abreast of shifts in the center of the art world. *Parachute* has continuously represented a crucial and dynamic flank within the realm of art publications, and firmly established itself alongside its counterparts.

As it now stands, this anthology serves as a kind of time capsule that, when opened, allows the reader the opportunity to glimpse back into the past and discover artists, ideas, and theories about art in their developmental stage as they first came into focus. It is fascinating to observe the initial impact and influence of some of these artists and concepts. In some instances, that impact has faded over time, while in others it remains as trenchant and timely today as it was when it was first addressed in *Parachute*. For some, the experience of reading these essays will prompt recollections of changes in the discipline that took place for over a quarter of a century. The experience will be different, but equally rich, for readers whose interest in art is more recent. For, from the start, *Parachute* gravitated toward the latest creative tendencies and critical approaches in art, and thus the essays featured in the following pages provide a useful genealogy of the emergence and development of new artistic practices and the extent of their repercussions.

The anthology is divided into four volumes: I. Museums, Art History and Theory; II. Performance and Performativity; III. Photography, Film, Video, and New Media; IV Painting, Sculpture, Installation, and Architecture. Within each volume the essays have been ordered chronologically in order to provide the reader with a sense of the development both of the "media" under consideration and of the particular focus of the art writing. Given that *Parachute* has constantly sought to erase and transgress conventional borders, the decision to construct categories following traditional lines of demarcation may at first seem contradictory to the overall mission of the magazine. Yet the categories have been erected with the hope that such divisions will aid in making the volume more accessible to the outside reader while still providing a source for the art specialist.

The volumes are to be taken as signposts or markers. As will be immediately evident, neither the categories, nor the media, nor the theoretical essays, are pure. Rather, they are continuously juxtaposed and blurred, thereby calling into question the very attempt to separate them into distinct practices. Moreover, the chronological ordering will aid the reader in discerning the parallel and divergent developments in different media. For instance, during the 1970s and early 1980s the magazine published an abundance of theoretical essays informed by post-structuralism, institutional critique, and psychoanalysis, as well as writings that attempted to rethink the medium of painting and the limits of perfor- mance and body art. The medium of photography received particular attention in the early 1980s, and those of film and video later in that decade and at the beginning of the next. More recently, texts that explore issues of postcolonialism, the idea of community, and the cultural politics of transnationalism are predominant, as is the focus on various forms of installation art and new media. Overall, the essays reflect the intellectual and artistic breadth and diversity of the first 25 years of *Parachute*.

* * *

The third volume focuses on texts that analyze photography, video, film, and new media. An important historical essay from 1981, Douglas Crimp's "The Museum's Old/The Library's New Subject" opens the discussion. Crimp uses the occasion of a Picasso retrospective at The Museum of Modern Art in New York to discuss the inherent differences between painting and photography in terms of ontological structure, reception, exhibition, and marketing strategies. In particular, Crimp is dismayed by the shift that he detects in the reception of photography from being considered as part of a "plural field," to its reduction to a "single, all-encompassing aesthetic." He goes on to see this new foundational basis for photography as "part of a much more complex redistribution of knowledge taking place through-out our culture." Crimp concludes that the entry of photog-raphy, a "radicalized art practice that truly deserves to be called postmodernist," into "the museum and the library's art division, is one means of photography's perversion of modernism."

Philippe Dubois' "Shadow, Mirror, Index. At the Origin of Painting: Photography, Video" also interrogates the ontological status of the photographic image in relation to the other arts. Dubois proposes a theory of photography and videotape based on the notion of the index as an epistemological rather than a semiotic category. He dis-cusses the two media with reference to how they incorpo-rate concepts of the "shadow" and the "mirror." These concepts, Dubois argues, depend not on resemblance, but on the principle of physical proximity—an immanent co-presence. Dubois thus traces the passage from the icon to the index historically, as a passage to modernity, and theoretically, from classical aesthetics to metaphor and trace.

In "A Notion of the *Corps-Cliché* in the 19th Century," French art historian Georges Didi-Huberman analyzes the

19th-century records of Charcot, which document the hysterical phenomenon that causes the body to become a graphic surface upon which the psychic malady of the ill person is literally inscribed. Didi-Huberman speculates whether or not these graphic inscriptions can be called "art," and wonders if there is a link between hysteria and photography. This essay brings together discourse theory, psychoanalysis, photographic analysis, and the history of body art, to construct a highly idiosyncratic yet useful historicist model of scholarship in art history. Guy Bellavance's "Photopolis, Photo-Police: Photography and the City" adopts a similar methodological approach. Bellavance links the representation of the city and the development of surveillance systems with the practice of urban photographers from Atget to Weegee, Thomas Struth, and Jeff Wall. Bellavance argues that the emergence of photography as an artistic medium signals a rupture in the art world that corresponds to how an urban mentality, with its overarching singularity, is at odds with the communal politics of the city. Bellavance concludes that as opposed to the singularity of the snapshot, the serial photograph articulates the diversity of a city. This essay appeared as part of a special issue of *Parachute* devoted to the city. As Pontbriand observed in her editorial statement to this volume, "to the rationalism of modern times now responds the organicity of today's city which behaves like a body: unpredictable, decaying, cancerous, spreading, difficult to cure yet resistant and always alive."[10]

Two essays in this volume focus in on recent photographic practices. One, by feminist film theoretician Laura Mulvey, examines *Magnificent Obsession*, a 1985 exhibition featuring the work of five artists. Mulvey draws connections between a photograph's stillness and the "aesthetics of melodrama," which "also give great weight to the frozen moment, the moment at which emotion exceeds expression in language and erupts into gesture." In a move that is as interesting as it is revealing, Mulvey, writing in 1986, concludes with a discussion of the cultural origins and national identities of the photographers as a means by which to enrich an understanding of their work. She argues that there is an "important interface, often overlooked in recent art theory, between personal desire, chances or accidents of individual biography and the forces of history that exert a powerful influence on someone's decision to become an artist and the kind of work that is then produced."

Many artists and art writers working in the late 1980s and 1990s seem to have taken the link that Mulvey posits between biography, chance elements, and artistic production to heart, as personal elements and subcultural milieus came to be foregrounded across the spectrum of aesthetic production. Nan Goldin has achieved celebrated status within the practice of photography precisely for exploiting such details and milieus. In "The Photography of Nan Goldin Is Touching," Larys Frogier argues that rather than representing particular bodies, Goldin sets out to make bodily contact. The artist's characteristic work, the author maintains, calls for a rethinking of bodily representation in photography with an emphasis on the haptic dimension. Here again, there is an attempt to override the visual and to push for an aesthetic theory that is not based on the primacy of vision.

Other essays deal with the flourishing media of film and video art. Many of the artists featured in these essays have subsequently received international recognition for the novel ways in which they developed their respective media. In the same vein, the authors of the articles on audio-visual productions are attentive to the thematics of the pieces, their method of exhibition, as well as the genealogy of the particular media in question. Considering what are still relatively new and undeveloped fields, the essays in this section are particularly useful as guideposts for how to approach these new media and the artists who work with them. Anne-Marie Duguet's "The Videos of Bill Viola: A Space-Time Poetic" analyzes the work of Bill Viola from the perspective of sound. Viola was then just beginning to receive recognition, though most of the writing on his work concentrated almost exclusively on visual aspects and ignored the acoustic dimension. Taking another tack, Duguet demonstrates that it is impossible to separate the two, and shows that Viola structures his images musically, creating an all-encompassing installation space that overwhelms the senses of the viewer.

The following essay, Peggy Gale's "Stan Douglas: *Evening* and Others," links this blurred video aesthetic to television. Gale uses Douglas' brilliant video project *Evening* (1994) as a springboard to track the steady transformation of television news broadcasts into entertainment. She also explores the ways this phenomenon has been treated in the work of a variety of artists including Antonio Muntadas and Dan Graham. The essay underscores the ever-tightening bond between television, mass entertainment, and contemporary aesthetic production.

Laura U. Marks' "Transnational Objects: Commodities in Postcolonial Displacement" addresses films and videos "produced in ['transnational'] contexts that breach the boundaries of nation and question nationalist narratives." Examining cultural objects framed in films such as Amos Gitai's *Ananas* (1983), Marta Rodriguez's *Love, Women and Flowers* (1989–1990), and Rea Tajiri's *History and Memory* (1991), Marks traces "the transnational and intercultural movement that produces transnational objects." Although she applies theories of transnationalism to film and video art, her thesis is applicable to other visual media. Among related issues addressed by Marks is the tension between transnationalism and globalization, and a recuperative theory of the fetish.

Jacinto Lageira's "Sight(s) and/or Sound(s): On Three Works by James Coleman" examines Coleman's work in terms of the series of polarities that the Irish artist constructs: continuity/discontinuity, synchronism/diachronism, constancy/rupture, and unity/pluralism. In addition, Lageira reflects on references Coleman makes in his work to the advent of sound in cinema in 1927, to Raoul Ruiz' *Hypothesis of a Stolen Painting* (1978), to the Kuleshov effect, and to plays by Samuel Beckett.

Jean-Charles Massera's "Intimacy, Greenery, and Dazzling Whiteness. Representations of Family Life in Eija-Liisa Ahtila's Video Works" offers an extremely detailed, psychoanalytically-based interpretation of two works by the Finnish artist. Massera demonstrates how Ahitla combines the documentary form with fiction, advertising, and the talk-show format to explore the infiltration of mass-media culture into the private sphere. Addressed in turn as voyeur, consumer, and confidant, viewers are faced with images designed to question how and to what degree these images shape our behavior. A psychological interpretation is also the basis for Jack Liang's "Another Day in Paradise: The Film and Video Work of Rodney Graham." Liang performs a close reading of Graham's audio-visual texts, finding within them a constant replay or looping back that the author then connects to Freud's repetition compulsion.

In two Special Issues devoted to "New Technologies" in 1997, *Parachute* investigated their effect on visual culture. Geert Lovink's "The Data Dandy and Sovereign Media: An Introduction to the Media Theory of ADILKNO" was published in this context, as was David Tomas' essay entitled "What Is a New Technology? Machine Drawings, Sentience, Intercultural Contact." In his short but immensely humorous account of the Internet, Lovink updates Baudelaire by creating a flaneur of the medium, proposing that "the net is for the electronic dandy what the metropolitan street was for the historical dandy." A footnote indicates that "ADILKNO is an abbreviation for the Society for the Advancement of Illegal Knowledge."

Tomas' essay continues the critical dialogue begun by Dubois, Didi-Huberman, and Bellavance that examines the relationship between an object and its representation in relation to the tools and media used to perform/enact that representation. The author begins his discussion by turning to the drawings of engineers as prototypes that "represent a zone of emergent possibilities." These hand-drawn, pencil graphics point to future ideas that function "through space and time"—they stand as a form of heuretics or creative imaginings. Tomas argues that such drawings are more than mere representations of machines; they stand on their own, in excess of the object they depict, as "alter egos" or "culture's representational shadow." He then extends his theory to include other new technological inventions such as photography, railway systems, cinematography, televison, and virtual reality. Tomas concludes by proposing expansions to the field of anthropology that would examine points of contact or interfaces between humans and new technologies, resulting in the translation of these technologies into cultural representational systems or "echoes of the mind." Fifteen years later, the field of media anthropolgy and technology has become a burgeoning one.[11]

* * *

The essays in this anthology indicate that *Parachute*'s initial pledge to its readers to function as "a magazine preoccupied with the tendencies specific to the times within an historical perspective … [focusing on] those who have made history and whose work remains important today," was consistently and perpetually fulfilled.[12] For over a quarter of a century the magazine played a crucial role by providing a critical voice in the increasingly expanding field of art. Having achieved what it initially set out to do, *Parachute* never settled into any form of comfortable complacency and suceeded in maintaining its critical edge. The journal continues to push the limits and to maintain its cutting edge identity. What is not revealed in these essays, however, is that over the years *Parachute* spread its mantle beyond the printed page and made possible a program of activities, including public symposia, exhibitions, and multi-disciplinary festivals.[13] The novel ideas and interpretive approaches presented within its pages have thus been further disseminated through other means.

As will become amply evident to anyone who reads through the essays in this anthology, *Parachute* dramatically evolved over the years. What commenced with a certain "urgency" about the need to relate art practice and theory, gave way to another central concern, namely that of discerning the points of intersection between art and the many crises in world politics faced in the new century. What is the role of art and culture in such a disastrous and potentially catastrophic world situation? Can art play a role in the construction of a cosmopolitan public sphere? Pontbriand and the editors subsequently devoted several special issues to this theme in the new series started after the turn of the millenium. In 2000 and 2001, the magazine published three volumes on "The Idea of Community." As Pontbriand, paraphrasing the Italian philosopher Georgio Agamben, put it in a public lecture in 1999: "The articulation of the self with community is a crucial issue which performative acts, with pragmatist underpinnings, such as those that we experience more and more with contemporary art, reveal in challenging ways."[14] Three years later Pontbriand coupled Agamben's theory of community with Jacques Derrida's concept of hospitality in the following way: "The idea of hospitality itself brings about a conception of the world as a place of hosting, of letting the other enter into one's privileged space."[15] Hospitality is culture; it generates culture and brings about the relationship to the other, the place of individuality and the meaning of collectivity. *Parachute* thus presented itself at the beginning of the 21st century as a community where the exchange of hospitality can take place.

Parachute has undergone several highly significant changes since its 25th anniversary. One criticism that may have been leveled at the early *Parachute* was that it was too focused on North America and Europe. However, as of the year 2000, *Parachute* has devoted one out of every four issues to a city previously considered to be on the periphery of the art world. These have included Mexico City in 2001, and Beirut in 2002. The magazine has thereby demonstrated its attentiveness to new zones of emergence and contact. Furthermore, since October 2000, each issue is based on a theme. These themes, according to the editor, are meant to be analytic and pragmatic—"to provide an analytical context in which to operate and regroup relevant art practices."[16] Ideally, it is important to remember, an art magazine will perform a double function: both to address the most significant contemporary art of its time and to feature writings by influential art critics and theorists. According to these criteria, the first 25 years of *Parachute* were remarkably successful. As the essays in this anthology make plainly evident, the magazine has served as an extraordinary vehicle for both communicating and shaping art theory and practice.

*   A more comprehensive version of the magazine's history by Alexander Alberro and Nora M. Alter can be found in the introduction to the first volume of the *Parachute* anthology [Museums, Art History, and Theory, 2012].

[1]   Editorial statement, *Parachute*, no. I (October/November/December 1975), p. 48.

[2]   Pontbriand became sole editor and publisher of *Parachute* in 1979 when Morin departed.

[3]   See Dan Graham, "My Works for Magazine Pages: 'A History of Conceptual Art,'" in Gary Dufour, *Dan Graham*, exh. cat., The Art Gallery of Western Australia, Perth 1985; reprinted in Brian Wallis, ed., *Rock My Religion: Writings and Art Projects 1965–1990/Dan Graham*, MIT Press, Cambridge, Massachusetts 1993, p. xviii–xx.

[4]   Editorial statement, *Parachute*, no. I, p. 48.

[5]   As of May 2002 the range of contributors included over 3,000 from Canada and Australia, Britain, France, Germany, Italy, Switzerland, and many other countries. Over 750 artists have been covered from Canada, and 750 internationally from across Europe, as well as Japan, South Africa, and Australia, among others.

[6]   Chantal Pontbriand, from "Echoes and Shifts" (1999), a lecture that was given at the symposium "Art at the Turn of the Century," held in the context of *Art Focus* at the Israel Museum on October 25, 1999. Published in French as "Echos, mouvances," in *Communauté et Gestes, Parachute*, Montreal 2000, p. 83. Unpublished in English.

[7]   For "heuretics," see Gregory Ulmer, *Heuretics: The Logic of Invention*, Johns Hopkins University Press, Baltimore 1994. The idea of establishing a connection between certain media and genres and the moment of their emergence was, of course, noted by Walter Benjamin in "A Small History of Photography" (1931), in *One-Way Street and Other Writings*, trans. Edmund Jephcott and Kingsley Shorter, Verso, London & New York 1979, p. 240–257.

[8]   Pontbriand, "Echoes and Shifts." See "Echos, mouvances," in *Communauté et Gestes*, p. 84.

[9]   Thus, one of the first interviews in *Parachute* was with Yvonne Rainer, followed by essays by artists such as Jeff Wall, Dan Graham, Rodney Graham, and others.

[10]   Editorial statement, "Virtual Cities," *Parachute*, no. 68 (1992), p. 4.

[11]   See for example *Media Archeology: Approaches, Applications, and Implications*, ed. Erkki Huhtamo and Jussi Parikka, University of California Press, Berkeley 2011.

[12]   Editorial statement, *Parachute*, no. 1, p. 48.

[13]   *Parachute* has organized two multi-disciplinary festivals, ten international symposiums of contemporary art and art criticism, and six art exhibitions.

[14]   Pontbriand, "Echoes and Shifts," in *Communauté et Gestes*, p. 86.

[15]   Pontbriand, "Changing Institutions for a Changing World," unpublished public lecture at the University of Gerona in Spain, March 2, 2002.

[16]   Ibid.

The Museum's Old/
The Library's New Subject

Douglas Crimp

Parachute, no. 22, Spring 1981

All the arts are based on the presence of man, only photography derives an advantage from his absence.
—André Bazin

For the 50th anniversary of The Museum of Modern Art, William S. Lieberman, sole survivor of the museum's founding regime associated with the directorship of Alfred Barr, mounted the exhibition *Art of the Twenties*. Presumably the exhibition's subject was chosen not only to commemorate the decade in which MoMA was born, but also because it would necessarily draw upon every department of the museum: film, photography, architecture and design, drawings, prints, and illustrated books, as well as painting and sculpture. And indeed, a major impression left by the exhibition was that aesthetic activity in the 1920s was wholly dispersed throughout the various mediums, that painting and sculpture held no hegemony at all.

The arts then clearly on the ascendant, not only in Paris but more tellingly in Berlin and Moscow, were photography and film, agitprop posters, and other functionally designed objects. With only a few exceptions—Miro, Mondrian, Brancusi—painting and sculpture appeared to have been very nearly usurped. Duchamp's *Large Glass*—not, of course, in the show—may well be the decade's most significant work, and one is hard-pressed to define its medium in relation to the traditional categories.

Art of the Twenties was therefore all the more interesting and appropriate for the museum's anniversary year, coming as it did at the end of another decade in which the energies of painting and sculpture had been displaced by other aesthetic options. And yet, if it is possible to assess the 1970s as a time of traditional painting's and sculpture's demise with the advent of postmodernism, it is equally possible to see it as the decade of an extraordinary resurgence of those modes, just as the 1920s can alternately be understood as a time of extreme conservative backlash in the arts, when, for example, Picasso returned, after the radical developments of analytical Cubism, to traditional modes of representation in his neoclassical period.[1] That radical moves should be accompanied by or cause retrenchment is not really surprising; but the degree to which such retrenchment is currently embraced and applauded, almost to the extent of obscuring whatever advances have been made, is alarming.

In MoMA's annual report for this past jubilee year, the museum's president and director give rather less attention to *Art of the Twenties* than to two of the year's other major events, both of which helped create the museum's first substantial operating surplus in its history. These were the sale, after many public-relations and legal difficulties, of the museum's air rights to a real estate developer for $17,000,000.00 as the most crucial aspect of the museum's expansion program; and the biggest blockbuster exhibition the museum has ever staged, *Pablo Picasso: A Retrospective*, which boasted nearly a thousand art works and over a million visitors. One other celebratory event was singled out by the museum's top officials as of particular importance, the exhibition of photographs by Ansel Adams, one of the founding fathers of MoMA's Department of Photography

—the first such department in any museum, as they proudly point out.

The big real estate deal, the blockbuster retrospective of the 20th-century's leading candidate for the title of artistic genius, the feting of the bestselling living photographer (a print of Adam's *Moonrise, Hernandez, New Mexico* recently sold for $22,000.00)—the significance of these events' conjunction can hardly be lost on anyone who is forced to cope with the realities of the current New York art world. Next to such momentous events, what had initially seemed so telling about *Art of the Twenties* begins to pale; perhaps the exhibition must after all be seen merely as the swan song of the early period of the museum and its curator, who has subsequently moved to the Metropolitan Museum.

The notion of art as bound by and deeply engaged in its particular historical moment, as radically deflected from the age-old conventions of painting and sculpture, as embracing advanced technologies for its production—all this could be swept aside, it seems, by a notion of art bound only to the limitations of individual human genius. Modern art could now be understood as art had always been understood, as embodied in the masterpieces invented by the master artist, Picasso—the man's very signature adorned the T-shirts of thousands on the streets of New York last summer, evidence, I suppose, that they had attended the spectacle and were proud of it, proud to have thus paid homage to such consummate genius. But they were themselves part of another spectacle, the spectacle of response. The myths, the clichés, the platitudes, the *idées reçues* about artistic genius were never so resoundingly reaffirmed, not only by the mass media, from whom it was to have been expected, but by the museum itself, by curators, dealers, critics, and, yes, by artists. The very suggestion that there could be something suspicious, perhaps regressive, about all of this was met with silent stares or open hostility.

A short five years ago, in a discussion of contemporary art intended for art school audiences, I wrote that Duchamp had replaced Picasso as the major 20th-century artist most relevant to contemporary practice. Today, it seems, I'd have to eat those words. Here, for example, is the recently successful young painter Elizabeth Murray: "Picasso is the avant-garde artist of our time... He truly says you can do anything."[2] Her fellow painter, the former critic Bruce Bolce, elaborates the same point:

> Picasso seems to have had no fear. He just did whatever he wanted to do, and obviously there was a lot he wanted to do… For me, to speak of what I find so astounding about Picasso is to speak of what is most fundamental to being a painter. Being a painter should be the easiest thing in the world because there are and can be no rules. All you have to do is to do whatever you want to do. You can just, and you must, make everything up.[3]

So this was the lesson of Picasso. There are no constraints, whether these are construed as conventions, languages, discourses, ideologies, institutions, histories. There is only freedom, the freedom to invent at will, to do whatever you want. Picasso is the avant-garde artist of our time because, after so much tedious discussion about historical determinism, about the death of the author, he provides the exhilarating revelation that we are free after all.

This creative freedom fantasized by young artists and confirmed for them by the spectacle of one thousand Picasso inventions is upheld as well by the art-historical community. A typical, if hyperbolic response is that of John Richardson writing in the favored organ of the US literary establishment, *The New York Review of Books*.[4] Calling Picasso "the most prodigious and versatile artist of all time," Richardson rehearses the biography of artistic genius from its beginnings in the transcendence of the mere child prodigy by "an energy and a sensibility that are astonishingly mature" through the "stylistic changes that revolutionized the course of 20th-century art" to the "poignant" late works, with their "mixture of self-mockery and megalomania." Richardson's assessment of Picasso is perhaps uncharacteristic in only one respect: he thinks that "up to the day of Picasso's death in 1973 the power was never switched off."

Absolutely characteristic, though, is Richardson's view that Picasso's is a subjective art, that "the facts of his life have more bearing on Picasso's art than is the case with any other great artist, except perhaps van Gogh." And so that we don't miss the meaning of any of these great works,

Richardson insists that, "every crumb of information should be gathered while there is time. In no other great life are the minutiae of gossip so potentially significant."

It is, then, as if Duchamp's readymades had never occurred, as if none of modernism's most radical developments, including Picasso's own Cubist collage, had ever taken place, or at least as if their implications could be overlooked and the old myths of art fully revivified. The dead author has been reborn; he has returned with his full subjective power restored, as the younger artist puts it, to make it all up, to do whatever he wants. Duchamp's readymades had, of course, embodied the proposition that the artist invents nothing, that he only uses, manipulates, diplaces, reformulates, repositions what history has given him. This is not to divest the artist's power to alter and expand a discourse, only to dispense with the fiction that that power arises from an autonomous self. The readymades propose that the artist cannot make, but can only take what is already there.

It is precisely upon this distinction—the distinction between making and taking—that the ontological difference between painting and photography is said to rest. MoMA's Director of the Department of Photography states it simply enough:

> The invention of photography provided a radically new picture-making process—a process based not on synthesis but on selection. The difference was a basic one. Paintings were *made* ... but photographs, as the man on the street puts it, were *taken*.[5]

But MoMA's jubilee photographer, Ansel Adams, is uncomfortable with this "predatory" view of photography. How could the artist Adams wants to call a "photopoet" be a common thief?

> The common term "taking a picture" is more than just an idiom; it is a symbol of exploitation. "Making a picture" implies a creative resonance which is essential to profound expression.

My approach to photography is based on my belief in
the vigor and values of the world in nature—in the
aspects of grandeur and of the minutiae all about us.
I believe in growing things, and in the things which
have grown and died magnificently. I believe in
people and in the simple aspects of human life, and
in the relation of man to nature. I believe man must be
a tree, both in spirit and in society, that he must build
strength into himself, affirming the "enormous
beauty of the world" and acquiring the confidence
to see and to express his vision. And I believe in
photography as one means of expressing this affirmation, and of achieving an ultimate happiness
and faith.[6]

There is really less contradiction of Szarkowski's ontological
position in Adams' Sierra Club humanism, however, than
there appears. For in both cases it is ultimately a matter
of faith in the medium itself to act as just that, as medium
of the artist's subjectivity. So, for example, Adams says:

A great photograph is a full expression of what one
feels about what is being photographed in the deepest
sense, and is, thereby, a true expression of what one
feels about life in its entirety. And the expression of
what one feels should be set forth in terms of simple
devotion to the medium—a statement of utmost
clarity and perfection possible under the conditions
of creation and production.[7]

Compare Szarkowski:

An artist is a man who seeks new structures in which
to order and simplify his sense of the reality of life.
For the artist photographer, much of his sense
of reality (where the picture starts) and much of his
sense of craft or structure (where his picture is
completed) are anonymous and untraceable gifts from
photography itself.[8]

By construing photography ontologically, as a medium
of subjectivity, Adams and Szarkowski articulate a

fundamentally modernist position for it, duplicating in nearly every respect theories of modernist autonomy articulated early in this century for the other arts. In so doing, they ignore the plurality of discourses in which photography has been a participant. Everything that has determined its multiple practice can now be set aside in favor of photography itself. Thus reorganized, it is readied to be funneled through a new market, ultimately to be housed in the museum.

Several years ago, Julia van Haaften, a librarian in the Art and Architecture Division of the New York Public Library, became interested in photography. As she studied what was then known about this vast subject, she found that the library itself owned many books containing original photographic prints, especially from the 19th century, and she hit upon the idea of organizing an exhibition of this material culled from the library's collections.[9] She gathered books illustrated with photographs from throughout the library's many different divisions: books dealing with archeology in the holy lands and Central America, ruined castles in England and Islamic ornament in Spain; illustrated newspapers of Paris and London; books of ethnography, geology, and geography; technical and medical manuals. In preparing this exhibition the library realized for the first time that it owned an extraordinarily large, rich, and valuable collection of photographs—for the first time, because no one had previously inventoried these materials under the single category of photography; until then the photographs had been so thoroughly dispersed throughout the library's vast resources that it was only with patient research that Julia van Haaften was able to track them down. And furthermore, it was only at about the time she installed her exhibition that photography's prices were beginning to skyrocket on the market. So, although now a book of original plates by Maxime du Camp or Francis Frith might be worth a small fortune, 10 or 15 years ago they weren't even worth enough to merit placing them in the library's rare book collection.

Julia van Haaften now has a new job. She is director of the New York Public Library's Photograph Collections Documentation Project, an interim step on the way toward the creation of a new division to be called Art, Prints, and Photographs, which will consolidate the old Art and Architecture Division with the Prints Division, adding to them photographic materials pulled in from all other library departments. These materials are thus to be reclassified according to their newly acquired value, the value that is now attached to the great artists who made the photograph. So, what was before housed In the Jewish Division under the classification "Jerusalem," will eventually be found in the Art, Prints, and Photographs Division under the classification "Auguste Salzmann." What was Egypt will become Beato, or du Camp, or Frith; Pre-Columbian Middle America will be Désiré Charnay, the American Civil War will now be Alexander Gardner, Timothy O'Sullivan, and others; the cathedrals of France will be Henri Le Secq; Switzerland will be the Bisson Frères; the horse in motion will be Muybridge, while the flight of birds will be Marey, and the expression of the emotions of these animals forgets Darwin to become Guillaume Duchenne de Boulogne.

What Julia van Haaften is doing at the New York Public Library is just one example of what is being done throughout our entire culture on a massive scale. And thus our list goes on, as urban poverty and immigration become Jacob Riis and Lewis Hine, portraits *of* Manet and Delacroix become portraits *by* Nadar or Carjat, Dior's New Look becomes Irving Penn, and World War II becomes Robert Capa. For if photography was invented in 1839, it was only *discovered* in the 1960s and 70s—photography, that is, as an ontology, photography *itself*. John Szarkowski can again be counted upon to put it simply:

> The pictures reproduced in this book (*The Photographer's Eye*) were made over almost a century and a quarter. They were made for various reasons, by men of different concerns and varying talent. They have in fact little in common except their success, and a shared vocabulary: these pictures are unmistakably photographs. The vision they share belongs to no school or aesthetic theory, but to photography itself.[10]

It was in this text that Szarkowski attempted to articulate the particulars of this "photographic vision" or photographic style, to define those things that are particular to photography and to no other medium. In other words, Szarkowski's ontology of photography understood it as a modernist medium, an art form that could distinguish itself in its essential qualities from all other art forms. And it is according to such a view that photography is now being redefined and redistributed. Photography will hereafter be found in departments of photography or divisions of art and photography. Thus ghettoized, it will no longer primarily be useful to other discourses; it will no longer primarily serve as information, documentation, evidence, illustration, reportage. The formerly plural field of photography will henceforth be reduced to the single, all-encompassing aesthetic. Just as when paintings and sculptures were culled from the churches and palaces of Europe and confined to the museums in the late 18ᵗʰ and early 19ᵗʰ centuries, they acquired a new-found autonomy, wrested from their functions in other discourses, so now photography acquires its autonomy as it too enters the museum. But we must recognize that in order for this new aesthetic understanding of photography to occur, other ways of understanding it must be dismantled and destroyed. Books about Egypt will literally be torn apart in order that photographs by Francis Frith may be framed and placed on the walls of museums. And once there, photographs can never look the same. Whereas we may originally have looked at Cartier-Bresson's photographs for the information they conveyed about the revolution in China or the Civil War in Spain, we will now look at them for the information they convey about the artist's photographic style.

This redistribution of photography's formerly multiple discourses, this formation of a new epistemological construct in order that we may now see photography, is only part of a much more complex redistribution of knowledge taking place throughout our culture. This redistribution has been given the name postmodernism, although most of the people who use the name have very little idea what, exactly, they are naming, or why they even need this new name. Postmodernism, in spite of the currency of its use, has thus far acquired no agreed-upon meaning at all. For the most part, it is used in only a negative sense, to say that modernism is over. And where it is used in a positive sense, it is used as a catchall, to characterize anything and everything that is happening in the present.

So, for example, Douglas Davis, who uses the term very vulgarly, but relentlessly, says of it:

> "Postmodern" is a negative term, failing to name a positive replacement, but this permits pluralism to flourish (in a word, it permits Freedom, even in the marketplace)… "Postmodern" has a reactionary taint—because "modern" has come to be acquainted with "now"—but the "Tradition of the New" requires a strong counterrevolution, not one more forward move.[11]

Indeed counterrevolution, pluralism, the fantasy of artistic freedom—all of these things are for many synonymous with postmodernism. And they are right to the extent that in conjunction with the end of modernism and the advent of postmodernism all kinds of regressive symptoms are appearing. But rather than characterizing these symptoms as postmodernist, I think we should see them as the forms of a retrenched, a petrified, frozen, reified modernism. They are, I think, the morbid symptoms of modernism's demise.

Photography's entrance into the museum on a vast scale, its reevaluation according to the epistemology of modernism, its new status as an autonomous art—this is what I mean by the symptoms of modernism's demise. For photography is not autonomous and it is not, in the modernist sense, an art. So long as modernism was a vital, operative paradigm of artistic practice, photography was necessarily understood as being too contingent, too dependent, too constrained by the world, which was photographed to achieve the self-reflexive, entirely conventionalized form of modernist art. This is not to say that no photograph could ever be a modernist work of art; the photographs in MoMA's *Art of the Twenties* exhibition were ample proof that certain photographs could be as self-consciously about photographic language as any modernist painting was about painting's particular conventions. And that is why the museum's Department of Photography was established in the first place. Szarkowski is the inheritor

of a department that ultimately reflected the modernist
aesthetic of Alfred Stieglitz and his followers. But it has
taken Szarkowski and his followers to retrospectively bestow
upon all of photography what Stieglitz had thought belonged to only a very few photographs. For photography to
be understood and reorganized in such a way is a complete
perversion of modernism, and it can happen because
modernism has indeed become dysfunctional. Postmodernism may be said to be founded upon this paradox: that
it is photography's reevaluation as a modernist medium that
signals the end of modernism. Postmodernism begins
when photography comes to pervert modernism.

If this entry of photography into the museum and the
library's art division is one means of photography's perversion of modernism, the negative one, then there is another
means of such perversion that may be seen as positive,
in that it establishes a wholly new and radicalized artistic
practice that truly deserves to be called postmodernist. For
at a certain moment photography enters the practice of art
in such a way that it contaminates the purity of modernism's
separate categories, the categories of painting and sculpture.
These categories are subsequently divested of their fictive
autonomy, their idealism, and thus their power. The first
positive instances of this contamination occur in the early
1960s, when Rauschenberg and Warhol began to slikscreen
photographic images onto their canvases.[12] From that
moment forward the guarded autonomy of modernist art is
under constant threat from the incursions of the real world
that photography has readmitted to the purview of art. After
over a century of art's imprisonment in the discourse of
modernism and the institution of the museum, hermetically
sealed off from the rest of culture and society, the art of
postmodernism begins to make inroads back into the world.
It is photography, in part, that makes this possible, while
still guaranteeing against the compromising atavism of
traditional realist modes.

Another story about the library will perhaps illustrate
my point. I was once hired to do research for an industrial
film about the history of transportation, a film that was to be
made largely by shooting footage of still photographs. It
was my job to find the appropriate photographs. Browsing
through the area of stacks at the New York Public Library

where books on the general subject of transportation were housed, I came across the book by Ed Ruscha entitled *Twenty-six Gasoline Stations*, the work Ruscha first published in 1963 consisting of photographs of just that—26 gasoline stations. I remember thinking how funny it was that this book had been miscatalogued and placed alongside books about automobiles, highways, and so forth. I knew, as the librarians evidently did not, that it was a work of art and therefore belonged in the art section. But now, because of the considerations of postmodernism, I've changed my mind; I know that Ed Ruscha's books make no sense in relation to the categories of art according to which art books are catalogued in the library, and that is part of their achievement. *Twenty-six Gasoline Stations* belongs right there where it is, next to all the other books about transportation.

The problem with that view of postmodernism, which refuses to theorize it and thereby confuses it with pluralism, is that it lumps together under the same rubric the symptoms of modernism's demise with what has positively replaced modernism. Such a view has it that the paintings of Elizabeth Murray and Bruce Bolce—clearly academic extensions of a petrified modernism—are as much manifestations of postmodernism as are Ed Ruscha's books—just as clearly replacements of that modernism. For they have escaped the categories through which modernism must be understood as they have escaped the museum, which arose simultaneously with that modernism and came to be its inevitable resting place. Such a view of postmodernism would be like saying of modernism at its founding moments that it was both Manet and Gérôme (and it is surely another symptom of modernism's demise that revisionist art historians are now saying just that), or, better yet, like saying that modernism is both Manet and Disdéri, that hack entrepreneur who made a fortune peddling photographic visiting cards, who is usually credited with the first extensive commercialization of photography, and whose utterly uninteresting photographs hang, as I write this, in the Metropolitan Museum of Art in an exhibition whose title is *After Daguerre: Masterworks from the Bibliothèque Nationale*.

[1] For a detailed discussion of this reaction in relation to the recent return to representational painting in Europe, see Benjamin H. D. Buchloh, "Figures of Authority, Ciphers of Regression. Notes on the Return of Representation in European Painting," *October*, no. 16 (Spring 1981).

[2] Lawrence Alloway, Bruce Bolce, Elizabeth Murray, et. al., "Picasso: A Symposium," *Art in America*, vol. 88, no. 10 (December 1980), p. 19.

[3] Ibid., p. 17.

[4] John Richardson, "Your Show of Shows," *The New York Review of Books*, vol. XXVII, no. 12 (July 17, 1980), p. 16–24.

[5] John Szarkowski, "Introduction to *The Photographer's Eye*," in *The Camera Viewed. Writings on Twentieth-Century Photography*, ed. Peninah R. Petruck, E.P. Dutton, New York 1979, vol. 2, p. 203.

[6] Ansel Adams, "A Personal Credo," *American Annual of Photography*, vol. 58 (1948), p. 16.

[7] Ibid., p. 13.

[8] Szarkowski, "Introduction to *The Photographer's Eye*," p. 211–212.

[9] See Julia van Haaften, "Original Sun Pictures: A Check List of the New York Public Library's Holdings of Early Works, Illustrated with Photographs, 1844–1900," *Bulletin of the New York Public Library*, vol. 80, no. 3 (Spring 1977), p. 355–415.

[10] Szarkowski, "Introduction to *The Photographer's Eye*," p. 206.

[11] Douglas Davis, "Post-Everything," *Art in America*, vol. 68, no. 2 (February 1980), p. 14.

[12] For further discussion of this founding moment of post-modernism, see my "On the Museum's Ruins," *October*, no. 13 (Summer 1980), p. 41–57.

Shadow, Mirror, Index.
At the Origin of Painting:
Photography, Video
Philippe Dubois

Parachute, no. 26, Spring 1982
Translated from the French by Bernard Schütze

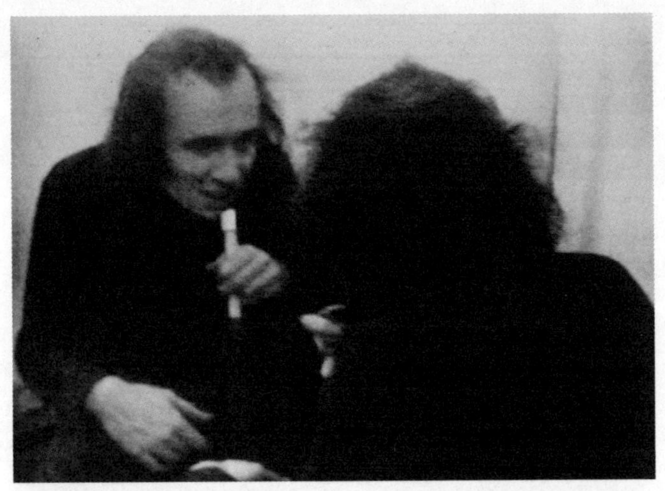

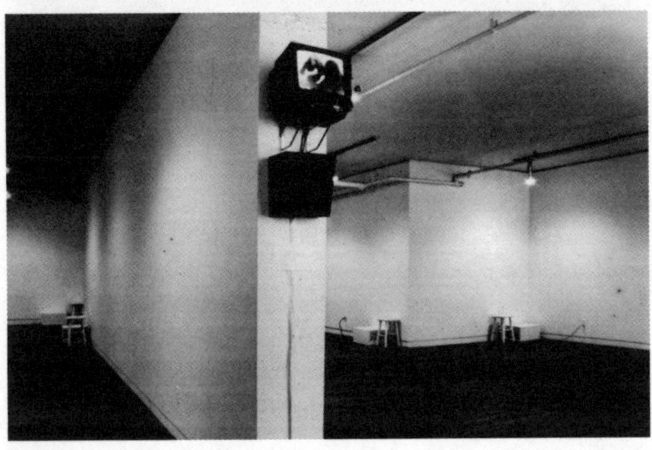

Vito Acconci, *Air Time*, 1973
Film still and installation view, video duration: 40'

The current notion of stylistic pluralism—one of the most resistant clichés of moribund American art criticism—must be replaced by a more effective mode of contemporary art: a description that takes the historical determinism at work within it into account. In order to do so, I have opened a new rubric, the art of the index, a term that could easily be replaced by another: the photographic.
—Rosalind Krauss[1]

Hence I will, primarily, discuss two relatively modern or contemporary artistic practices here: *photography* and *video art*. I will discuss them only from the point of view of their relation to a fundamental conceptual category: that of the *index* in Charles S. Peirce's sense (by opposition to the icon and the symbol).[2] This category of the index will itself be considered through only two important tropes (among others possible[3]), two models of the double: the *shadow* and the *mirror*.

In accordance with Peirce's definitions, these are in fact two forms of representation that only exist in the *presence* of their referent: between the image in the mirror (or the cast shadow) and the object to which they refer, there is first and foremost the idea of resemblance, the principle (the necessity) of a rapport which is that of a physical nearness, of a real proximity and an immanent copresence. Peirce:

> Index. A sign, or representation, which refers to its object not so much because of any similarity or analogy with it, nor because it is associated with general characters which that object happens to possess, as because it is in dynamical (including spatial) connection both with the individual object, on the one hand, and with the senses or memory of the person for whom it serves as a sign, on the other hand.[4]

This study is hence to be comprehended as forming part of a broader work on the index conceived as an epistemological (rather than semiotic) category. This means that it is a coming to terms with in a positive way (rather than simply in a negative manner as has too often been the case) with the emergence of new forms of representation in contemporary art. The category of the index, by theoretical implication and by the philosophical opening it allows, becomes a singularly privileged and effective instrument. In order to situate the present proposal I will briefly outline the overall perspective that guides it.

One can consider that one of the underlying tenants of this global project is contained in the idea of a passage from the category of the icon to that of the index, a passage that is viewed not only as an *historical* characteristic of modernity, but also more generally, as a *theoretical* displacement, where an aesthetic (classical) of mimesis, of analogy and resemblance (*metaphoric order*) gives way to an aesthetic of the trace, contact and referential contiguity (*metonymic order*). Such a perspective, where the evolution of modern art is seen as an appearance, development, and systemization of practices operating primarily on an indexical mode, is without doubt not completely new. Rosalind Krauss' recent studies have, to my knowledge, gone the furthest in this area.[5] Studies on which one could expand and develop: starting with Duchamp and photography, to bring together the entire problematic of painting as a trace, in a wide sense that includes the imprint, tracing, molding, numerous works associated with land art and conceptual art, and the increasingly radicalized forms of this logic of the index, such as the readymade, body art, installation, and performance in which the referent itself becomes its own representation, and where the physical proximity between the sign and its object is one of total identification.

But where one must be particularly careful, precisely from an epistemological point of view, is in the relation between history and theory. It is in this that my analysis notably differs from Krauss' approach. In order to avoid any finalism, I propose to reverse the evolutionism of the history of painting, which underpins this perspective, to show that in its first moments, in its primitive phase, painting itself, *as a theoretical apparatus*, was fully caught up with the question of the index, i.e. the question of presence and the contiguity of the referent, as much so, if not more so than with the question of resemblance. Through this gesture of reversal I, in a sense, cancel the historicist and teleological dimension of the problematic: the category of the index can here function *only* as theory. And it is in this sense that this text's subtitle with all its quotation marks needs to be understood: "At the 'origin' of painting: photography, video."

I therefore advance my thesis right from the start: photography and video art are two theoretical forms of artistic thinking that reconnect, *as indexical practices*, with the theoretical form of painting seized in its "originary" moment (in the phantasm of its origin). This transhistorical affirmation of an aesthetic of the index that places analogical—detached, autonomous—(the art of the icon) representation in parenthesis, marked the necessity of a referential inscription in the history and theory of art, that is to say the irreducible implicit force of the *pragmatic* dimension of the work of art.

I. At the "Origin" of Painting: Fables, Absent Models, and Prototypes

I will first proceed through evocations, flashes, quotations of a series of *texts*, well known by art historians, that all refer to the inevitably mythic question of the "origin" of painting by each time assigning it an explicit relation to the logic of the index, under the cover of the imprint, the tracing, and especially that of the shadow and the mirror. In all cases, *the representation was born through contact*. This is what these primitive images say to us, these founding fables, these lost prototypes, which are themselves so *eloquent* that one can dispense with commenting on them.

Lascaux or the Birth of Art

The men of the Magdalenian Age, particularly those in Lascaux, probably used the same method as that employed by todays Australians, which consists of placing a colored powder in a hollow tube and then blowing through it. In this way they achieved *stenciled hands*, which are quite numerous throughout the whole group of caves: the hand was placed on the cave wall and one blew all around it. In Lascaux this practice was generalized for flat pigments.
—George Bataille[6]

In Lascaux, that is at the historical "origin" of painting, this primitive "stencil" technique, which closely resembles tracing and the imprint, was used generally. This indexical relation of physical proximity and contiguity between the sign (the painted hand) and its object (its cause: the hand to be painted) could not be more narrow, direct, and applied (the hand was applied). The resulting image is literally a trace, a transposition, a vestige of a vanished hand that had been there. Note how in this process the technique simulta-neously involves the presence of a screen that serves as an inscription surface (the cave wall) and the projection (by way of blowing), a source (the tube as a hole and focus point) of a matter which is to color, draw, and fix the whole (the powder). The resulting image of a contour by contact thus appears as a cast shadow, but a shadow in negative,

a white, hollow, emptied figure, a non-painted painting
(the outline was blown around) obtained through subtrac-
tion, by the preservation of a virgin space that is very
precisely the one that was covered by the referent. One can
sense it coming: it is already, in a certain way, the entire
photographic apparatus that is at work here. The Lascaux
stenciled hands can be easily compared to this form of
photography which is strictly indexical, but which, as such,
clarifies the ontology of all photography, a form that Man
Ray called "rayographs" and Moholy-Nagy "photograms":
photographs made without a camera by placing opaque and
translucent objects directly on photosensitive paper,
exposing this composed whole to light, and then developing
the result. Mimesis has no place here (these contact photographs have often been qualified as "abstract compositions"): the only important thing is the depositing of the
object on the surface: resemblance—such an easy thing for
photography—is erased before the pressing necessity of
contiguity. The distance between the sign and its object is
here reduced to its minimum.

A History of Shadows

Pliny dedicated the 35th book of his monumental *Naturalis
Historia* to a "history" of painting, a history that was not so
much factual as directly articulated around the mythological,
and a certain form of the imaginary. He is inevitably confronted with the question of the origin, and its impossibility:
"the question of the origin of painting is obscure," he
states. One could even say that it literally remains *in the dark*
(*dans l'ombre*). In fact, Pliny goes on to say that, beyond
the broad variety of interpretations (relating this origin to the
Egyptians and then the Greeks), almost all commentators
agree on at least one, absolutely determining, point: that
is that painting is born at the moment *"that one began to outline
the contours of the human shadow."* This is, in a very classical
sense, the *princeps* operation, the inaugural gesture that
painting poses not only in its "origin" but also, as we will see,
in its "essence," and which will be taken up as a founding
fable both in the very numerous texts on painting—
and sometimes with singular and interesting variations
(Quintilian, Plutarch, Vasari, Alberti …)—as well as in

painting itself as a theme or iconographic motif (for example, [Joseph Benoît] Suvée's painting *Uitvinding tekenkunst* [The Invention of Drawing],[7] or David Allan's engraving, *The Origin of Painting*[8]).

But Pliny goes beyond this well-known principle of the drawing of the shadow. He details this origin and substantiates the fable. Pliny tells the *story* of the daughter of a potter from Sicyon, called Dibutades, who is in love with a young man. One day he has to leave for a long voyage. During the farewell *scene* (from the outset one can see to what extent this story is already on the level of representation, staging, narration, and fiction), the two lovers are in a room lit by a fire (or a lamp) that projects their shadows onto the wall. In order to conjure the forthcoming absence of her lover and to conserve a physical trace of his actual presence, in this pivotal moment fraught with desire and fear the young woman has the idea of using charcoal to represent his silhouette as it is projected on the wall: in this ultimate and flamboyant instant, to abolish time and fix the shadow of he who is still there but will soon be gone.

From this unforgettable initiation scene, we will only retain certain basic elements that we will continue to encounter. In order for there to be a projected shadow, and thus for painting to be able to exist, there must be, as for the Lascaux hands, a *screen*, a partition, a receiving and intersecting plane (wall, canvas, paper …) which will serve as a surface of inscription; and here too a *projection*, but this time one of *light*, which presupposes a light *source*, a focal point, something that acts as the origin of the ray (the fire, the lamp), and which determines a direction and an organization of space *through* light. Finally, this projected figure, this pure index that only exists in the presence of its referent, must still be *doubled by a drawing* that *fixes* it through a direct tracing.

A full set of differences has established itself in relation to the stencil technique. To begin with, the matter projected on the screen changes status: the colored powder is here replaced by light itself. This has the notable consequence of limiting the coloring to a pure play of *black and white*, of *immaterializing* this very matter that has become impalpable, as well as allowing it to be propagated through self-radiation: the shadow is "natural" and the "breath" of man as a motor origin is no longer necessary. In addition, the very process of the shadow's appearance is *instantaneous*, it appears all of a sudden through the luminous impulsion (while the powder projection was progressive and appeared part by part). These modifications bring us closer and closer to the photographic apparatus: an indexicality operating through the interplay of black and white, an instantaneous capture of the image without the intervention of human mediation, and above all, it appears literally as a *writing through light* (the very etymology of the word *photo-graphy*).

What differentiates this origin of painting through shadow drawing and photography is finally the problem of *fixing*, a crucial problem because this poses the question of the index's relation to temporality. In fact, between the projected shadow and its traced *drawing*, beyond the *spatial* relation of co-presence, what is at play here is the *temporal* relation to *duration*: the shadow itself is, as we have stated, fleeting; it has no other time but that of its referent. In this sense it is an almost pure index: the principle of the physical connection between the sign and its object function in space *and* in time. As Leonardo da Vinci, who gave this question of the shadow much thought, stated: "[shadows] always come in company, joined to bodies."[9] The shadow always affirms a *"this is here."* While the shadow *drawing*, as well as photography, always affirms *"that-has-been"* (see Barthes). The pure referentiality of one is opposed to the necessary precedence of the other. The shadow drawing refers representation to a before, to a previous cause, which is to be here and now called up by the sign. The essential, of course, is that the referent passed *through* the shadow, that it was mediated by this pure index, that it is its copy by contact. But at the same time this passage implies a thorough change in temporality; drawn, it is inscribed in duration and a fixed state once and for all. In a way the drawing tears the shadow from the time of its referent to fix and stop it in a time proper to it. Through its inscription the shadow loses its temporal indexicality and refers its spatial indexicality to the past. This loss of indexicality, this gain of iconicity and temporal autonomy—which, while conserving its real connection to the referent is given as necessarily anterior, as an origin that has always been *surpassed*—clearly corresponds to photography's great fantasy: to both affirm the existence of the referent as an irrefutable proof of that which has been, hence to make it eternal, to fix it beyond its own absence; and by the same token, to designate this mummified referent as a representation that is ineluctably lost and inaccessible for the present as such: in the same movement it is forever frozen in a sign and returned as a referent to an inexorable absence, oblivion, lack, and death. There is the fantasy of murder, of surpassing chronic time (it is its inversion that makes the *Portrait of Dorian Gray* so fascinating) and the fantasy of theft, the rapture of the image from its own body precisely because it is fixed and will survive, will surpass it. Whether it operates through drawing or photography, this is where the process of fixing of the index leads.

Admittedly, their technical means are not exactly the same (in one instance it is the manual outlining in black of a contour, in the other the photochemical development with developer and fixer), but beyond this technological gap, in both cases, the characteristic marks of the fixing process meet, in that, for the most part, they run counter to those that defined the appearance of the image, that is, they no longer correspond to an indexical logic: shadow *drawing* and photographic *fixing* make use of a concrete and palpable matter (charcoal, silver nitrate) rather than light; the image to be fixed on the support that does not appear in a single instant but proceeds through progressive elaboration (drawing and development demand a certain lapse of time, which can even, as in the second case, be strictly determined); etc. In other words, photography understood in terms of its visual result, and the representation of the shadow as a supposed origin of painting, are only strictly indexical in their first constitutive phase, in the *conditions of the production* of the sign (the direct transposition of a referent on a contiguous screen through an optical play of luminous projection). But as soon as the image-index produced in this way is inscribed for good, is fixed for memory, that is as soon as it seeks to surpass its referent, to become eternal, to be frozen in representation, hence to substitute itself, as an arrested trace, to become an ineluctable absence, this image loses part of what made up its indexical purity, it loses its temporal connection. The index becomes partially autonomous. It opens itself to iconicity, that is to say, to death. The iconic fixing in killing the direct relation to referential time marks the beginning of representation's death work—it *mummifies*.

Finally, a last and brief remark on Pliny's fable concerning the relation of the image to *desire*, and the role of the index therein. The amorous circumstances in which the mythic story of the birth of painting unfolds, and by which it is directly motivated, are obviously not innocent. In particular it is clear that this indicates a clear *congruence between desire and the index*. What the fable puts forth is that from the point of view of desire, the representation counts more as a trace than as a resemblance. For the lover that seeks to conjure the imminent absence of the one she loves, the important thing is to find a sign that emanates directly from him, which would be a testimony of the *real* presence of the referential body. The physical proximity that defines the specific status of the index corresponds perfectly to the requirements of the amorous relation. The lesson of the fable is summed up in this: mimesis comes after contiguity, desire first goes through metonymy, and painting is born as an index because desire founds it.

In echo to this desiring dimension of the primitive myth of the painted shadow, I will, without commentary, cite a passage that is quite close, but which in this case relates to the amorous dimension in *photography itself*. This text, written in 1843, is the extract of a letter on photography written by Elizabeth Barrett and addressed to her friend Mary Russell Mitford.[10] It makes explicit everything we have said here and in fact defines what shall become one of the most fundamental psycho-social aspects of the entire photographic tradition. The rehearsal of the "primitive" scene goes as follows:

> I long to have such a memorial of every being dear to me in the world. It is not merely the likeness which is precious in such cases—but the association and the sense of nearness involved in the thing … the fact of the *very shadow of the person* lying there fixed forever! It is the very sanctification of portraits I think— and it is not at all monstrous in me to say, what my brothers cry out so vehemently, that I would rather have such a memorial of one I dearly loved, than the noblest artist's work ever produced.

Before finishing with these shadow stories, I will evoke yet
one more interesting variant of this founding myth that in
fact defines the other great version of this same story. Vasari,
for example, right at the beginning of the "Preface" to his
Lives of the Artists echoes this variant:

> But it is my opinion that design, which is the founda-
> tion of both arts, and the very soul which conceives
> and nourishes in itself every part of the intelligence,
> came into full existence at the time of the origin
> of all things, when the Most High, after creating the
> world and adorning the heavens with shining lights,
> descended through the limpid air to the solid earth,
> *and by shaping man, disclosed the first form of sculpture
> and painting* in the charming invention of things. Who
> will deny that from this man, as from a living example,
> the ideas of statues and sculpture, and the questions
> of pose and of outline, first took form?
> [...]
> According to Pliny, the art of painting was introduced
> in Egypt by Gyges of Lydia who, while near a fire,
> observed *his own shadow* projected on a wall, and
> suddenly *(subito)* drew his own outline *(contormò se
> stesso)* with a stick of charcoal...[11]

This version introduces at least two noteworthy modifications in relation to the preceding story: first it introduces
the *reference* to God and to *the genesis of man* as an original
model of representation; second, while referring to the same
text by Pliny, it transforms the shadow portrait of the *other*
into a shadow *self-portrait*. We will follow the successive
implications of these two changes.

To take the representation of God's creation of man
as a model is to explicitly refer the birth of painting (and
sculpture) to the ancient myths of origin ("in the beginning
of all things"), and to place God in the position of the Great
Original Painter. By extension it is precisely not to make
every painter a god, a *creator ex nihilo*, but a subject that
has already been created and who only imitates, copies,
reproduces (imperfectly the work and gesture of the Great
Genitor, using the same materials that emanate from
His Creation [*creature non potest creare*], said Saint Augustin).

Destined to be but the repetition of an origin, reproduction rather than creation, the reworking of an inaccessible model that is always already there, it is the very activity of representation that is thus inscribed in a logic of an indexical type. The index is no longer the index as such, the pictorial sign, but the act of painting proper, conceived as a tracing and a memory, as a relay and revival of the Divine Creation from which it *really* proceeds (in the order of belief) since the painter is a creature of God and works with that which He has given him.

On the second point, which of course also recalls Apuleius' well-known shadow portrait, one can first discern that in making representation auto-referential, the fable explicitly situates the very origin of painting in *narcissism* (the desire for the other is a desire for oneself)—which directly returns us to the first point and what is implicit in it: this absolutely original self-portrait that was the creation of man in the *image of his Creator*, as it is written in the book of Genesis.[12] We will shortly return to this fundamental problem of narcissism in more depth.

This narcissistic drift of the "first" painting toward the shadow self-portrait clears the path for a *paradox*: it is known that every self-portrait condenses two very distinct instances of the representational process: the object to be painted and the painting subject. In the self-portrait of *painting*, this condensation is already replete with problems, both theoretical and practical, linked to the fact that the subject who takes him or herself as an object, if s/he wants to be accurate, must paint him or herself painting, i.e. to include in the enunciated the process of its enunciation. This is the basis of the paradox and every self-portrait has to confront it with cunning.[13] With the *shadow* self-portrait this problem of paradoxical inclusion of the enunciation in the enunciated becomes practically insurmountable because of the total physical connection that unites the sign and the referent. The representation cannot be accomplished because of the shadow's indexical nature (spatial and *temporal*). In fact, in the very process of fixing the shaded form with charcoal (a process, as we said, that takes place progressively and in time), the object to be painted, the shadow itself, is modified, and moves slowly as the drawing advances (because, as we have also said, the shadow has a temporal attachment to its referent). The subject may try as s/he will to limit the movements of his or her body; there will always be something (an eye, an arm) that will escape this rigidity if s/he wants to carry the inscription through. The drawing hand, in particular, will never be able to draw itself drawing: in order to do so it would have to stop, to fix its shadow, but this would also stop the drawing. Or it would run after itself in vain; no matter how fast it would never be able to catch up. In short, as an index, this hand can never really succeed in attaining the coincidence, the condensation, the superimposition of instances that theoretically founds self-representation.

Two French-speaking Swiss artists, Jean Otth and Gérald Minkoff, each separately produced several video experiments that work directly with the problematic of the impossible indexical self-portrait by using means that are specific to the electronic medium, in particular those exclusive to close circuit video in which the *camera recording* and the *projection* on a screen are rendered *simultaneously*—this is exactly what characterizes the spatial connection of the shadow: video thus makes it possible, as opposed to photography and cinema, which can never suppress their delay even if they can reduce it (Polaroid), to *fully engage the paradoxical logic of the index* (we will get back to this in detail).

Jean Otth, for example, made a video where one sees him from the back in front of a black canvas onto which a powerful projector casts his shadow. He vainly attempts to trace with chalk the outline of this shadow, which keeps escaping, which never lets itself be circumscribed or fastened. This ceaseless effort of representation finally results in nothing more than a doodle of overlapping lines. Furthermore, Otth does not undertake this attempt at a self-portrait by looking directly and frontally at his shadow and his hand sent out in pursuit of it, instead he looks at this hand, this shadow and the whole scene on a video monitor, placed beside him, which transmits what we, the viewers, see from a point of view situated behind. (The viewer, the camera—the view of the scene—is located approximately at the same place from which the light casts the shadow onto the black screen.) In other words, through the scopic mediation of the video monitor, both to visually follow the movement of his hand and to see himself, he becomes the viewer of himself as a painter in the process of representing himself—in the same manner that we see him from the location of the light source that gives birth to the shadow figure. In using the video monitor as a generalized intermediary of the gaze, the installation as imagined by Otth knowingly complicates the play of superimposed instances: in this circuit, so aptly qualified as *closed*, as the artist says,

> the monitor, the unique reference, brings together in the same time and space the subject (the model), the painter (the operator), the support (the canvas), the signs (chalk intervention), and the entire medium (camera and monitor).[14]

In joining the indexical force of the shadow and video, the paradoxical condensation is here transformed into a veritable flattening of instances.

For his part, Gérald Minkoff, in the 1971 installation presented at the Galleria dell'Obilisco in Rome, or in the video entitled *Palindrome*, has approached the impossible self-portrait in a similar way, but this time not by playing directly on his shadow—nor with his reflection in a mirror which has the same indexical qualities as the shadow, on top of inverting left and right—but by replacing this shadow through its simultaneous image on a video monitor. These works show

> (his) hand which tries in vain to draw itself drawing on a video monitor, by turning its back upon itself, since the screen is not a mirror and it can neither face itself nor face a reality which escapes its will (it is a mise en abyme or an infinite regression of the referent in the representation).[15]

It thus becomes evident that what is given as the origin of painting is in fact the *history of a figurative impossibility*. One cannot theoretically represent one's own shadow, and the entire history of representation consists of a travesty, a bypassing and a filling-in of this lack and this original defect, in order to sidestep, trick, and find substitutes for them.

In fact only one thing could make the condensation of the shadow portrait's instances possible: the representation would have to take place all at once, so that the image of the shadow be seized, petrified, and paralyzed: frozen as such on its support. It is, moreover, in this sense that one must understand the unexpected *subito* that found its way into Vasari's text ("he *suddenly* drew his own contour"). The duration of the process of inscription must be reduced to a unique seizing and arresting gesture (seizing life and fixing it dead) (*prise de vie et arrêt de mort*). The shadow must be *thunderstruck*. However, this instantaneous fixing is an impossible task for drawing and its manual carrying out, while *photography*, as we know, is able to do this. The time— a fraction of a second—it takes to expose the film, to freeze the image of its shadow on the emulsion (even including the image of the photographic camera), is all it takes to accomplish this *impossible representation* (see for example Arthur Tress' book *Shadow*, which is entirely made up of such shadow self-portraits).[16] In the time of a flash, a lightning flash, the thunderclap of this ruthless shadow mouth grabs and keeps everything it reaches out for, aggresses, absorbs, and seals every reference, and thus puts photography's petrifying effects to work. *The indexical Narcissism of the self-portrait can theoretically be accomplished only in photographic petrifaction.* Photography is *this* origin of painting.

Narcissus and His Mirrors

We will remain in the mythological realm, in the narration of origins, and will continue to *face* painting. We will not leave the field of the index behind. We will simply take on another major figure and other references; the shadow will be replaced by the mirror (the image in –) and Pliny and Vasari will be followed by Alberti, Philostratus, and Ovid. To do this it will suffice to follow the traces of a hero and a concept: Narcissus. During this trajectory we will once again encounter photography and video.

Leone Battista Alberti, at the outset of his famous *Della Pittura*, in following the tradition of all treatises, also concerns himself with the question of the origin of painting: "this painting, which like friendship, is said to render the absent itself present."[17] Like everybody else, he indicates the origin through the representation of the shadow, and vaguely evokes several historical antecedents. However, Alberti does not continue down this path. His project is not of a historical or anecdotal nature. Rather, it resides in a non-factual apprehension of painting, as a theoretical apparatus with its specific epistemological stakes. It is from this obviously fundamental perspective that Alberti, in a well-known and often cited passage, calls up the figure and the entire fable of Narcissus, for this allows him to seize painting not so much in its "origin" as in its "essence." Here is the famous passage:

> For this reason, I say among my friends that Narcissus, who was changed into a flower, according to the poets, was the inventor of painting (*inventore della pittura*). Since painting is already the flower of every art *(la pittura fiori ogni arte)*, the story of Narcissus (*tutta la storia di N.*) is most to the point. What else can you call painting but a similar embracing (*abbracciare*) with art of the surface, here, of the spring (*quella ivi superficie del fonte*)?[18]

I will certainly not propose a new commentary on this difficult text (for further reading refer to Hubert Damisch's excellent article "D'un Narcisse à l'autre"—see note 18). I will merely insist on the last sentence, whose meaning must be clarified in order to continue with my proposal. I will particularly point out the very imporant *abbracciare*, which is to be understood in all its dimensions, that is at least in its dual spatial and amorous sense: to embrace (a surface) with the *gaze*, to encompass and completely circumscribe—a narcissism and desire for totality—and to embrace (a body) with *hands* and *mouth*—narcissism and autoeroticism. An image of this polysemic *abbracciare* can, for example, be obtained by contemplating Caravaggio's *Narcissus*, which is coiled upon itself and entirely constructed on a circular pattern—it is a specular desiring. In addition I will also underline the insistence, in Alberti's text, on the *surface* which seems to be marked by an ambiguous status whose fundamental importance will become apparent: *the spring,* or, if one may, the *water-painting (tabl-eau)*.

Having paved the intital way, and since Alberti invites us to do so, we will now turn toward this "story" of Narcissus with a little more precision. What is the relation of painting to the narcissistic myth? Among the diverse classical "sources" of the fable (Ovid of course, but also Conon, Pausanias, Plotinus, Pliny, Philostratus…) we will retain the last author, lesser known no doubt, but particularly interesting from our perspective.

Philstratus' text *(Imagines* I, 23) concerns us foremost in that it is the only one to evoke the story of Narcissus *through the intermediary of painting*. The work conforms entirely to the literary genre of *ekphrasis* that consists of prose works that describe works of art whose subject matter is generally mythological. Whether the paintings described really exist or not is of no importance; what is important is the description itself as a discursive genre. In other words, and herein resides the interest of this text presented as a *gallery of portraits*, the evocation of mythological subjects is imaginatively always traversed by the question of pictorial representation.

The 23rd portrait of *Imagines* is presented like a painting illustrating the myth of Narcissus. Philostratus' description begins with an absolutely decisive sentence that will bring the entire apparatus of painting into play. Here one immediately understands how it prolongs and clarifies Alberti's final formulation on the dual surface: "This fountain paints the features of Narcissus *in the same manner* that the painting paints the fountain, Narcissus himself, and his entire story."[19] Such an opening forcefully poses the ramifications of the problematic in a single stroke: *here we have Narcissus facing the spring; the viewer facing the painting; and in each case it is the same relation that unites one with the other*.

The consequences of such an affirmation are enormous. If the image that Narcissus observes in the fountain is his own "painted" reflection and if the painting, like the fountain, is also a painting—"reflection"—then what is reflected there will always be an image of the viewer that observes it and who observes him or herself in it. It is therefore always me who sees myself in the painting I look upon. I am *(like)* Narcissus: I believe that I am seeing another but it is always an image of myself. What Philostratus' definition finally reveals is that *every gaze on a painting is narcissistic*.

What allows this formulation is in fact the super-imposition of the two instances, or rather the two levels of representation of which one includes the other. *Level I* (intradiegetic): Narcissus looking upon himself in the fountain as a play of mirrors *in* the universe of representation. The indexical relation is here entirely integrated in the enunciated and the painted story. The *face-to-face* encounter that is implicit in self-reflection in the mirror is looped upon itself, enclosing the two diegetic protagonists that are Narcissus and his reflection. We, the viewers, are excluded from this relation, out of play, ob-scene. We are missing and become a neutral third term: we are positioned as a " s/he" voyeur of the "I/you" couple. We are kept at a distance (iconic) of *their* connective relation (indexical). *Level II* (extradiegetc): the viewer looking at (him/herself) the painting, at this play of mirrors which is no longer that of representation but that of representation itself as a pragmatic process. The narcissistic relation here operates in the enunciation, in the pictorial discourse; and we are no longer cut off from this relation, on the contrary we are fully and truly implicated in it; the face to face relation with the painting positions us as protagonists in their own right ("I" faced with *our* "you").

Philostratus' maneuver, as mentioned before, is to superimpose these two levels, to posit an equivalence between a narcissism of the enunciated and a narcissism of enunciation. By way of the Narcissus myth one encounters the entire (paradoxical) play of the superimposition of instances that founded the shadow self-portrait. Here the mirror has simply replaced the shadow.

In a general manner the condensation of levels put into play by Philostratus has the effect of *troubling* representation, which is thereby struck with ambiguities that can slip into confusion. For example, in his *epkphrastic* discourse Philostratus describes some minute, apparently insignificant details that are of interest only to the extent that they allow the descriptive discourse to play, precisely, with the levels of representation and to introduce ambiguity as though it were a *trompe l'oeil*:

> Faithful to truth the painting shows the dew drops
> suspended from the petals: a bee lands on the flower;

> I cannot say whether it is the bee that is fooled by the painting or if it us who are fooled into believing that the bee really exists.

Things will get even more complicated when Philostratus, seemingly putting an end to these driftings, comes back to his subject (Narcissus) and appears to denounce these representational illusions and deceptions. He lectures Narcissus in a determined attempt to neatly differentiate these levels:

> As for you young man, it is not a painting that is causing your illusion, it is not the colors or the deceptive wax that keep you enchained; can you not see that the water reproduces you according to your contemplation of yourself; you do not see the artifice of this fountain, and yet to realize this you need but bend over, to change your expression, to move your hand, to change your attitude; but you are like someone who just met a companion, you remain immobile and wait for what will follow. Do you really believe that the fountain will speak with you? But Narcissus does not listen to us at all: the water has captivated his eyes and ears…

One can observe the subtlety of this play of slippery shifts: all the while indirectly affirming the specular equivalence between the painting and the fountain (in the same way we may be fooled by the image of the bee on the flower, Narcissus is fooled by his image reproduced in the water), Philostratus is moralizing Narcissus through his "do not be confused" lecture and thereby playing the role of the one who is not fooled by the representation. Yet the entire discourse is a *direct personal address* to the character. Throughout the passage he does not cease to address him: "can't *you* see that the water reproduces *you* … *you* do not recognize the artifice of this fountain … *you* remain immobile … "
In other words, while denouncing the illusion of Narcissus who mistakes his reflection for a "real" person, in his own discourse Philostratus directly addresses the *image* of Narcissus as though it were a "real" person that can be spoken to. Philostratus, the viewer, falls into the very trap

that he denounces the other of not seeing. It is a paradoxical situation of floating categories. Philostratus can only balk at this paradox since he ineluctably arrives at this quasi-Möbian question that he addresses to Narcissus: "Do you really believe that the fountain will speak with you?" (!). This proposition marvelously synthesizes the entire circular apparatus in which the enunciated and the enunciation are reflexively self-implicated in the contradiction. To find a way out there is only one solution: the commentator must move his tale back into the third person, which he does immediately after his very paradoxical question: "But, Narcissus does not listen to us at all." To find his way out of the paradox one must *exit* the index, leave behind the game of pure deictics, and come back to narration. To remain there would be to get lost, like Narcissus.

This game of personal pronouns, this direct addressing of Narcissus by the narrator as a reflection of the specular address of Narcissus to himself, is also something we find, in almost identical form, in Ovid's version of the fable (*Metamorphoses* book III, line 430 and onward). Ovid echoes Narcissus' famous monologue in which he slips from a narrative "he" to a dialogic "you" in the designation of his reflection.

> I am enchanted and I see (*video*), but I cannot reach what I see and what enchants me [such is narcissism: I see (myself), therefore I am not (*video ergo non sum*)], I cease to be, I am parted from myself—deep in error is this lover—and it increases my pain the more, that no wide sea separates us, no road, no mountains, no walls with locked doors. We are only kept apart by a little water! [Where one can see the logic of the *index* being indicated and made a theme as such, the principle of *the joint*, of the sign's physical proximity to its object, in opposition to the idea of a *separated sign*.] Whenever I extend my lips to the clear liquid, *he* tries to raise his lips to me. *He* desires to be held. You would think he could be touched: it is such a small thing that prevents our love [the screen, the surface]. Whoever *you* are come out to me! Why do you disappoint me, you extraordinary boy? Etc. [The rest of the "monologue" continues in the I/you form.] [20]

Here we see Ovid himself, caught up in his own narration just after having, as the story's exterior narrator, provided the "truth" of his character who cannot know it for himself. ("Unknowingly he desires himself, and the one who praises is himself praised, and, while he courts, is courted, so that, equally, he inflames and burns… ") Ovid goes from this "he" of truth to an apostrophe and to a "you," a direct address of illusion, and this passage corresponds exactly to the *emergence of an indexical logic* in the apparatus:

> What *he* has seen *he* does not understand, but what he sees he is on fire for, and the same error both seduces and deceives his eyes. *Fool*, why try to catch a fleeting image, in vain? What *you* search for is nowhere: turning away, what *you* love is lost! What you perceive is the shadow [Ovid refers to the reflection as a shadow several times][21] of reflected form: *nothing of you is in it. It comes and stays with you, and leaves with you*, if you can leave!

This is the foundation of the matter: *narcissism is the index*, the principle of the subject's real adherence to him/herself as a representation in which the subject can only lose him/herself and founder—*except if one leaves the index*, except if one breaks this circular and specular relation of co-presence to oneself as other, except by renouncing the deictic (auto-dialogue "I"/"you") to enter into the narrative ("s/he"). In the field of indexical representation (painting in its mirror stage) one of course encounters this elementary polarity of the dialogical couple (I/you) as attached to its subject, that is to say as inscribed in the very constitution of subjectivity. According to [Emile] Benvéniste:

> Language is only possible because each speaker positions him or herself as a *subject* by referring to him or herself as the *I* of his or her discourse. From this fact the *I* is posed as another person, the one which, in its exteriority to "me" becomes an *echo* to which I say *you* and that says *you* to *me*.[22]

Brunelleschi's Installation

Let us now look at this singular apparatus that is foremost technical, but also theoretical: Brunelleschi's very well-known machine (machination) which is said to be at *"the origin of perspective"* (the title of the article that Hubert Damisch devoted to this apparatus and to which we refer the reader for a more in-depth analysis).[23] This mirror "installation," this *camera lucida* , is know to us only through the texts of commentators. In order to evoke this *vanished prototype* we will follow, like everybody else, Manetti's minute description:

> He [Brunelleschi] first demonstrated his system of perspective on a small panel (*une tavoletta*) about half a *braccio* square (between 25 and 35 cm). He made a *representation* of the exterior of San Giovanni in Florence [the building in question is the Florence Baptistry situated just in front of the cathedral], *encompassing* as much of that temple *as can be seen at a glance* [compare with Alberti's *abbraciare*] from the outside. In order to paint it, it seems that he stationed himself some three *braccia* inside the central portal of Santa Maria del Fiore [the Florence *Duomo*]. He painted it with such care and delicacy and with such great precision in the black and white colors of the marble that no miniaturist could have done it better [...]
> And he placed burnished silver where the sky had to be represented, that is to say, where the buildings of the painting were free in the air, so that the real air and atmosphere were *reflected* in it, and thus the clouds seen in the silver are carried along by the wind as it blows.
> Since in such a painting it is necessary that the painter postulate beforehand a *single point* from which his painting must be viewed, taking into account the length and width of the sides as well as the distance, in order that no error would be made in looking at it (since any point outside of that single point would change the shape of the eye), he *made a hole in the painted panel at that point* in the temple of San Giovanni,

which is directly *opposite the eye* of anyone stationed
inside the central portal of Santa Maria del Fiore, for
the purpose of painting it. The hole was as tiny
as a lentil bean on the painted side and it widened
conically like a woman's straw hat to about the cir-
cumference of a ducat, or a bit more, on the reverse
side. He required that whoever wanted to look at
it place his eye on the reverse side where the hole was
large, and bringing the hole up to his eye with one
hand, to hold a flat mirror with the other hand in
such a way that the painting would be reflected in it.
The mirror was extended by the other hand that more
or less approximated in small *braccia* the distance in
regular *braccia* from the place he appears to have been
when he painted it, up to the Church of San Giovanni.
With the aforementioned elements of the burnished
silver, the piazza, the viewpoint, etc., the spectator
felt he saw the actual scene when he looked at the
painting. I have had it in my hands and seen it many
times in my days and can testify to it.[24]

This is a *witness* of the *princeps* experiment through which
perspective was born as a theoretical construction. This
complex apparatus raises numerous crucial questions that
are not directly linked to my proposition (see Damisch).
I will focus on some simple notations, apparently selective
and quite descriptive, but which will take on all their
meaning when put in relation with photographic and
videographic constructs that will be discussed later.
  Brunelleschi's machinery is an installation made up
of two surfaces: a painted representation (the *tavoletta*, at the
same time a square, a frame, a window, and a painting) and
a mirror that *faces* it. Of the painting proper one first notices
that it already integrates portions of the mirror (burnished
silver), and thus reserves its place for the sky in the representation.[25] This mixture inscribed in the very constitution
of the support obviously implies that the mirror and the
painted panel have the same representative status: the entire
surface of representation, in all its ways, must *reflect* its
referent (its "actuality"). From a theoretical point of view
the important thing is therefore primarily the *indexical*
function of the representation. Of this representation we

are told that it was constructed so that one "saw the actual scene": in other words, here we have a strictly perspectivist construction, with a perfectly established *point of view*, "a single point" *referentially* determined since it is placed "inside the central portal" of the *Duomo* etc.; and also with a *vanishing point*, symmetrically situated in relation to the former (projectively speaking) on the other centric axis of the visual pyramid. It can thus also be precisely located not in the space of the referent, but in the space of the representation: "*a hole in the painted panel at that point* in the temple of San Giovanni … "

Now, the vanishing point inscribed in the representation is in fact—and this is where the Brunelleschian installation begins to unveil its singular force—designated in a very particular way because it takes on the form of a *hole*, which pierces the panel itself. And it is this peephole ("*opposite the eye*") coupled with the play permitted by the *mirror* directly *facing* the painting that will make the whole machine work. The hole, the blind spot of the apparatus in so far as it pierces the painting itself and through which the panel can be *glimpsed, materially brings about* the total superimposition of the *point of view* and the *vanishing point*. It is in every sense the "point of the subject" of which Pellerin Viator speaks. And this coincidence, this identification is made visibly possible only through the intervention of the mirror, which in facing the painted image refers the front of the panel to its back, where the peeping eye can seize it.

In other words, in this installation, the viewer—and there can never be more than one, and who is one-eyed on top of it—does not see the painting directly, but only its inverted reflection in the mirror. The viewer does not face the work for s/he is behind it. The viewer is faced with a mirror, which itself faces the "right side" of the painted panel, which is pierced to allow the back and forth movement of the gaze that peers through it. The viewer thus appears to be expulsed to the outside and back of the painting. As though the apparatus functioned only between two surfaces, two images that echo each other, and which in this specular back and forth appear to loop the circuit of representation on itself; they apparently put this autonomous narcissistic circulation of the painted image and this indexical meta-representation through the mirror in parenthesis. It is as though there were no outside to this machine, except though this single rift, this *vanishing* of the system, which is its empty center. For *everything* of course passes through this hole. This veritable knot in the negative is the condition of the work's very possibility; and as such, as a condition of possibility, it must officiate *in absence*. This is how the viewer, facing the mirror while at the same time peering through the hole, sees the reflection of the painting, but *does not see him- or herself* in the act of viewing. One can weigh the full difference with the gaze of primary narcissism. Finally the Brunelleschian installation makes the *eyeless gaze possible;* and it is this gaze that constitutes painting.

I borrow this entirely provisional term of this singular "reflection" from Damisch:

> Brunelleschi's experiment was organized around an inverse of Lichtenberg's paradox: how can one see oneself in a mirror *with one's eyes closed*? If this first paradox—how facing a mirror, being caught in its field can one look without seeing oneself there?— found its solution in perspective in Brunelleschi's experiment, Lichtenberg's was countered not long after: *photography soon made it possible for anyone to take his own portrait, just as in a mirror even when one's eyes are closed.* [26]

II. Photography

Throughout this journey that began with Lascaux and the originary myths of representation through the projected shadow, we have occasionally made links and connections with photography. In the following pages I would like to come back to this question in a more systematic manner. I will approach the matter according to a double movement, first *historical* and then *theoretical.* To begin with I will use a variety of texts and experiments related to the technical appearance of the photographic apparatus, I will show how it literally came out of the dark (*sorti de l'ombre*) and can be precisely situated as a continuation of the stories (*histoires*) mentioned at the beginning of this text. I will then draw on recent considerations of the theoretical status of the "photographic" to return to the question of the index, to underline to what extent it is co-substantially and ontologically linked to photography. As a further step, I would have liked to illustrate this general proposal with a series of selective analyses of photographic works in which the shadow and/or mirror play a central role (Arthur Tress' *Shadows*, Michael Snow's *Authorization*, Denis Roche's "self-timer delayed self-portraits" etc.) I have neither the time nor the space to develop these analyses here. However, the third section, "Videos," will, for its part, be exclusively built up on the basis of specific works whose simple description will suffice to make the theoretical models work, since the foundations will already have been laid.

Today everyone is aware that the photographic apparatus consists of a double, or rather triple process: *a purely optical process* which is, grosso modo, that of the *camera obscura* (or *lucida*): an image-capturing apparatus that transposes a referent into its representation; and a *double physical and chemical process* of *printing* and *fixing* the image on a support.

As far as the optical apparatus itself is concerned I will be very brief. It is known that it is far older than photography itself, that it was already frequently used in the 17th century in the form of the "magic lantern," before becoming the *camera obscura* (see Athanase Kircher, *Ars Magna Lucis et Umbrae*, 1646, and Johannes Zahn, *Oculus artificialis ...*, 1702[27]). We also know that the same kind of apparatus used *to capture* images to be painted, was also used to *project* images, which had been painted or drawn beforehand, on a screen. The taking and projection of images were already linked and passed through the same "box," which thus functioned as a transformation and exchange unit.

One of the most common forms of this optical machinery was the *portable darkroom*, for example the one drawn by Kircher in his *Ars Magna*, which is very big, since a man can stand up inside the room, from where he can easily see and draw the inverted images projected there. The function of these apparatuses was precisely this: to make it possible to draw or paint the referent on a screen-support through a *direct transposition*. In his box the painter needed to do no more than recopy, reproduce, trace the image that was "naturally" projected within it. One can understand that these machines had to be portable: since the *physical presence* of the referent to be painted was necessary, and this could not always be moved in front of the eye-hole of the apparatus; hence the whole installation itself had to be moved (in front of a landscape for instance). In short, we see that such apparatuses are *entirely ruled by the principle of the index* both on the level of the image's appearance in the box, which can only function through contiguity with its referent, and the level of the fixing through drawing or painting of this natural image, which proceeds by tracing, by a contact copy. In this sense the *camera obscura* is nothing more than a "mechanical" refinement of the shadow drawing of the lover in the fire-lit room. The principle is the same, it has only been slightly codified, cubed, and improved. The improvement continued through knowledge derived from optics and dioptrics (the control of the sharpness of the image through a more and more elaborate set of lenses placed before the hole; a mastery of lighting conditions; etc). Our modern camera bodies, with automatic exposure and interchangeable lenses are but the latest development along this line.

As for the *camera lucida*, of course it also works according to the same indexical logic. Its principle is even simpler than its *obscura* sister: it is nothing more than an eyepiece equipped with a mirror and a lens attached to the end of an immobile stick which is itself fixed to a drawing table. The "painter" need only place his eye on the eyepiece to frame his/her object and to let his/her hand simultaneously trace on the paper what the eye sees. Here there is no screen, no projection. There is no tracing and no intermediary. It all goes directly from eye to hand. It is as though the body, or at least the brain of the painter, functioned as a box (*camera obscura* or *lucida*?), as a visual resonator. In fact, with the *camera lucida* one finds what were to become two important characteristics of photography: on the one hand the optical apparatus as *a prostheses of the eye*,

> One can compare the portraitist who views the model in front of him or her exclusively with the eyepiece of his or her *camera lucida* (as is shown in the illustration of the cover of Roland Barthes' book on photography) with these statements by Cartier Bresson and Minor White, and with a Minolta ad:

> Henri Cartier-Bresson: "I had just discovered the
> Leica. It became the extension of my eye, and I have
> never been separated from it since I found it."
> Minor White: "I m always mentally photographing
> everything as practice."
> Minolta ad (1976) "It is hard to tell where you leave off
> and the camera begins. A Minolta 35 mm SLR makes
> it almost effortless to capture the world around you…
> Everything works so smoothly that the camera
> becomes part of yourself. You never have to take the
> eye off the viewfinder to make adjustments… When
> you are the camera and the camera is you."[28] Etc.

and on the other hand, as a corollary, the optical apparatus
as a *cut of the real* (the image sampling, selection, and framing
function of photography). For why should the draftsmen look
through his or her small apparatus to see that which s/he
could see directly, and better—that which is there before
his or her eyes—if it were not precisely that the mediation
of the apparatus provided him or her with a *frame*, that is to
say with a space of representation, axes, and relations, a
composition? It is of course futile to insist on the importance
of this problematic and the countless discourses it has given
rise to in all forms of representation, whether in painting
(the painting as frame, Alberti's window, Dürer's perspective
device, Leonardo's mirror, etc.) or photography (the cut, the
edge, the crop, the shot, the capture, the extraction, the
abstraction, the fragmentation, the isolation, the stopping,
the grid, the layout, the freezing, the enclosing, the internal
arrangement, etc.) or even in literature in its visual presentation on the space of the page (the "*cadroir*" in Denis
Roche's *Dépots de savoir et de technique*).[29] In short, besides the
indexical value of the trace, the imprint, the testimony of the
real (which has been the sole concern in this article and to
which we shall return from a more theoretical point of view),
and also besides the possibility of the *mechanical reproducibility* of the work (Benjamin), the function of *cutting and framing*
the real no doubt constitutes a third major characteristic
of photography.

If we now turn to the more specific problems of the
medium, such as that of the *printing* and *fixing* on a support

of the image obtained through optical devices, we shall have a particularly clear confirmation of the workings of the index in the constitution of photography.

I would like to present two apparently very close illustrations, and yet in-between them the entire passage from painting to photography is at stake. It is, moreover, here that we will reencounter the question of the projected shadow, in the way we presented it, following Pliny, as a model at the "origin" of painting. Let us begin with the first of the two illustrations reproduced at the beginning of this article.

This image represents one of the great portrait traditions of the 17th and 18th centuries. The very coded "installation" is presented in the following way: the model to be portrayed takes their place on a seat. S/he is asked to remain as still as possible. The session, as one knows, will take *some time*. A light source (in this case a simple candle) is placed on one side of the model. The effectiveness of this source is increased both by its lighting power and directionality. Thus oriented toward the seated subject, it projects its rays on a screen placed perpendicularly on the other side of the model (on the side of the profile in the shadow). The respective distance of the light source and the screen in relation to the model has been determined in such a way that the distanced light, while near enough to retain its power, projects a shadow on the screen that is as close as possible to the size of the model (this is why the screen is so near the face to be portrayed: the shadow is always bigger than its referent and grows increasingly so as the receiving plane recedes from the object—this is an elementary law that Leonardo had already clearly formulated[30]). This screen (canvas or paper) also serves, on its other side, as the *inscription surface* of the image. This dividing support must thus be relatively transparent, or rather translucent,[31] so that the shadow of the model, projected on the backside of the screen, can be seen *through* the screen. At this point the painter, who is placed on the front side, will need do nothing more than trace, report, and mark the projected shadow from the *backside*. In this apparatus one finds all the fundamental elements of the founding experiment of painting mentioned by Pliny, except for the amorous relationship (can we be certain?). One considerable

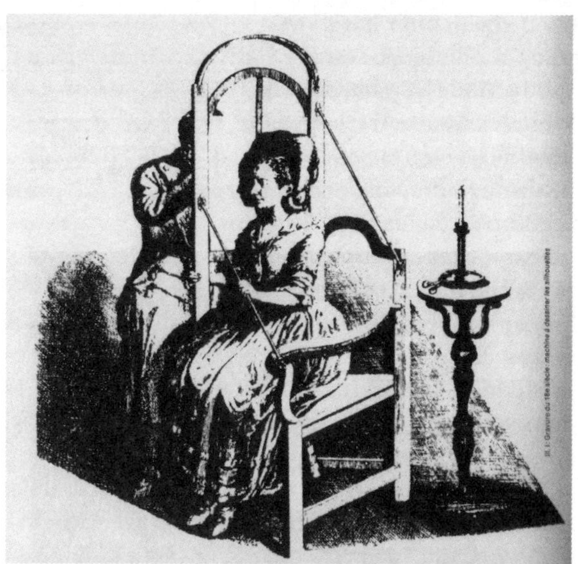

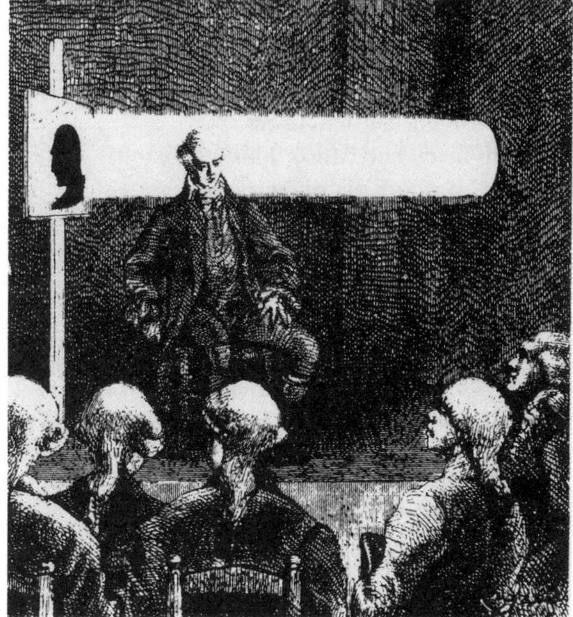

Machine used to draw a silhouette, engraving, 18th century

Device used to "photograph" a silhouette on paper treated with silver nitrate, engraving, late 18th century

difference here, and this is something that brings us back to Brunelleschi's machinery, is that the painter has moved to the *other side of the support*, they are no longer on the side of representation but have moved behind the painting which they can only see inverted through a hole and by way of a mirror. This same insidious modification has hence entered representation: in fixing itself through drawing on the recto of its verso the shadow has been inverted, exactly like the reflection in a mirror. Strange paradoxes can arise from this inversion. Kant spoke of them as the property of bodies' *mirror incongruence* in space.[32] I cannot develop these lengthy and complex problems here.

Let us now turn to the second illustration. At first glance it resembles the previous scene (a seated model, directional light, a screen, a shadow). Yet something very important separates the two engravings, something which founds photography in relation to drawing: here, the shadow projected on the screen *imprints itself*; the "painter" does not intervene at all in this inscription and they thereby cease to be a painter. This second illustration, therefore, recalls the discovery of the *photographic printing* process: a piece of paper, a support covered with a film of silver nitrate which is sensitive to light and its variations; it records them in its own materials through gradations of black and white. This self-inscription of the referent on its support of course makes one think of the typical indexical model of Christ's direct impression on the holy shroud: Veronica's veil, this exemplary archeiopoetic image (*sinu manu facta*—made without the intervention of the hand) is, in a way, the prototype of photography, its archetype, its origin myth.

We know that the "inventor" of this process, he that the history of photography has recorded as the first to have undertaken experiments to produce images through the action of light on silver nitrates, is the late 18th-century physician Thomas Wegwood. His *shadowgraphs*, as he aptly called them, were obviously taken up again in France a quarter of a century later first by Niépce and shortly afterward by Daguerre. In parallel, in Great Britain, William Henry Fox Talbot also sought to perfect this device. It is also known that at the beginning of their research they were confronted with the thorny problem of *fixing*. As Fox Talbot recounted in an explicitly titled 1839 text,[33] while he arrived at "producing a sort of image or drawing of a shadow that in a certain way resembled the object from which it derived" through the sensitization of a support, it was essential to conserve these images in a folder and to view them only in candle light because in daylight the same natural process that formed the image destroyed it by blackening the paper.[34] In other words, the process through which the image is revealed to us is also the one that destroys it. The process that brings photography into *being* carries its own *death* within it. If one wants to avoid this self-devouring, if one wants the image to be conserved, one must intervene, one must cut, one must find a means to stop the movement before its completion: *the process itself must be petrified*. It is only after much trial and error that Fox Talbot, like Niépce and Daguerre, succeeded in perfecting the *fixing* procedure that arrests the process whereby nitrate becomes sensitive to light. It is only upon arriving at this final stage that Fox Talbot could shout out:

> The phenomenon which I have just described appears to me to partake of the character of the *marvellous*, almost as much so as any fact that research in physics has brought to our knowledge. The most *transitory* of things, a *shadow*, the proverbial emblem of all that is *fleeting and momentary*, may be *fettered* by the spells of our natural magic, and may *be fixed forever* in the position which it seemed only destined for a single instant to occupy.[35]

Photography has also never ceased to be confronted with the problem of *time*. It in fact has in every sense of the term made a fixation of it—still image, petrified shadow, photography, or the mummification of the index. This is how the *history of photo-petrification* is constituted.

To come back finally to the question of the index and photography from a more theoretical approach, beyond any historical or technical consideration, I would like to very briefly quote some general theoretical texts on photography, texts that all touch upon, whether explicitly or not, the principle of an indexical logic. These texts, of which each deserves a more in depth analysis, will close this second part of the article. First of all we will recall that the photographic sign can obviously be considered as an index *in full*, for as Charles Peirce himself unambiguously stated,

> Photographs, especially instantaneous photographs, are very instructive, because we know that in certain respects that they are exactly like the objects that they represent. But this resemblance is due to the photographs having been produced under such circumstances that they were physically forced to correspond point by point with nature. In that respect then, they belong to the class of signs known as the index.[36]

It is certainly not one of Peirce's lesser merits to have surpassed the primary and short-sighted conception of photography as mimesis in his analysis of the theoretical status of photography. In doing so he exploded the real epistemological obstacle that is the so-called "perfect" resemblance of the sign with the real. If he could explode the obstacle in this way it is because he took not only the sign as such into consideration, but also and above all the very *mode of production* of the sign; that is he realized that he could not define this sign other than through generative *circumstances. One cannot think photography outside of the process of its taking, therefore outside of its referential inscription and pragmatic efficiency.*

This is a fundamental proposition that is, moreover, clearly reaffirmed by all those who have anything substantial to say about photography, from André Bazin in his text on "The Ontology of the Photographic Image," which remains one if the clearest and stimulating reflections, even if it dates from 1945:

> The originality of photography is not to be found in the result achieved, but in the way of achieving it [...] One might consider photography in this sense as a molding (the molding of death masks for example), the taking of an impression, by the manipulation of light [...] This production by automatic means has radically affected our psychology of the image. In spite of any objections our critical spirit may offer, we are forced to accept as real the existence of the

object reproduced, actually represented. Photography enjoys a certain advantage in virtue of its transference of reality from the thing to its reproduction. (Here one should really examine the psychology of relics and souvenirs, which likewise enjoy the advantages of a transfer of reality stemming from the "mummy complex." Let us merely note in passing that the Holy Shroud of Turin combines the features alike of relic and photograph.)[37]

to Denis Roche, who more vehemently alludes to it in his preface to *Notre Antéfixe*, when he discusses photography from the point of view of a daily practitioner as (yes, exactly) literature:

> The question [of photography] is obviously not so simple. A hackneyed concept always resurfaces: representation [...] everybody who discusses photography speaks of it as another painting: take Delacroix, Walter Benjamin, Moholy-Nagy, or Gisèle Freund, one is still caught up in worn out quarrels about the imitation or non-imitation of nature, what does or does not make photography an art like painting, or on the contrary, something entirely different from painting, etc., etc. When one should instead rub one's nose in it, see things from close up, in the moment when the action takes place, and not in the product of this action, or in a stray hybrid of the two, the crazy developer bathing the passing wind [...][38]

Hence photography is in fact ontologically, existentially, ineluctably indexical, and this as much from the point of view of the photographer as from the point of view of the viewer of photographs. The referential inscription is at play on all sides. And, precisely, from the point of view of the viewer, if there is someone who has not ceased to explicitly affirm this indexical referential dimension it is Roland Barthes. This affirmation, which was also present in his 1961 texts,[39] runs from start to finish of the book *Camera Lucida*: "The photograph," says Barthes, "is literally an *emanation* of the referent."[40] Barthes sees only this in photography: "Myself, I saw only the referent, the desired object, the beloved body."[41] One would have to cite the entire book, which is but a hymn to this function. I will limit myself to a single, well-known, passage, which will serve as the final word:

> First of all I had to conceive, and therefore if possible, express properly how the referent of photography is not the same as the referent of other systems of representation. I call "photographic referent" not the optionally real thing to which an image or sign refers, but the *necessarily* real thing which has been placed before the lens, without which there would be no photograph. Painting can feign reality without having seen it [...] Contrary to these imitations, in photography I can never deny *that the thing has been there.* There is a superimposition here: of *reality* and of the *past,* and since this constraint exists only for photography, we must consider it, by reduction, as the very essence, as the *noeme* of photography… The name of photography's *noeme* is therefore: *that-has-been.*[42]

Video

If I have approached photography from a theoretical and historical angle rather than from an analysis of selected works, and if the indexical accent was above all placed on the relation between the shadow and photography, in this third section I would like to operate in the opposite manner: to pay more attention to the game of mirrors in specific video works.

In what follows I do not propose to theorize the problematic of the index and the mirror in video art. In this regard one can find particularly pertinent elements of reflection (notably those drawing on the Lacanian theses of the mirror stage) in studies such as Rosalind Krauss' "Video: The Aesthetics of Narcissism,"[43] or more recently Nicole Widart's "Video As an Aesthetic Between Two Mirrors."[44] In parallel, on the margins of this theoretical discourse, I would rather very simply, almost descriptively evoke, in so far that these works are by themselves their own commentary, and so to speak their own theory, a series of tapes or installations whose very mode of operation will immediately reveal, without having to clarify them as such, the entire network of oblique relations that links them with the material explored beforehand. I will leave the *reader* with the task of cross-checking and weaving the links together: it is the *work* of reading.

To begin let us take Vito Acconci's tape titled *Air Time* (1973). A stationary 40-minute shot in which Acconci is seen from the back, in front of a mirror whose edges we do not see, in which we see the artist's reflection. He addresses his own reflection through the intermediary of a microphone in a long monologue, which obviously directly recalls Narcissus "addressing" his own reflection in the spring and/or that of the commentators (Philostratus, Ovid) "addressing them-selves" to the Narcissus of their narration: the same drifting of identity between the subject and his image, simultane-ously the Same and the Other. The same hesitation—held here for almost three quarters of an hour and pushed, exacerbated, to the limits (acted?) of the *schize* (split) and collapse—between misapprehension and recognition of oneself. The alternation, same deferred play between the alter and the ego (*altermoiement*) in the discursive instances of the monologue between the deictics "I" and "you" referring now to the reflection and now to the subject. The same fascination and the same compulsive effort to reach for an (impossible?) identity unit. Above all, there is this idea of the apparatus' circularity, of its complete enclosure, its sealing off, which is as much visual, temporal, and discursive (see Benvéniste and the specular circularity of the "I"/"you" couple proper to every subject). As Rosalind Krauss states, in *Air Time* Acconci does nothing other than "to play out the drama of the shifter in its regressive form."[45] *Acconci is there*, facing his other self (Ch. S. Peirce: "the index afirms nothing: it only says: *there*. It seizes your eyes and so to speak forces them to look at a particular object, and that is all." CP 3.361). For 40 minutes he speaks to it and to himself. The reflection can only mimic Acconci, but it does it implacably and ineluctably. Nothing escapes it. Nothing escapes us. The camera is focused on Narcissus and his double. The face-to-face encounter embraces (*abbracciare*) the entire surface (mirror, screen). Nothing is exterior to it (one does not see the camera reflected). Nothing exists nor has existed outside of this frantic, tense duel between identity and difference, which could go on infinitely, outside of time —here a "white" time—in this enclosure coiled about itself. This first work plunges us (regressively?) into a totally primary, culturalized narcissism, performed by Acconci's work, but where video is not yet used for its own ends by employing the means specific to it.

Let us now take another videotape—by Lynda Benglis titled *Now* (1973). This tape also plays with a face-to-face encounter with oneself; except here the mirror gives way to a large video screen where a prerecorded tape shows Lynda Benglis' head in profile as it goes through a variety of movements and actions. In front of this recorded image, which functions as a background, there is the same profile of Benglis *live* and inverted left to right, which moves in the same manner as the other profile, accompanying it and miming it in strict mirror synchronicity. The two profiles are thus adjusted through an effect (not only visual) of superimposed layers, which produce a manifestly autoerotic coupling (the *abbracciare* is quite literal here: to embrace one's own image). The relation with Acconci's work is clear, it is one of both likeness and inversion: inversion because here it is not the "mirror" that imitates the "real," but on the contrary the "real" (Benglis live) which mimes its image—but this is precisely to produce, beyond the difference in supports and the gap between levels of representation, a rather strict *mirror effect* (everything is put in place in this perspective: the prerecorded right/left image had to be inverted because the mirror inverts these positions. Video, for its part, in principal renders them without inversion). Here video intervenes in full, but it is taken in a strategy (of *détournement*?) whose main goal is to make it function exactly *like* a mirror. This is Narcissus backward.

Furthermore, the implicit force of the *indexical* play of this narcissistic apparatus is also marked through a new discursive use of the deictic expressions. Several times during the face-to-face encounter of the profiles, one hears Benglis' voice ordering "Now!" or questioning "Is it now?" Since we do not know whether this voice emanates from the live image of Benglis or the prerecorded one, we can only be taken in by this game of a *floating temporal reference of speech*. Once again, as in the ambiguities occasioned by the slippage between levels of representation, there is a

superimposition of the moments through the play on
temporal shifters.

Let us now take Ulrike Rosenbach's *Glauben sie nicht,
dass ich eine Amazone bin* (Do Not Believe that I Am an
Amazon). At the start of this 1975 video tape there is an
action, a simple but significant one: Rosenbach is face-to-
face ("as an Amazon," that is to say in white tights and
armed with a bow and arrows) with a circular target that
bears the haloed head of the Virgin, a fragment from Stefan
Lochner's famous gothic painting *The Madonna in the Rose
Garden*. Rosenbach will shoot 15 arrows toward this figurative
target, which make a dead sound as they plant themselves in
her face. In and of itself the gesture is already highly
symbolic (woman as martyr, sacrificed for a future power, or
the feminist shooting down the image of the masochist
woman, etc.).

To this basic performance, two synchronized video
cameras are added. One is focused on the target and the
other on the face of the archer. There is also a single
monitor that *simultaneously* shows in *double exposure* what the
two cameras are recording. In other words, what one sees
on the screen are the two superimposed faces (they resemble
each other) of Rosenbach shooting, and the Madonna who
is pierced by the arrows. Here the superimposition of events
is very pronounced: on the monitor, victim and henchman,
Virgin and feminist are joined as one. And since the two
images are simultaneous, singular paradoxical effects ensue:
the arrows' departure point (which is also the point of
view of the representation: insistence on the eye that aims
and the arrow that marks the gaze and traces the axis of
the visual pyramid) coincides with its point of arrival—the
vanishing point—not only *in space*, but also in time (the
duration of the arrow's flight is smothered and reduced to
a point: the instant, that of its fixation, its "tchac" signaling
its petrification). With this arrow-gaze which kills instantly
from a distance, with this target that is circular like a shield
(or an eye) whose virginal figure identifies itself, through
the grace of electronics, with that of its murderess, and thus
reverses the trajectory-gaze of the arrow, how can one in
fact not think of the (Caravaggian) apparatus of the mirror-
shield bearing the head of the Medusa?[46] Autoeroticism here
becomes self-mutilation.

And that is not all: in the second half of the tape, perhaps less successful on an aesthetic level, but which nonetheless adds a new dimension to the work, it is the viewer themself—at first outside of the game, simply as a voyeur—who will be taken in by the machine. The camera is displaced in relation to the axis of the arrow-gaze, and is placed exactly along *the axis*. It is therefore us, the viewers, who will receive the arrows (the mortifying gaze). The super-imposition of these instances is again heightened by a third term: the Madonna, the archer, and the *viewer* are now joined as one. To produce such an effect one can imagine only one technical set up: the lens of the camera is placed exactly in the center (empty) of the target and *it films* (us watching) *from the outside, via the hole* that has been made in this center. Here we have Brunelleschi's apparatus integrated into the workings of a video-Medusa.

It is certainly not possible to account for the relation between shadow, mirror, and video without evoking the names and the works of two major artists in this context, artists who have built their work on these relations, with an intelligence, a coherence of thought, and a plastic perfection rarely attained in this field: Peter Campus and Dan Graham. From Campus we will chose the first of his *Three Transitions* (1973). This is a singular metamorphosis. The initial apparatus is not that different from Rosenbach, though it is somewhat more "pared down," stripped of the ideological charge and endowed with a drive whose effec-tiveness is even more implicitly forceful. Here there are also two cameras that simultaneously record the action and render it synchronically on a single monitor that superim-poses the two images. Except that the maneuver is more subtle: the two cameras that face each other directly (their visual axis leads straight from one to the other, like a vanishing point linked to its point of view) do not record each other because between the two, exactly in the middle, in the position of the painting that cuts the visual pyramid, Campus suspended an opaque gray screen made of canvas or paper. On the monitor one at first sees nothing but a unified gray surface whose edges are off-screen. At this point Campus enters the field (on only one camera because the other is masked by the dividing "wall"). He moves toward the "back" of the image and stops just in front of it (at this point the viewer does not yet know that what s/he sees is the result of the superimposition of the two cameras facing the separating screen. Campus controls his position: he is well in the middle of the frame (of the visual field pyramid). The operation itself only begins at this point: equipped with a knife hidden in his hand, still facing the screen and with his back to the only camera that still does not see him, he pierces the separating screen, and, very, very slowly, enlarges the resulting *hole*. He ends by passing his hand through to the other side and thus increases the rip; his arm is followed by his head, and finally his entire body, until he has fully passed the "wall," like Alice passing through the looking glass. One imagines what this will create on the video monitor that superimposes the two visions: the little hole at the start, which is invisible for camera one (masked by the artist's body), is the first thing camera two perceives from the other side of the screen. In the double exposure, since Campus is well in the center of the frame, this hole appears in the middle of his back. And when his hand passes through the screen, it emerges in the middle of his own back just like his arm, followed by his head, and then his entire body. On the video screen the viewer thus observes a strange and gripping spectacle of a man that climbs out of himself, who emerges from his own body. This is an image of radically spectacular effects: seeing Campus literally being turned inside out like the finger of a glove, self engendering himself through a hole installed in the materiality of his own body. And the same time that he gives birth to himself (for camera two) he is swallowed by his own opening (for camera one). This is an absolutely co-substantial appearance, disappearance of the same in and by the other, like a Möbius strip interiorized in his own body. He is swallowed and generated. And it this corporealization of narcissism that invests this electronic metamorphosis with all its forceful drive.

From Dan Graham let us choose what is without doubt his best-known installation: *Present Continuous Past(s)* (1974). Since the work has already been abundantly commented upon and "interpreted," let us remain on the base level of a mechanical description. The installation is once again, essentially based on a face-to-face encounter between a mirror and a video installation. The work is presented as a large, approximately square room with white walls, like a television screen; it is a real "*camera lucida*." Two of the adjacent walls of the room are entirely covered by a large mirror. A video monitor recessed in the wall facing one of these two mirror walls shows images that a camera, placed just above it, records through a hole in the wall. The visual field of the camera covers the totality of the mirror wall that is facing it and which embraces the whole space. It is the *abbracciare* of the narcissistic gaze.

As with Brunelleschi's machine, here we have a *camera lucida* where everything is played between two face-to-face images that reflect each other. The very obvious difference between the two devices is that in Brunelleschi's case the viewer is outside the painted representation on the reverse side of the panel; s/he looks through the hole to see the image reflected back by the mirror. With Graham it appears that the viewer is *in-between* the two images. But what needs to be emphasized is that the "viewer" does not at all have the same status in the two cases: with Graham s/he is the object of the representation; it is s/he that must be "painted" on the video monitor; it is s/he, and s/he alone that is on view, and who must see *him-* or *herself* while, as we witnessed with Brunelleschi, it is the viewer who looks through the hole at the mirror facing him- or herself, and who *cannot see him- or herself there* (the eyeless gaze). It is as though Graham, in using his own means, has integrated Narcissus into Brunelleschi's apparatus by introducing the viewer *into* the box, and by the same token, making him or her the object of representation, that is to say by *integrating* both *the referent and the gaze* in the machine. In any case, the function of the exterior gaze continues to exert itself even in the video installation where the subject is on the inside: on the reverse side of the wall of representation there is indeed a hole, and a gaze: that of the camera that sees the screen from the exterior in the mirror facing it, and only through this intermediary. One could even consider that this camera eye is even more powerful than that of Brunelleschi's viewer, in so far as it *reverses* what it sees in the machine, thus heightening the circular back-and-forth between mirror and video. (In this respect one could spend a lot of time musing about this *photograph* of Graham's installation taken through a hole at the Otis Institute Gallery, in September 1975).

In fact, as described so far, one could think that this installation is but a "banal" apparatus that generates the classic mise en abyme: the camera records everything in front of it and transmits it directly on the monitor. But what is happening on the monitor, which is reflected in the mirror facing it, and with the camera filming everything that appears in this mirror (a reciprocal self-implication: is the essence of every paradox, where each instance also includes the other), is that the camera (re)films that which it transmits. It is an endless loop.

This (commonly applied) principle is used by Graham, but with a fundamental perversion that ultimately makes it possible for him to *appropriate time*. Technically speaking the perversion is the *apparatus of delay*. That is to say, while most artists use video for one of its great specificities, that is the possibility of synchronizing recording and transmission, Dan Graham for his part reintroduces a delay between the two phases (as in photography or cinema), albeit a slight delay fixed at eight seconds, but whose consequences, coupled with the paradox of the mise en abyme, are dizzying.

In fact, that which appears on the screen is therefore the past, that which was recorded eight seconds ago. Since this is transmitted (with the aforementioned delay) this means, that by way of the mirror, which is simultaneous and always in the present, this will be recorded again on the second degree, and thus retransmitted for a second time, but this time with a delay of 16 seconds between it and the first event. This twice delayed retransmission will itself be rerecorded after another relay via the mirror and retransmitted with a delay of 24 seconds, and so forth without end. In other words, this means that once the viewer has been filmed by the camera—let us not forget that as soon they enter the room they are on screen since the camera's view embraces the entire room—they can be certain of reappearing on the screen every eight seconds, and this *ad infinitum* (virtually in any case).

Such is the full diabolic trickery of this machination: the viewer must actively participate, it is s/he who is literally the object of the work, it is s/he who makes up the image at the same time that s/he looks at it (reflexively). But once s/he shall have entered the installation, *there is no exit*. S/he is literally boxed in, once and for all caught by a succession of representations that will never let him or her go—a prisoner of the abyme. S/he is trapped by the joint action of the paradox of reciprocal inclusion and the delayed recording of cyclical repetition. Video and the mirror unite their effectiveness to master time and institute a perpetual machinic narcissism.

This text is the development of a paper given at the colloquium *L'Objet théorique en "art"* (*The theoretical object in "art"*), July 1981, Semiotic Centre of the University of Urbino.

[1] Rosalind Krauss, "Notes on the Index," in *The Originality of the Avant-Garde and Other Modernist Myths,* MIT Press, Cambridge, Massachusetts 1985, p. 196.

[2] Unless otherwise specified, all quotations from Peirce are from Charles Sanders Peirce, *Collected Papers of Charles Sanders Peirce,* ed. Charles Hartshorne and Paul Weiss, Harvard University Press, Cambridge, Massachusetts 1931–1958. Hereafter abbreviated as CP in the text.

[3] For example the theoretical form *ruin* (as *trace, vestige, remains,* etc.) can also be considered as part of the indexical category. One knows how prominent a role has been reserved for it in art history. For more on this subject see my article "Figures de ruine. Notes pour une esthétique de l'index," *Rivista di estetica,* no. 8 (1981).

[4] Though Peirce was the first to have thus theorized this triadic classification of signs, and clearly mastered the concept of the index, he did, however, not invent it, for there are many traces of this concept in reflections on language prior to his. For example, in the Port Royal *Logique ou l'Art de penser* one already finds a very clear distinction between what Arauld and Nicole term the "signs *separated* from things," and "signs *connected* to things." For his part Quintilian, in a certain way, considered every sign an index: "signs are *indexes or vestiges* whereby one understands other signs."

[5] Rosalind Krauss, "Notes on the Index."

[6] Georges Bataille, *Lascaux. Or the Birth of Art: Prehistoric Painting,* trans. Austryn Wainhouse, Skira, Paris/Geneva 1955.

[7] [Joseph Benoît] Suvée, *Uitvinding tekenkunst,* 1791, Groenigenmuseum, Brugge, Belgium.

[8] David Allan, *The Origin of Painting,* 1745, National Galleries of Scotland, Edinburgh.

[9] Leonardo da Vinci, Ms 2038 of the French National Library (sheets 21,22,29,30).

[10] This letter by Elizabeth Barrett is quoted in the brief anthology at the end of Susan Sontag's *On Photography,* Dell Publishing Co., New York 1974, p. 183.

[11] Giorgio Vasari, *Lives of the Artists,* trans. George Bull, Penguin Books, New York 1965, p. 21.

[12] "What is it that the Bible us tells in stating that God made man in his image other than that man is the self-portrait of Jehovah? Of which God? That of the God sculpting his own image in the clay, that is the image of a creator in the very act of creation." Michel Tournier, *Des Clefs et des Serrures. Images et prose,* Chêne/Hachette, Paris 1979, p. 99.

[13] For more on the question of the self-portrait see René Payant's current studies, in particular "Picturalité et autoportrait: la fiction de l'autobiographie," in *Degrés* (*Langage et Ex-communication*), no. 26–27, Liège symposium proceedings, 1981.

[14] Jean Otth, "Le portillon de Dürer," in *Vidéo-corpus (la vidéographie dans tous ces états)*, dossier no. 10, Institut d'études et de recherches en information visuelle, Lausanne 1979, p. 48–49.

[15] Gérald Minkoff, "Copernic=ciné corp," in *Vidéo-corpus*, p. 43–44. See also *Gérald Minkoff—vidéo 1970-1975*, exh. cat., Internationaal Cultureel Centrum, Antwerp 1975.

[16] Arthur Tress, *Shadow*, Avon Publications, New York 1975.

[17] This context inevitably recalls Pliny's fable referred to at the beginning of this text.

[18] Leone Battista Alberti, *On Painting*, trans. John R. Spencer, Yale University Press, New Haven 1970, p. 64. The question raised here is further developed in Hubert Damisch's "D'un Narcisse, l'autre," in *Nouvelle Revue de Psychanalyse (Narcisses)*, no. 13, 1976, p. 113–114.

[19] This and the following quotations are from Auguste Bougot, *Philostrate l'ancienne, une Galerie antique*, Paris 1881.

[20] Ovid, *The Metamorphoses*, trans. A. D. Melville, Oxford University Press, Oxford 1986, p. 64–66.

[21] For example, "While he drinks he is seized by the vision of his reflected form. He loves a bodiless dream. He thinks that a body, that it is *only a shadow*." Ibid.

[22] Emile Benvéniste, "De la subjectivité dans le langage, (1958)," in *Problèmes de Linguistique générale I*, Gallimard, Paris 1966.

[23] Hubert Damisch, *The Origin of Perspective* (1987), trans. John Goodman, MIT Press, Cambridge, Massachusetts 1995.

[24] Antonio di Tuccio Manetti, *The Life of Brunelleschi*, intro. and critical text by Howard Saalman, trans. Catherine Engass, Pennsylvania State University Press, London 1970, p. 42–44.

[25] On the deictic and indexical status of this mirror in *painting* see Hubert Damisch, *A Theory of Cloud/Toward a History of Painting* (1972), trans. Janet Lloyd, Stanford University Press, Stanford, California 2002, p. 139–140.

[26] Damisch, *The Origin of Perspective*, p. 125–126.

[27] There are several works on this question. Among the most recent ones see Jacques Perriault, *Mémoires de l'ombre et du son. Une archéologie de l'audio-visuel*, Flammarion, Paris 1981.

[28] These quotations (Cartier-Bresson, White, Minolta) are from Susan Sontag, *On Photography*, p. 184–202.

[29] Denis Roche, *Dépôts de savoir & technique*, Collection "Fiction & Cie," Seuil, Paris 1980. The "*cadroir*" is mentioned on page 16.

[30] For example see the note "How the projected shadow is never the same size as its cause." Ms 2038, National Library of France, 29v.

[31] In fact, if it were completely transparent (like a glass plate), this support-screen would make the installation resemble something that is comparable to the well known technique described by Leonardo da Vinci: "To accurately represent a scene take a glass plate as large as a royal folio paper and adjust it well before your eyes, that is *between your eye and what you seek to represent*. Now, remove your eye two-thirds of a *braccia* from the glass and *fix* your head using an instrument so that it cannot move; close or cover an eye and with a brush or a pencil of well ground red chalk, *draw what is visible beyond on the glass, then reproduce it by pressing the glass on a sheet of paper*, then transfer it to superior quality paper and paint it if you wish." Ms 2038, National Library of France, Nat. 24r.

[32] The referenced text is Immanuel Kant's "Concerning the Ultimate Ground of the Differentiation of Directions in Space," in *The Cambridge Edition of the Works of Immanuel Kant, Theoretical Philosophy, 1755–1770*, ed. and trans. David Walford and Ralf Meerbote, Cambridge University Press, Cambridge 1992.

[33] William Henry Fox Talbot, "An Account of the Art of Photogenic Drawing or the Process by which Natural Objects May Be Made to Delineate Themselves Without the Aid of the Artist's Pencil," January 31, 1839, paper to the Royal Society of Great Britain.

[34] Ibid.

[35] Ibid.

[36] Charles Sanders Peirce, *Philosophical Writings of Peirce*, selected, ed., and intro. Justus Buchler, Dover Publications, New York 1986, p. 106.

[37] André Bazin, "The Ontology of the Photographic Image," in *What Is Cinema*, vol. 1, trans. Gray Hugh, University of California Press, Berkley 1967, p. 12–16.

[38] Denis Roche, *Notre Antéfixe*, Collection Textes, Flammarion, Paris 1978, p. 14–15.

[39] For example, Roland Barthes, "le message photographique," in *Communications*, no. 1, 1961.

[40] Roland Barthes, *Camera Lucida* (1980), trans. Richard Howard, Farrar, Strauss and Giroux, New York 1981, p. 126.

[41] Ibid., p. 19.

[42] Ibid., p. 76.

[43] Rosalind Krauss, "Video: The Aesthetics of Narcissicsm," in *October*, no. 1, 1976, p. 54–64. Reprinted in Gregory Battcock's critical anthology, *New Artists Video*, Dutton, New York 1978, p. 43–64.

[44] Nicole Widart, *Vidéo: une écriture entre deux médias*, typed Master's thesis, Université de Liège, section Information et Arts de Diffusion, 1980, 140pp.

[45] Rosalind Krauss, *The Originality of the Avant-Garde*, p. 197.

[46] For more on this subject see Louis Marin's fine analysis in *Détruire la peinture*, Galilée, Paris 1977.

A Notion of the *Corps-Cliché**
in the 19th Century
Georges Didi-Huberman

Parachute, no. 35, Summer 1984
Translated from the French by Harvey L. Mendelsohn

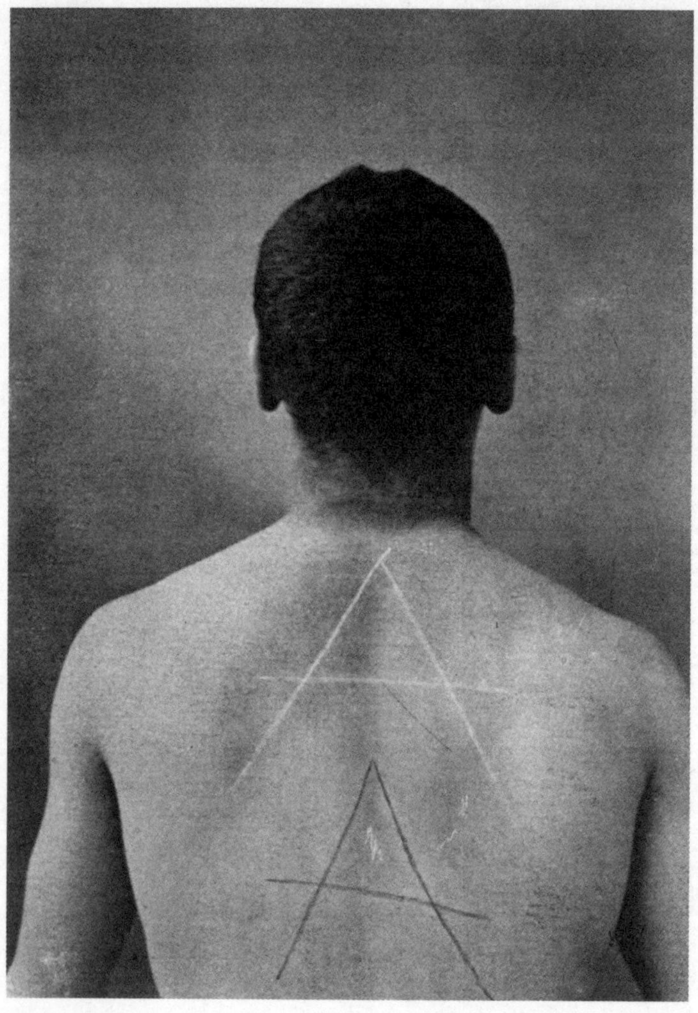

Illustration from *Nouvelle iconographie de la Salpétrière*, "dermographisme rouge et blanc," T. XXIII, Masson & Cie Éditeurs, Paris 1910

The Subject Impressed/Imprinted in Her Symptom

In the field of experimentation on hysteria in the 19th century, there is an extraordinary elective affinity between *symptom* and *figuration*. This affinity (the functioning of this affinity) has perhaps not been without influence on our current understanding of both the symptom and its figuration. This is the case despite, or perhaps because of, the Freudian revolution itself. For in the 19th-century clinical practice systematically *put to work* [*mis en oeuvre*] this structural affinity. It was thus constantly experienced for lack of having been thought about. And it was put to work in the sense in which Claude Bernard defined such an operation, specifically, as a key stage in the experimental method, in as much as the latter is not simply a matter of observation but rather of observation that has been "provoked." In other words, it is, first of all, *the art of obtaining the facts*, and, secondly, *the art of putting them to work*.[1] We already see here the two words "art" and "work." The clinical study of hysteria raised, in an exemplary fashion, the problem of *art* every time it raised the epistemological problem of the *symptom*.

On the one hand, it has been shown that the very elaboration of the notion of hysteria by Charcot occurred within the element itself (in the Hegelian sense) of figuration; its conceptual means, as well as what was at stake, were those of figuration. Charcot put to work a whole figural domain (photographic, sculptural, schematic, etc.) in order to establish firmly a clinical notion that was itself conceived in terms of a tableau (in all the senses of the word, notably that of a syn-optic dreamed of as pan-optic).[2] On the other hand, and as it were reciprocally, in adopting this figurative approach to the symptom, clinical study gave rise to perhaps the first of the great psychopathological theories of art (which at the time took the name of "studies in the medical criticism of works of art"): as early as 1857 Charcot published an article on ancient marble statuary,[3] and became interested in the iconography of possession and ecstasy. Starting in 1888, the medical publications at the Sâlpetrière hospital include a not insignificant number of texts devoted to the history of art. Already in 1887 Charcot and Richer published their astonishing and famous book *Les Demoniaques dans l'art* [The Demoniacs in Art], followed two years later by their study *Les Difformes et les malades dans l'art* [The Deformed and the Sick in Art],[4] in which the point, literally, was to see and analyze hysterical symptoms "at work" in the painting.

This masked and served a fantasy, namely that everything visible looks like something recognizable so that it becomes legible. Examining the experimental protocols in detail, one sees that this fantasy came to function as a categorical imperative. I would like to show, using a very specific example, how the photographic process was very often at the heart of this dialectic. I have already attempted to show how, starting from the status of *visible proof*, it came to function as the *production of the visible*, and as the production of a formal existence [*formalité*] of the symptom itself through the use of hypnosis. One can perhaps see here how this extreme attention to and experimentation with the visible could give rise to the invention (in both the archeological and rhetorical senses of the term) of something like the status of the body as a photographic surface.

In this context, a fundamental notion already existed that tied together these two prodigious phenomena of photography and hysteria. (Historically, the symptom has almost been defined by an inability to understand it materially; it has always been a *malum sine materia*.) It is a question of the notion of "impressionability" [*impressionabilité*]. In both cases the spectacular and mysterious occurrence of the visible is only a surface phenomenon, or so it seems, but the surface is endowed with sensibility. Since the 16th century, persistent attempts had been made to autopsy the cadavers of hysterics, but nothing was ever found *inside*. We can state, in a summary fashion, that in the 19th century the notion of impressionability took over from the no less magical and impalpable one of "hysterical" vapors. It was Briquet, who, in 1859, gave the hypothesis its full scope:

> 1. Impressionability, augmented by the affective element of the nervous system, constitutes the basis of the predisposition to hysteria. 2. Hysteria is almost a particular characteristic of the female sex, because of the predominance in it of this affective element.
> 3. Nevertheless, hysteria can exist in a man, but on condition that this same predominance exists.
> 4. The reason for this particularity is not to be found in the female genital apparatus; it is found in the mode of sensibility proper to women… As a result one can consider hysteria to be the consequence of the suffering [*souffrance*] endured by the portion of the encephalon destined to receive affective impressions and sensations.[5]

Such a notion of hysteria, understood both as a disease and as a prodigious display of impressionability, thus made it possible, in 1859, to understand for the first time its most extraordinary symptomatological quality, i.e., that of being able to reproduce exactly, but without any concomitant lesion, all the other diseases. Considering impressionability as the "basis" of hysteria would account for its virtually absolute mimetic capacity. It is worth noting here that this text is exactly contemporaneous with Baudelaire's essay in which he castigated photography for its ability to provide an "exact reproduction of nature."[6]

The Hysterical *Symptôme-Cliché*

Briquet's text, however, appeared a full 20 years after the famous report by Arago on the daguerreotype (July 3, 1839). It also preceded, by just about 20 years, the publication, by a physician at the Saint-Antoine hospital in Paris, of an unheard of and extraordinary case of "vasomotor problems of the skin observed in an hysterical woman."[7] This publication is remarkable, first of all, for being the very first of its kind,[8] and secondly, for the appearance in it, as if spontaneously, of two astonishing phrases used in naming the person afflicted with this symptom: *femme-cliché* and *femme autographique* [where a *cliché* in French can designate the negative of a photographic image, as well as a plate which is a negative image used for printing; and an *autographie* is a copy made by printing].

This is a young woman whose life, as it is told to us, appears to be dominated by a kind of occult power of the interior over the periphery. Her entire symptomatology could be read as trajectory of destiny (the death of her father) toward the visceral foundation (the appearance of her menses, epigastric constrictions), and from the visceral foundation toward corporal "surfaces" that are panic-stricken (convulsive movements, grimaces, neuralgias) or deprived (loss of consciousness, deafness, anesthesia). Anesthesia of the entire cutaneous surface appears to be a major trait of this symptomatology: moreover, this was not just frequent in hysteria—in the 19th century it was still considered one of its characteristic traits. "One can move from one end to the other along the skin of her limbs, of her stomach, of her breasts, and of her face without her feeling the least pain."[9]

This loss of *sense* is apparently symmetrically matched by a fabulous capacity of the skin to *reproduce exactly* urticaria [or hives] when it is touched. This is a "curious and very strange urticaria, because it can be limited so closely to the place touched that one can trace whatever characters one wants on this patient's skin."[10] Everything appears to indicate that the skin has lost its sensation, but, in return, it has become stigmatized through the absolute graphic reproducibility of the mark, of the signifier, of the "character" that anyone at all might care to trace on it, and *to record* [*clicher*] on it. The skin has lost its sense in order to welcome the Other's meaning [*sens*].

Thus we get these terms: *femme-cliché* (woman-printing plate) and *femme autographique* (woman-copy)—with the obvious ambiguity of the latter term. If hysterical *autoscopy* (seeing one's own face from within) arises in some way from the most excessive of appropriations (this would be an "identification" having traversed, and destroyed, all the structures of reflexivity), on the contrary, in what Dujardin-Beaumtez calls "autographie," the relationships of the interior to the exterior, of the subject to the Other, are rendered exceedingly complex, and permit no circulation at all of sameness [*mêméte*: identity of character during the life of an individual (auto)]. Indeed, the corporal surface specifies its subject only to become the apparent surface of inscription of the desire of the Other. This symptom is an effect of writing whereby the writer exists only in a perpetual reflection of existence and identity. The skin itself writes itself "on" itself, or rather the writing comes to it "from within"; it is both surface *and* subject of the inscription. But it only exists as such in writing itself through an Other: the skin receives the meaning of the inscription only from an "outside." More precisely, the coming into being of this "auto-graphie" functions as the quasi-visceral horripliation in response to (the slightest contact with) the Other.

The nomenclature of the "autographie," moreover, will evolve. Terms that will be used include "factitious," "graphic," and "nervous" urticaria, "vasomotor dermoneurosis," "cutaneous stereography," "stigmatographism," and there are more. The terminology becomes more or less fixed around 1890, settling on the expression "dermographia," or preferably, *dermographism*.[11] Also at this time the phenomenon, considered in 1879 to be "very curious and extremely rare," embraces a much wider nosological domain. The thesis that Barthélémy devoted to dermographism in 1893 already contained 70 case descriptions.[12] In a 1901 publication we read that the symptom is really "not rare if one takes the trouble to seek it out."[13]

Beside the problem of nomenclature, there remained the question of finding out what subjective process gave rise to this "sensitive" or "printing" quality of the skin, and this question remained wholly unanswered. Or rather it remained indecisive in its very formulation: it never ceased attempting to go beyond its initial field of experimentation, namely hysteria, while never ceasing to return to it. Certainly, as a malfunctioning of the "vasomotor nerves of the skin," dermographism requires a "nervous system that is especially susceptible, impressionable, and upon which an impression has been made [*impressioné*]," wrote Berthelemy.[14] It may therefore be considered as having an elective affinity with the female sex, because the latter's "nervous system is more vibrant, more impressionable"[15]— in other words, more susceptible to hysteria. For, after all, following Briquet, hysteria was conceived only on the optico-photographic model of what Barthélémy himself called an "enlarging apparatus of nervous impressions."[16] One should also note, in the expositions of the case studies, the recurrent aesthetization of the problem, in which a criterion of what I might call *venustà* [beauty] comes to be closely linked to that of hysteria: it is often stated that the skins most susceptible to being imprinted upon [*clichées*] are the finest, the whitest, the smoothest.[17]

Meanwhile, there were attempts to conceive of dermographism outside the "hysterical monopoly," in the words of Chambard, who detected it in 1889 in an "alcoholic imbecile."[18] Generally speaking, this migration beyond the field of hysteria occurred in three directions. The first was to find greater *truth* in the symptom, by which I mean that one sought the *symptôme-cliché* in that element of which it could be considered an exact reproduction. Thus the doctors Féré and Lamy write that "we find a predominance [of the phenomenon] in two categories of patients: on the one hand, hysterical women; on the other, individuals already suffering from true urticaria."[19] A second direction of research involved subsuming the notion into the vast domain of *animality*. It is true that animals, no less than hysterics, are eminently hypnotizable: "beings that are no doubt inferior to the human species, but endowed like them with sentiments." This is what Barthélémy remarks in a chapter of his book in which he describes an exemplary *symptôme-cliché* provoked in a thoroughbred (for "thorough-breds have even more nerves and blood under the skin than the others"); and, as proof, Barthélémy wrote the word "Satan" in capital letters on the animal's flanks.[20] Finally, this extension of the dermographic field almost robbed it of its very existence as a symptom, leading it toward inexist-ence, or at any rate toward *epiphenomenality*. Because it covered a relatively fluid nosological field, at the boundary of neurology and dermatology, dermographism was thus reduced to the status of syndrome (a symptom common to several illnesses) of pure "effect" (as opposed to a "charac-teristic trait") of "simple epiphenomenon."[21]

Dermographism is perhaps only a simple surface effect. But it is an effect, a spectacular one, of the touch of the Other, and even, it is clear, of his/her gaze. As such it already arises from a structure of the hysterical phantasm. And this does not go unremarked in the "literature" in ques-tion; for hysteria does not cease to make surreptitious reappearances there. Accordingly, an epileptic who has dermographism is assumed to display the incorporation of an *hysterical trait* in the general symptomatology of his epilepsy.[22] Although Barthélémy dismissed hysteria to a certain extent when he proposed that, in addition to impressionability, intoxication is a factor in the genesis of the dermographic syndrome, he brought it back in the end when he decided to consider the problems of hysteria themselves on the model of an auto-intoxication.[23] Finally, dermographism was thought by most of the authors to be a means, a path, an inclination toward hysteria; for the subject endowed with this figural capacity of the tegument will be unavoidably inclined, they say, to simulate the other derma-tological maladies. Henceforth clinicians, suspecting this to be the case, will attempt to detect in the visible evidence of the *symptôme-cliché* the desire to *figure* another illness. "How well all that accords with hysteria!" exclaimed a physician concerning a *homme-cliché* who counterfeited scarlet fever one day and smallpox or measles the next.[24]

The Skin as Magic Writing-Pad

The occurrence of the graphic element manifested by the *symptôme-cliché* is therefore to be understood as an intrusion, possible at any moment, of the fictional in the "the truth of the body." An untroubled practice of medicine would be happy to proceed on the assumption that the symptom *never lies*, that it speaks for the subject, telling the truth about him/her, even if the latter is not assumed to master it or to know it. It is obvious why the hysterical symptom, which has at its root the deception of the subject and of its Other, has served, in the words of Freud himself, as the *bête noire* of medicine. Inasmuch as it is a graphic effect, the *symptôme-cliché* is therefore by nature a prey to fiction, to writing, to figuration. And what Freud calls hysterical figurability will function, in any case, whether as cause or effect, as the very element of this wondrous phenomenon of the body/surface.

This is a figurability of the antithesis, of the *antithetical passage*.[25] In the phases of what the physicians themselves call the "development" of the dermographic print [*cliché dermographique*], one actually observes a double passage. On the one hand, the cutaneous surface goes from the *white* of its normal state to the *red* of the localized trace, and the latter in turn (all the while remaining a trace, that is to say a difference) returns to *white*. On the other hand, simultaneous to this color metamorphosis, another passage occurs, which goes from *deep* within (vasomotor system of the dilation and contraction of the subcutaneous blood vessels) to the surface (coloration of the trace), and from being just at the surface takes form on it in *relief*. For as it whitens, the trace becomes raised in a process that may be compared to horripilation, a condition of the skin comparable to goose bumps, that is to say it takes the form of a *cliché* in the typographic sense of the word. (In engraving, the cliché is a metal plate with characters in relief that may be used to print all the copies of a typographical composition.) What Dujardin-Beaumetz calls the trace's "white protrusion" ["*saillie blanche*"] produces a relief that becomes "increasingly prominent until it attains a thickness of a millimeter and half."[26] Barthélémy will considerably outbid this figure, reporting a case where the number reached as much as six millimeters.

But the real one-upmanship occurs, rather, in the descriptive categories themselves, which continue to evolve. More precisely put, the vocabulary used to describe the phenomenon will make a bold display of all the subtleties and riches of a *pictorial* semantics, repeatedly trying to come to grips with the notion of an *ekphrasis* of the change in color, one of the key aspects of which obviously concerns the question of *the crimson coloring [incarnat]*.[27] This should not astonish us, inasmuch as the *symptôme-cliché* touches very closely on ancient figural phantasms. For it *gives body to the characteristic [trait]*, to the trace; it "brings out" the design, puts it into relief, by means of a process that is simultaneously the *very process of producing the color*: the rising of the blood, in a localized area, toward the surface, *from the interior*. This is what Hegel called the "interior animation" of the hue in the incarnation [*incarnat*], which for that reason functions, according to him, as the very ideal of pictoriality in its sensitive materials.[28] The troubled emotions [*le trouble du sang*] at the heart of a living being, the blood's symptomatic rising toward the bodily surfaces, should therefore be understood as the culmination of a pictorial mimesis; at the same time this is the way in which physicians (Meinert for example) have very often attempted to account for the etiology of mental illnesses. These two constellations meet, one might say collude, in dermographism.

The symptom's transformation into metaphor, however, was still crystallizing around the word *cliché*. The notion of typographic relief is of course fundamental: the amplitude of the relief functions here as the criterion of the symptom's intensity or purity; the basic form of dermographism is "flat" [*plate*], while the term "grand dermographism" is applied to the most prominent form.[29] And if the duration of the dermographic effect is extremely variable, ranging from half an hour to several days, the process's indefinite reproducibility is not the least of its magical aspects. It is both typographic magic (low relief) and photographic magic, exhibiting the immediate impressionability of a film surface. It lies between optics and textuality. The notion of writing [*graphie*] here encompasses both the signature of original, figurative (*Bilderschrift*) writing, and the repetition, the persistence, of *stigma*, including its possible conversion into textuality, into meaning.

We thus have something like a *Wunderblock*, a magic writing pad, and in fact it was precisely this device, lying between the optical and the scriptural, that Freud employed as metaphor for the workings of the psyche.[30] Here the dermographic symptom constitutes, as it were, a portrait of the layering, of the exfoliation, of the insanity even of a notion of the subject. For in the very way that it operates, it destroys (as does the *Wunderblock*), the notions of exterior and interior, for example, the speck [*gramme*] that appears there produces "the space and the body of the sheet itself," and it also produces something like a "stratification of surfaces in which the relationship to the self, the interior, is only the implication of another surface."[31] It produces the trace and the very moment of its erasure. It is an act of engraving in which the surface never ceases to return to its virgin state, to its capacity to receive a new impression [*clichage*].

What the physicians do not discuss with regard to dermographism is the *memory effect* that such an "intradermic"[32] writing can generate beyond the time of its erasure. Hysteria is a sickness characterized by *forgetting the impossibility of forgetting*, and it was Freud who detected the effects of this phenomenon and who worked out its structures. I cannot resist conjecturing that the sign written on the skin of an hysterical woman displaying dermographism could have *returned*, at some moment, as a symptom, since every trace, despite, or because of its having generated the time of its erasure, remains capable of acting subsequently. The exchange routes of the interiors and surfaces are in themselves impenetrable. Lannois reports the case of a young woman of 23 who became dermographic at the very moment at which she was freed from what until then had been devouring her from the inside—several meters of a worm; then, "we easily wrote her name on her chest, her back, and her forearms."[33]

The Game of the Trait and the Game of the Pose

The attempt to deprive dermographism of its status as symptom was perhaps made in order to have it considered, instead, as a syndrome, but even more so as a symbol. Moreover, no one was particularly concerned with its therapeutic treatment; at the most, Barthélémy suggested that the *femmes-clichées* be given a brimming glass of Coca-Cola.[34] Dermographism came to be seen as having a kind of secondary status: rather than as a symptom it was thought of as "representing the basis of another symptom" (hysteria, epilepsy, dementia praecox). In other words, in clinical discourse it functioned above all as a basis of representation.

Consider, now, the representation—this puts itself to work [*se met en oeuvre*], creates the milieu [*se met en scène*]. Everything written in the wake of Dujardin-Beaumetz's original publication is simply a relentless series of experimental variations, responding, perhaps, to some deep curiosity: what are the limits of the body's wondrous capacity to accept and to produce a *cliché* of every trace made on it? The essence of the dermographic effect was sought by means of a controlled variation of the modes of producing a *cliché*: blunt points, fingernail tips, pins, "thermal excitations" (freezing and burning), electromagnetic exposure using Duchenne de Boulogne's famous "electric paint brush" of galvanic currents, etc. The impact of this key notion of impressionability can be gauged in reading the accounts of the Salpetrière physicians, in which one senses their vague disappointment in not having obtained any effect through the use of x-rays.[35] This, however, did not keep researchers from systematically looking for the "elective zones" of dermographism, just as they simultaneously sought to construct a map of the "hysterogenous zones." Several went so far as to try to detect the *cliché* effect in the interior of the mouth.[36]

Now, putting to work this experimental variability led to the symptom (or the syndrome) being considered in terms of a *technè* [craftsmanship]. In other words, the notion of *cliché* was subtly displaced from being the paradigm of the spontaneous *effect* (observed on the skin) to being the paradigm of an *art* (to provoke, to produce such an effect on the skin). The impression [*clichage*] has thus returned to its oldest meaning. "The impression [*clichage*] is the art of obtaining imprints (in the form of depressions or hollows, or in relief) by pressing molds down" on a metal brought to an intermediate state between fusion and its natural hardness.[37] Here "imprint" has become a generic term encompassing the notion of tracing as *Bilderschrift*. What one observes, then, in studying the actual protocols of this experimental variability is a miming of a reinvention of writing. For it is extremely interesting to note what was being written on such *corps-clichés*.

At first, this is a pure game of the trace, of difference expressed on the foundation of the skin, in short, a pure exercise of making a mark. Next, and logically so, it is a game of difference in the materiality itself of the tracing: what may be called raised dermographism is distinguished from the "flat" variety, and red (resulting from vasomotor dilation), from white (resulting rather from a constriction). The phenomenon of contradictory figurability allowed Doctor Roudnew to produce simultaneously a white *cliché* and a red *cliché* on the back of the same subject.[38] This recalls the experiments in which Charcot literally divided the subject he was experimenting on, imposing a cataleptic state on half of her body, and producing a state of lethargy in the other half.[39]

One can see that with his red and white dermographism Roudnew was beginning to construct an alphabet, as the *Bilderschrift* goes from being a mark to writing. Elsewhere we read: "I traced several designs at the same time to fix the ideas, specifically, the first four letters of the alphabet, once on the same shoulder, and another time half on each shoulder."[40] But the meaning becomes more precise, if I may put it that way, or at the very least what is at stake does. An observation made by Lannois, which begins with the words "a certain A.D., 33 years of age … " is accompanied by a double photograph showing this *femme-cliché* bearing, on her chest, the word "ANGELINE" written in capital letters, while on her back, between her shoulders, is prominently displayed "DONADIEU."[41] A double impression [*clichage*], therefore, and an extreme moment of portraiture; for the subject of the photograph has created on her own skin the impression of her full name, which the text, deontologically, had reduced to her initials.

In other cases it is not the subject's name that becomes the *cliché*, but rather its truth, by which I mean its truth according to the Other, i.e. the photographer or the physician. I mean its diagnostic truth, or rather the knowledge supposedly displayed by it [*supposé savoir*], traced at the level of the skin, like a sentence.[42] But the effect of this knowledge [*effect de savoir*] did not fail to produce consequences that the authors themselves term "picturesque": one woman displayed the image of coins; another was covered with fantastic, "kabbalistic" inscriptions;

another bore the figure of the *sigillum diaboli*, the hand of the devil or the name of Satan; another was simply riddled with little ornamental needle marks; and, finally, another woman was returned to her husband, who, taking advantage of the opportunity, "from time to time wrote his name on his wife's skin."[43] All this business about the "picturesque" is not, however, bereft of meaning, because what all this is about ultimately is very clear. *It is about turning the body into an icon, and signing it.* The "autographic skin" is an appeal to the meaning of the Other; the Other (the perverse Other) simply profits from it. It is a figurative and indentificatory bonanza. And what is written on the *sujet-cliché*'s back is neither more nor less than the name of the physician, the "subject who is supposed to know" [*sujet-supposé-savoir*], who at that moment dreams that he is like the artist, *the fictor, the author of the subject.* Thus Doctor Eli Châtelain did not hesitate to sign and date the iconic body of his *sujet-cliché*, while he was photographing it for the great museum of clinical practice.[44]

The dermographic phenomenon is therefore not only that of rendering contact visible. It is also that of rendering visible the discourse of the Other—his/her writing, his/her signature. In this process, the letter is deployed, as it were, photographically, whereby the emitter of the trace (the *sujet-cliché*) receives from the Other his/her own message, but in an inverted form: in order to exist I desire you as my master, my author, my painter (you are therefore the guarantor of my fictive existence [*existence-fiction*], of my non-existence). Inversion also enters into the definition of the *cliché*, even the optical and photographic definition.[45] It is constantly at work in the link of the hysterical phantasm and the deviant phantasm. In this sense, the *symptôme-cliché* should be considered an effect of the contract of the photographic pose itself, about which Balzac rightly said that it was a "disease of the brain."[46] This is because the pose is always struggling with its two essential limits: melancholy and hysteria. The *symptôme-cliché* should be seen as a kind of inscribed delay (*hysteresis*) of a crisis linked to the phenomenological structure of the pose.

In this context, moreover, pose and hypnosis overlap. Barthélémy noted that the dermographic subjects were eminently hypnotizable. He even caused the dermographic state using hypnosis.[47] The *symptôme-cliché* could therefore be considered the effect of a kind of *haptic*, or tactile hypnosis, if I might put it that way. One is not surprised to encounter here a basic phantasm of the photographic process in the 19th century, namely that of the look that touches [*regard-tact*], of the look that shocks [*regard-choc*], of the luminous blow, of contact at a distance—something that the physicians and photographers often reveled in to the point of abuse.[48] This is the ancient paradigm of *achiropoïèsis*, of acting and touching others, and of making images, without using one's hands. The medical photographs of dermographism never show the instrument responsible for the trace, or the hand of the physician.

An observation of Barthélémy's seems to me to tie together, in an exemplary manner, all these factors. The case is that of a woman whose hysterogenous zones he is seeking to find. Dermographism is detected. She undergoes experiments on her feet, her hands, her breasts, "also on her face." The dermographic state presents itself, clearly, as a latent hysterical crisis. But with the crisis there also appears a painful latency in which the humors mount in her—tears, blood. But there is still something else to note: all this occurs when one looks at this woman from behind. For the glance doesn't need the eye to be present; it simply registers here the efficacity of a phantasm of the Other as one who touches in the act of looking [*voyant-touchant*]:

> [A] bizarre, disagreeable, enervating sensation, stronger than her will, is experienced by the patient if one looks at her *from behind*. If one persists in doing this, tears appear, and if one rubs her vigorously, then there is no doubt that a crisis will occur. Her period begins at that very moment.[49]

APPENDIX

Notes on the Vasomotor Problems of the Skin Observed in an Hysterical Woman (*femme autographique*)

Presentation given at the Société Médicale des Hôpitaux, in the session held on Friday, July 11, 1879.
By Doctor Dujardin-Beaumetz, physician at the Saint-Antoine hospital.

I have the honor of presenting to the Société des Hôpitaux a very curious case, and an extremely rare one—since I have found no other example in science—of cutaneous vasomotor problems in an hysterical woman whom I am observing at this time in my department at the Saint-Antoine hospital. But, before going further and submitting this woman to the various experiments that I will perform here for you, allow me to give you in its entirety the report of our observations as they have been recorded by my intern, Mr. Dubar:

Observation. – Hysteria; loss of general sensitivity over the whole surface of the skin; vasomotor problems allowing characters that are traced on her skin to appear in raised relief for a period of several hours. Catalepsy.

Julie Jagoret, 29 years of age, day laborer, enters the Saint-Antoine hospital on June 30, 1879, salle Saint-Agathe, no. 16, in Doctor Dujardin-Beaumetz's clinic.

She is a woman of delicate complexion, and above all of a very pronounced nervous temperament. Her father died at the age of 51 of a chronic chest ailment; her mother, who died at the age of 52, had nervous attacks. She had four brothers and a sister, all of them now deceased: some from consumption, others from tubercular meningitis. The last one, who succumbed to typhoid fever, was a somnambulist. He was in the habit of running over roofs at night. Thus, all the children in this family displayed very weak constitutions and, without a doubt, a disposition to neuroses.

The patient whom we are observing has shown, since her earliest youth, a predisposition to nervous ailments of all kinds.

At the age of nine, she became deaf in both ears, and this deafness, which was not accompanied by discharge from the auditory canals, or by a sore throat, disappeared after a few months.

At the age of 12 she suffered from severe chorea that completely deprived her of sleep for more than a month and that did not disappear for two and a half years. Even today she still has a few very minor facial grimaces.

At the age of 16 she began to menstruate. The patient reports that the very day her period began her father died, and that the sorrow this event caused her provoked her first fit of hysterics. She lost consciousness for three days and nights, and her parents told her that during all this time her whole body shook violently. During this period she followed a treatment that brought good results, because for two years she had no more hysterical fits and enjoyed good health. From this time on her menstruation has always been normal.

At the age of 18, the death of one of her brothers provoked a second crisis, which was extremely violent and lasted for nine days. It appears that she was bled, on the arm and on the ankle, and this relaxed her completely.

From this time on her health has been very satisfactory. She was able to work, and even engage in quite tiring occupations. She remained very nervous, impressionable; she did have, quite infrequently, however, minor hysterical fits when someone angered her; but she was not in pain.

During the first months of the year 1878 she began to experience vague pains in her chest and stomach. These pains continued to increase, reaching a point that brought her, in March of that year, to enter the Saint-Antoine hospital, in Doctor Ball's clinic. She stayed there a month and then left, because, she says, she did not want to submit herself to the treatment she was receiving.

Several months after leaving the hospital, without any treatment, her pains disappeared as if by magic. No longer suffering, she believed she was completely cured. However, about every two months she suffered an attack of hysteria, displaying very pronounced spasms. But she paid no attention to these, attributing them to various annoyances. Toward the month of May 1879, her chest and stomach pains reappeared; at the same time her limbs felt very weak. She could hardly walk. Soon she lost her appetite. She entered the hospital on June 30.

The nervous ailments that this patient presents are very complex. We have already mentioned a certain number of nervous incidents in other members of her family (her parents).

Here we shall enumerate only the symptoms we observe at present—which are none other than those of a very pronounced hysteria—limiting ourselves to pointing out and emphasizing most especially a bizarre phenomenon, one that is at the very least exceptional, if not unique, in the annals of science.

Her general sensitivity is profoundly altered. The entire cutaneous surface is the seat of a total anesthesia. One can move from one end to the other along the skin of her limbs, her stomach, her breasts, and her face without her feeling the least pain. Nevertheless, in these cases she does perceive a slight pressure, which proves that the sense of touch is not completely destroyed. Sensitivity to cold, to heat, and to tickling is likewise not in evidence. With regard to the mucous membranes, we do not observe any phenomenon of this kind.

Her sense of touch is very diminished. In fact, the patient manages to sew only with the greatest difficulty. She drops the needles, and, if she does not pay great attention, if she takes her eyes off her work for only a moment, she continues to make hand and arm movements but without the needle between her fingers, and consequently does so with no result, which greatly irritates her. There is no plantar anesthesia; she senses the ground perfectly well and is aware of its nature. On several occasions, during the same day, the patient has the sensation that a ball is rising up from her epigastrium to her throat. It is at these moments that the epigastric constriction increases more than is normal and she vomits. At the present time we no not observe any problems with her sense organs. We attribute the dizziness that she experiences when she stands up after having bent down to pick up an object to anemia.

In addition to these problems regarding sensation, there are intercostal and lumbar neuralgias, and pains in her legs.

No appreciable diminution of mobility has been observed, and her muscular force is undiminished.

We now arrive at the most interesting point of our observations, namely the description of a completely extraordinary phenomenon, the nature and pathogenesis of which remains quite obscure to us.

When one traces a line on the external integument with a fingernail or an instrument with a blunt point, after a few seconds one sees a red trail [*traînée*] appear; then this redness expands and forms a rectangular patch; and finally, after two to five minutes, a white elevation appears along the entire length of the line traced on the skin, and steadily increases in relief, ultimately reaching one and a half to two millimeters. This state of affairs endures for three to six hours, sometimes even for 12 hours, and then everything disappears.

One can vary the experiment in a thousand ways, producing the most varied designs on the skin, writing names of ten to 15 letters; wherever the blunt instrument is applied a white relief forms, and all around it, to a distance of four to five centimeters, there is a red patch. This patch always displays a notable increase in temperature, readily detectable to the touch.

When the phenomenon reaches its fully developed state, when the patch and the reliefs are completely constituted, the portion of the skin on which they are located very much resembles a typographic setup [*cliché*]; hence the name *femme-cliché, femme autographique*, by which she has been known ever since she entered the department.

The patient experiences no subjective sensations at the site of the patch.

How can one interpret this phenomenon? There is no doubt that a substantial vasomotor problem exists here. The redness that appears at the beginning is wholly dependent upon it. But is it possible to explain the white relief on the skin in the same manner? This relief, as we have seen, is considerable, since its thickness can reach as much as two millimeters. We have often seen, in observing hysterical women, that urticarial patches arise in response to various pressures and irritations, or to the application of a magnet. There is no doubt that a very great analogy exits between this development of an urticaria and the appearance of lines in white relief on our patient. We will not enter into a deeper discussion of this here. Our teacher, Doctor Dujardin-Beaumetz, has reserved the presentation of the arguments that militate in favor of this opinion for himself.

In summary, then, we have here a woman of 29 years of age who presents all the characteristics of hysteria and who displays a general loss of cutaneous sensitivity; one can pierce [*piquer*] her as deeply as possible, and move across her thighs and arms without detecting any manifestation of sensitivity in her. The sense of touch, as well as sensitivity to heat and cold, are also abolished. But these are facts commonly observed among hysterics, and I will not dwell further upon them. However, I should tell you that all the attempts we have made, whether using the entire metalascopic series, or with magnets or electricity, have failed to modify this lack of sensitivity.

The interest of the case that concerns us at present lies in the fact that when one presses down on the skin with a little vigor, especially with a hard object, one sees at the end of several minutes an elevation emerge that corresponds very exactly to the point that was touched; and this elevation, which lasts a more or less long time, is at first well delimited, with very clear borders, then continues to spread out, finally disappearing after four or five hours. The place that is touched in this way is red, and the skin is warmer there.

The visual aspect of the skin totally reproduces the urticaria, but this is a curious and very strange urticaria, since it can be so restricted to the point touched that one can trace any characters one wants to on the skin of this patient and in this way see the names and words thus inscribed rise up on the skin to such a degree that not only can one read them very clearly; it would also be possible to print actual proofs from them. Accordingly, my colleague and friend Doctor Mesnet has suggested giving this patient the nickname *femme autographique*, and I accept this ingenious denomination.

Despite the increase in the temperature of the skin, and despite its congestion and redness, sensitivity does not return under the influence of this momentary excitation.

I have looked for analogous cases, and I have not found any that may be compared with this one. However, in the case of another female patient, also an hysteric, I had noticed that pin pricks, or the application of a magnet produced, at points of the skin touched in this way, phenomena completely analogous to those that we see here. I had this patient brought back, and I tried to reproduce characters, but I obtained no results. Professor Vulpian, who examined this patient, told me he had observed the same phenomenon in a man who presented no sign of hysteria.

I should note that since the medical journals have reported this phenomenon, Doctor Goubeyre has told me he has observed two analogous cases, and he even was kind enough to show me a young hysterical woman, though one who exhibited no anesthesia, upon whom one could also trace characters and see them appear in raised form on her skin.

Finally, my colleague Mr. Duguet showed me a young man in his department who displayed the same phenomenon, but in a much less intense manner. I may add that one of my students, Mr. Cuévas, who plans to gather together all these facts in his inaugural thesis, told me has observed an analogous case in the department of Mr. Hérard.

Let us return now to our patient. I have experimented with very many different means in order to see if I could modify this vasomotor problem. I began first of all with the method suggested in Germany by Frantzel and Ernst Schwimmer for curing urticaria, namely atropine injections; then I tried electricity, applications of different metals using Burq's method, magnets—nothing worked. And today, after the patient has been under our observation for more than six months, the vasomotor problem is just as evident and just as intense as it was when she entered the hospital. My colleague Mesnet, who was kind enough to supervise the patient during the holidays, made a series of very interesting observations on her, giving her cherries, strawberries, currants, and shrimp, all of them apt to produce urticaria; by giving her these foods he was always able to induce an outbreak of urticaria.

I wish to call the Society's attention to two major points of our observations. First, the case of this hysterical woman would lend itself marvelously to all those fantastic accounts that led people to believe in witchcraft and in miracles; in particular this phenomenon corresponds in several ways to those observations of stigmatizations that were so much talked about in another age. The second point is more interesting. Seeing the considerable influence that pressure and touch exert on the vasomotor circulation of the skin, one wonders if analogous problems would not occur along the cerebro-spinal axis, and if, under the influence of certain factors, the vasomotors of the nervous centers would not undergo analogous modifications.

This patient has very clear and very pronounced attacks of hysteria, but she exhibits the following important phenomenon. If you make her stare at a precise point for several minutes, that is sufficient to cause her immediately to have a cataleptic attack that quickly terminates in a true attack of hysteria. The patient feels this influence to such a degree that she never speaks without lowering her eyes and refuses to stare at objects. One may therefore offer the hypothesis here that vision has the same influence on the vasomotor circulation of the brain that contact has on cutaneous circulation, and that it is this influence that gives rise to attacks of hysteria.

There are a number of points here that ought to be examined more deeply, and that will require new studies and new research. However that may be, I believed I should publish this phenomenon, which increases the number of truly bizarre cases of hysteria, and which confirms what was said by one of our teachers, namely, that in the realm of hysteria, nothing is impossible.

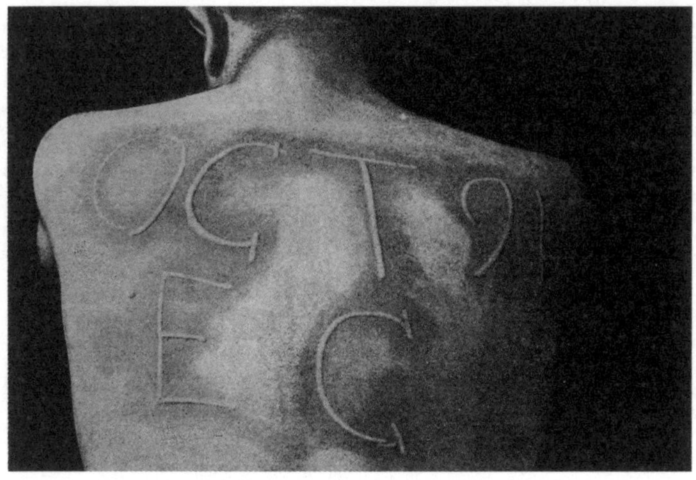

Illustration from Eugène Châtelain, *Journal des maladies cutanées et syphilitiques*, T. III, Paris 1891

* For the sense of the word "cliché" here, i.e. a metal plate used in printing, see the author's remark in the text: "In engraving, the cliché is a metal plate with characters in relief that may be used to print all the copies of a typographical composition."

[1] Claude Bernard, *Introduction à l'étude de la médecine expérimentale*, Baillière, Paris 1865, p. 24.

[2] See Georges Didi-Huberman, *Invention of Hysteria: Charcot and the Photographic Iconography of the Salpêtrière* (1982), trans. Alisa Hartz, MIT Press, Cambridge, Massachusetts 2004.

[3] Jean-Martin Charcot and Amédée Dechambre, "De quelques marbres antiques," in *Gazette hebdomadaire de médecine et de chirurgie*, T. IV, no. 25, 1857.

[4] Charcot and Paul Richer, *Les Démoniaques dans l'art*, Delahaye et Lecrosnier, Paris 1887, reprinted Macula, Paris 1984; *Les Difformes et les malades dans l'art*, Lecrosnier et Babé, Paris 1889.

[5] Pierre Briquet, *Traité clinique et thérapeutique de l'hystérie*, Baillière, Paris 1859, p. 161 and 601.

[6] Charles Baudelaire, "The Salon of 1859" ("The Modern Public and Photography"), in *Art in Paris, 1845–1862*, trans. and ed. Jonathan Mayne, Phaidon, London 1965, p. 149–155.

[7] Georges Dujardin-Beaumetz, "Notes sur des troubles vaso-moteurs de la peau observés sur une hystérique (femme autographique)," in *L'Union médicale*, no. 144, December 9, 1879, p. 917–922. See appendix attached to this text, "Notes on the Vasomotor Problems of the Skin Observed in an Hysterical Woman (*femme autographique*)."

[8] One finds several clinical notations of the phenomenon in Pierre Rayer, *A Theoretical and Practical Treatise on the Diseases of the Skin* (1826), Carey and Hart, for G. N. Loomis, Philadelphia 1845; as well as in Villan and Bateman (1841), W. Gull (1859), etc. But these notations are short of Dujardin-Beaumetz's strict nosological denomination.

[9] Dujardin-Beaumetz, "Notes on the Vasomotor Problems of the Skin Observed in an Hysterical Woman (*femme autographique*)."

[10] Ibid.

[11] See V. Cornu, *Contribution à l'étude de la dermographie (urticaire graphique, provoquée)*, Jouve, Paris 1890; Toussiant Barthélémy, *Étude sur le dermographisme ou dermoneurose toxivasomotrice*, Société d'éditions scientifiques, Paris 1893, p. 13.

[12] Ibid.

[13] M. Lannois, "Dermographisme chez les épileptiques atteints d'helminthiase intestinale," in *Nouvelle iconographie de la Salpêtrière*, T. XIV (1901), p. 297.

[14] Barthélémy, *Étude sur le dermographisme ou dermoneurose toxivasomotrice*, p. 14.

[15] Ibid., p. 35.

[16] Ibid., p. 98.

[17] Ibid., p. 27–28.

[18] E. Chambard, "Dermoneurose stéréographique et érythrasma chez un imbécile alcoolique," in *Archives de Neurologie*, T. XVII (1889), no. 49, p. 8–21.

[19] Ch. Féré and H. Lamy, "La Dermographie," in *Nouvelle iconographie de la Salpêtrière*, T. II (1889), p. 284.

[20] Barthélémy, *Étude sur le dermographisme ou dermoneurose toxivasomotrice*, p. 38–40.

[21] Ibid., p. 12–13.

[22] Lannois, "Dermographisme chez les épileptiques atteints d'helminthiase intestinale," p. 207.

[23] Barthélémy, *Étude sur le dermographisme ou dermoneurose toxivasomotrice*, p. 37.

[24] E. Boix, "Contribution à l'étude de l'œdème bleu hystérique," in *Nouvelle iconographie de la Salpêtrière*, T. IV (1891), p. 76. Barthélémy, *Étude sur le dermographisme ou dermoneurose toxivasomotrice*, p. 129–130; and M. Féréol, "Dermographisme ou autographisme," in *Bulletin de la Société médicale des Hôpitaux de Paris*, 3rd series, T. VII, session of November 21, 1890, p. 888.

[25] Sigmund Freud, "Hysterial Phantasies and their Relation to Bisexuality" (1908), http://postausderprovinz.files.wordpress.com/2013/10/sigmund-freud-complete-works.pdf; Didi-Huberman, *Invention of Hysteria: Charcot and the Photographic Iconography of the Salpêtrière*, p. 161–172.

[26] Dujardin-Beaumetz, "Notes on the Vasomotor Problems of the Skin Observed in an Hysterical Woman (*femme autographique*)."

[27] Barthélémy, *Étude sur le dermographisme ou dermoneurose toxivasomotrice*, p. 25–26; Lannois, "Dermographisme chez les épileptiques atteints d'helminthiase intestinale," p. 209; Féré and Lamy, "La Dermographie," p. 285; F. Allard and H. Meige, "Effets produits par les différents modes d'excitation de la peau dans un cas de grand dermographisme," in *Archives générales de médecine*, 8th series, T. X (1898), vol. 2, p. 40–42.

[28] G.W.F. Hegel, *Aesthetics. Lectures on Fine Art*, trans. T.M. Knox, 2 vols., Clarendon Press, Oxford 1975.

[29] Barthélémy, *Étude sur le dermographisme ou dermoneurose toxivasomotrice*, p. 18, 23–26.

[30] Freud, "A Note upon the 'Mystic Writing Pad'" (1925), http://postausderprovinz.files.wordpress.com/2013/10/sigmund-freud-complete-works.pdf.

[31] Jacques Derrida, *Writing and Difference* (1967), trans., intro. and additional notes Alan Bass, Routledge & Kegan Paul, London 1978; http://www.clas.ufl.edu/users/burt/Writing_and_Difference__Routledge_Classics_.pdf.

[32] Barthélémy, *Étude sur le dermographisme ou dermoneurose toxivasomotrice*, p. 33.

[33] Lannois, "Dermographisme chez les épileptiques atteints d'helminthiase intestinale," p. 212–213.

[34] Barthélémy, *Étude sur le dermographisme ou dermoneurose toxivasomotrice*, p. 139 (or rather, more precisely, Kola-Coca).

[35] Allard and Meige, "Effets produits par les différents modes d'excitation de la peau dans un cas de grand dermographisme," p. 42–50; Féré and Lamy, "La Dermographie," p. 286–288; Barthélémy, *Étude sur le dermographisme ou dermoneurose toxivasomotrice*, p. 66–80.

[36] Féré and Lamy, "La Dermographie," p. 284.

[37] R. de Valicourt, *Nouveau manuel complet (…) du moulage et du clichage des médailles*, Librairie encyclopédique de Roret, Paris 1875, p. 339.

[38] M. Roudnew, "Dermographisme rouge et blanc," in *Nouvelle iconographie de la Salpêtrière*, T. XXIII (1910), p. 197–210.

[39] Didi-Huberman, *Invention of Hysteria: Charcot and the Photographic Iconography of the Salpêtrière*.

[40] J. Delboeuf, "Autographisme," in *Revue de l'Hypnotisme*, T. VI (1982), no. 9, p. 258–259.

[41] Lannois, "Dermographisme chez les épileptiques atteints d'helminthiase intestinale," pl. XXVI.

[42] L. Trepsat, "Un cas de démence précoce catatonique avec pseudo-œdème compliqué de purpura," in *Nouvelle iconographie de la Salpêtrière*, T. XVII (1904), p. 193–199 and pl. XXVII. Barthélémy, pl. XIV; J. Séglas, "Démence précoce et catatonie," in *Nouvelle iconographie de la Salpêtrière*, T. XV (1902), p. 330–348 and pl. XLV.

[43] Barthélémy, *Étude sur le dermographisme ou dermoneurose toxivasomotrice*, p. 63–64. Chambard, "Dermoneurose stéréographique et érythrasma chez un imbécile alcoolique," p. 15.

[44] E. Châtelain, "Pseudo-urticaire dermographique (urticaire factice, dermographie, autographisme, etc.)," in *Journal des maladies cutanées et syphilitiques*, T. III (1891), p. 547–555.

[45] E. Latreille, *Almanach-manuel du photographe*, Mallet-
Bachelier, Paris 1858, p. 28 (many thanks to M. Wiedeman
who brought this text to my attention).

[46] G.F. Nadar, *Quand j'étais photographe*, Flammarion,
Paris 1900, p. 8.

[47] Barthélémy, *Étude sur le dermographisme ou dermoneurose
toxivasomotrice*, p. 81–99.

[48] Didi-Huberman, *Invention of Hysteria: Charcot and the
Photographic Iconography of the Salpêtrière*.

[49] Barthélémy, *Étude sur le dermographisme ou dermoneurose
toxivasomotrice*, p. 163.

Magnificent Obsession
Laura Mulvey

Parachute, no. 42, Spring 1986

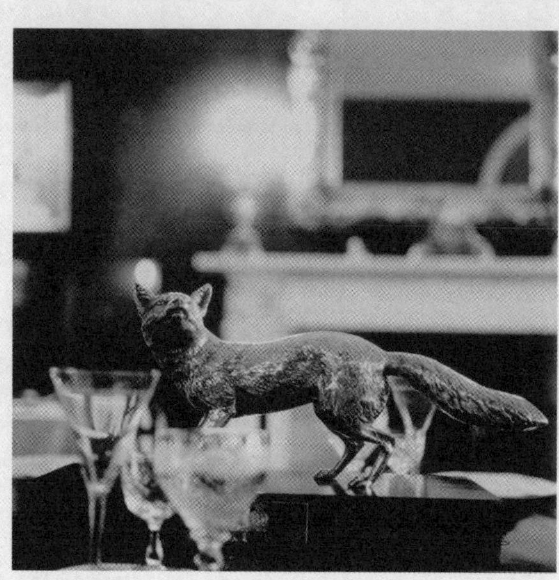

Pleasure as a serious Pursuit
for the Unemployed.

Karen Knorr, *Country Life*, 1983–1985

Magnificent Obsession is an exhibition
of photography that shatters
preconceptions of what a photograph is or should be (Architectural
Resource Centre, Toronto,
20 May–8 June, 1985; Galerie Optica,
Montreal 5–26 October, 1985).
The fantasy of a privileged insight
that tears the mask away from
perceived reality gives way to
another reality, that of the mask
itself and the reality of fantasy.
Photography is generally assumed
to be primarily anchored to the
visible. The pleasurable paradox,
familiar to the cinema, that the
photographic image can be organized to express an abstract idea,
an argument, the interior world of
desire and imagination, seems
strange to still photography.

The cinema is a medium of
sequence, event, and fiction.
Expectations of the still image, on
the other hand, have grown from
an aesthetic of transparency, autonomy, and homogeneity within
the single whole. It is clear, at first

glance, that the aesthetics of the works on exhibition here are derived from opposition to general expectation, and have grown from counter strategy. They break the rules. All use words, not as caption, but as a parallel to the image, to defy autonomy; all are stylized to denaturalize transparency; all use series to break out of the confines imposed by the autonomous single image.

The five artists—Karen Knorr, Mark Lewis, Geoff Miles, Olivier Richon, and Mitra Tabrizian—studied together at the Polytechnic of Central London in the 1970s, the period when a conjuncture between feminist politics, psychoanalytic theory, and deconstructive aesthetics combined to produce a radical avant-garde across the visual arts. Feminism established representation as a terrain for political struggle, and questions about images of women necessarily spilt over to raise wider issues about the image and authenticity. Psychoanalysis provided the language and concepts to expand the sexual politics of representation to include, for instance, desire, the look, and fetishism. The photograph, in particular, lost its innocent one-to-one relation to reality once it was understood to be that every relation that concealed its compromised position within the social system [was] under radical attack. Perhaps, in retrospect, the inclusion of theory within practice could be taken as both a mainspring and hallmark of the British radical avant-garde of the 1970s, producing, as a result, works that were considered as "difficult" as the theory that informed them. Theory forced a rupture with the established aesthetic conventions of the autonomous image, but it also provided a framework for an alternate aesthetic. So, for instance, by including references to psychoanalytic theory, Victor Burgin, Mary Kelly, or myself in the films that I produced with Peter Wollen, insisted on a deconstructive theoretical practice in the early days of the movement, but also established the possibility of a word/image juxtaposition that could become infinitely more flexible and varied.

These photographs are the work of a next generation, no longer strictly bound by the confrontational aesthetics of the 1970s. The formal influences are there, there is a continuity of interest and concern, but there are important and marked differences, particularly with respect to realism and pleasure. It is as though the long, hard battle against the transparency of realism and the spectator pleasure inscribed by tradition and convention (of which the use of woman's image is emblematic) has broken down and reached the end of the road. Out of the debris a language and imagery can emerge that are no longer primarily concerned with an either/or dichotomy. But there is no spirit of compromise nor even synthesis here. The values and desires of this group have developed out of the process of working their original influences through, to the point of distance and displacement, where "pleasure" and "realism" are material for irony and play. In this sense, the exhibition has an art historical perspective, quite apart from the intrinsic interest of the individual work, in that it records the way a specific movement can grow, change, and develop, avoiding the dangers of fossilized repetition and purism. The work, however, still seems difficult, apparently demanding an initiated reading. Confrontational, negative aesthetics can draw on the act of opposing convention as a source of meaning and significance. The next step is harder. It is easier to oppose and deconstruct than to construct alternatives and to capture the spectator's imagination while maintaining a radical approach to spectatorship and address. Riddles and enigmas offer the spectator the lures and pleasures of decipherment, while demanding active participation and work in creating the text's meaning. These photographic series all revolve around clues, and clues to meanings, that form a mode of address that ask the spectator to find and follow them into an emotional or intellectual response. The play with enigma and riddle is an invitation to search for an entry point—through association and personal reverie— that may vary for each individual spectator. This is not to say that there is no precise line of argument laid down or programmed into the work by the artist, but the aesthetic strategies allow flexibility, detours of the imagination, oblique approaches to penetrate an intention which is not reducible to personal self-expression, but revolves around collective, shared cultural interests and concerns.

An important clue is contained in the exhibition title. *Magnificent Obsession* is named after Douglas Sirk's 1953 melodrama in which the heroine loses and regains her sight. The reference to vision makes an initial link with photography, but there are further implications in the title. The word "obsession" invokes the psychoanalytic underpinnings to photographic practice, so important to this movement. Victor Burgin has commented on the close relationship between the photograph and the fetish: "The photograph, like the fetish, is the result of a look which has, instantaneously and forever, isolated, 'frozen,' a fragment of the spatio-temporal continuum." Although these photographers have moved into series, out of the "fragment," there is a sense that, in Karen Knorr's words: "image-makers must accept compromise with fetishism." The camera's almost natural function as instrument of the photographer's voyeuristic power, to be handed on to the spectator, provides both a point of resistance and departure for Geoff Miles' *The Trapper's Pleasure of the Text* (1985). And there is also the characteristic obsession with meticulous details of image, print, and finish. But whereas an awareness of photography's relation to processes originating in the unconscious and the instincts inflects the work in the direction of theory and self-reflexivity, the accompanying word "magnificent" clearly rejects the austerity and asceticism in favor of a grandeur of visual scope, from the sheer size of Mark Lewis' prints to Olivier Richon's use of color and front projection to Mitra Tabrizian's film noir lighting.

The title *Magnificent Obsession* places the show squarely in juxtaposition to the melodrama as a genre, throwing new light on the aesthetics of photography as well as challenging the critical orthodoxy that the photograph is essentially objective. The photograph's stillness is usually related to a moment in time recorded by the shutter, light, and movement combined by the photographer's eye. The aesthetics of melodrama also give great weight to the frozen moment, the moment at which emotion exceeds expression in language and erupts into gesture, heightened by the mise-en-scène. Fassbinder, in his remakes of the Sirkian melodramas, would occasionally hold a scene in tableau, in the manner of the 19th-century theatrical melodrama, where gesture, music, and staging played a crucial role, decisively separating the genre from literary theater. The photographs in this show formalize their "stillness" in relation to these melodramatic codes. The moment caught is dramatic rather than natural. Miles and Lewis use the further reference to gesture and stasis by incorporating a statue or shop-window dummy into the image. Tabrizian and Richon use the look itself as the point that holds time in check. In *Country Life* (1983–1985) Knorr substitutes objects for gestures that evoke the perpetual masquerade of aristocratic living. Peter Brooks has said of the melodrama:

> In the gap of the language code, the grandiose melodramatic gesture is a gesturing toward a tenor that is both grandiose and ineffable. Consequently it is inadequate to speak of decoding such a gesture; we must rather decipher it, follow its directions, rename its indications in our translations.

The image, then, triggers the spectator's stream of consciousness into an internal verbal interpretation. The same process is brought into play here, as by its very nature the photograph is mute. These artists provide the trigger images that provoke curiosity and reverie. The words do not supply the image with an explanation, but add another discourse, equal to the others.

Spectator decipherment also depends on "reading" the mise-en-scène. There are moments when the scene as a whole, staging, characters, lighting, must share the weight of representing a meaning, which is diffused because it is too unspeakable or too excessive to be conveyed in words. This visual representation of meaning, blatantly constructed and non-naturalistic, is strongly invoked here with direct reference to Hollywood codes in Mitra Tabrizian's *Correct Distance* (1985–1986). Roland Barthes, approaching the visual representation of meaning from another vantage point, uses semiology to rediscover the diffused language of advertisements that now make a bridge between the codes of melodrama and the still photograph. In placing themselves under the aegis of melodrama and also overtly acknowledging the influence of Barthes, the artists in this group have combined references to strands of popular culture in a surprising and innovative manner. It is important, at this point, to remember that this stylization, diffusion of significance, reliance on mise-en-scène, and use of character is also the result of a collective revulsion against a concept of the photograph's natural essence. André Bazin states in *The Ontology of the Photographic Image* (1945):

> Photography affects us like a phenomenon in nature,
> like a flower or a snowflake, whose vegetable or
> earthly origins are an inseparable part of their
> beauty… The aesthetic qualities of photography are
> to be sought in its power to lay bare the realities…
> Only the impassive lens, stripping its object of all
> those ways of seeing it, those piled up preconcep-
> tions, that spiritual dust and grime with which my
> eyes have covered it, is able to present it in all its
> virginal purity to my attention and consequently to
> my love.

For this group, the photograph is a screen that blocks. It is
not a transparent screen that carries the imprint of "realities"
and maintains the belief that something truly lies beyond.
Following Mario Pernilo, Richon describes the theologies of
representation to give the argument context:

> For the iconophile, the image is a good appearance,
> which must reveal and translate a profound reality:
> God. St. Thomas Aquinas claimed that the respect
> paid to an image should equate the respect paid to
> the model. Against this, the iconoclast considers the
> image as a bad semblance that can only mask and
> distort the profound reality of God. Calvin condemned
> the use of icons because, among other things, they
> lessen our fear of the Divine, rendering his presence
> too familiar. Iconophiles and iconoclasts are obsessed
> with models, Origins, and fascinated by Deep
> Meanings. They are both asking: what is behind the
> image, what is the meaning behind it, what is the
> image's behind… What they will eventually find is
> precisely what they wish to disavow, that behind the
> veil of the surface there is nothing, the function of
> the veil being to hide nothingness: to put something
> in the place of nothing.

Fiction and fantasy undercut and replace authenticity.
These images do not represent the world but reveal the
symptoms of material repressed in the unconscious or
ideology. The realities represented here are enacted because
they are precisely not visible to the naked eye or lens. It is

these aesthetic considerations that generate the gesture to narrative that marks all these works. Pronouns imply characters and, in sequence, they then evoke a fictional world or diegetic space. These works do not in fact tell stories as such. They materialize cultural worlds, redolent of myth and social fantasy, that are opened up for the spectator's curiosity and desire.

Mitra Tabrizian, through generic lighting, mise-en-scène, and heightened gesture, evokes the codes, characters, and conventions of Hollywood film noir. This "world" is conjured up as the cinematic site of the femme fatale, who connotes woman as enigma, threatening active sexuality, and androgyny. In the movies, the story must, in the last resort, distance itself and close off identification with this figure who is doomed to an ending of failure and probable death. The still image, however, can generate identification and represent enigma without recourse to narrative closure. The *femme fatale* acts as a trigger image for individual fantasy, free-floating and trans-sex, activated by the narrative codes but not contained by them. The world of film noir is also another world, an underworld, closer to repressed, unspoken desires than genres based on a rigid system of masculine/feminine binary opposition. The evocative figure of the femme fatale has reappeared in contemporary advertising, which has recycled her independence and allure to appeal to modern women's fantasy of sexual and economic freedom. In deconstructing this "post-feminist" imagery, Tabrizian draws attention both to the roots of this particular glamour in the psychoanalytic sense—the magical attraction, for both sexes, displayed by the phallic or androgynous woman—and to the present formal traits in advertising photography: irony, intertextuality, and nostalgia.

Karen Knorr transforms the social, documentary reality of aristocratic high-life into a personified fantasy that suggests a world as remote and contained as a fiction. Codes, cultural tradition, gesture, objects, and settings are clearly enunciated in the milieu itself to define and distinguish a special elite status, and more significantly, a tradition. Tradition acquires visible, material presence in its chosen mise-en-scène, which fossilizes and represents the position as perpetually alive in the present. The *Gentlemen* series (1981–1983) emphasizes this double presence in its use of the club portrait as characters in their own right, and as framing context to the photographed portraits. *Country Life* (1983–1985), more obliquely than *Correct Distance*, also brings a narrative genre into play. The detective novel was born at the same time as photography, and is equally tied to obsession with material evidence as clues. In this series possessions are evidence of mastery, and clues to the nature of the masters. The spectator is drawn into observing behind the closed walls inhabited by a privileged elite, whose privilege is precisely maintained in isolation, the mark of real and actual political and economic ascendancy. At the same time, the photographs suggest a more immediate suspended narrative. Significant events may have just taken place. Once again, the spectator is offered a closed world for fantasy and curiosity.

Olivier Richon's "world" of the Orient is also closely tied to the origins of photography. The juxtaposition between 19th-century academic painting, then, and the photograph, now, depicts the relation between the two as a phantasmatically recreated myth. The moment when academic painting appeared stylistically as the precursor of photography is doubled with another point of mythic origin: that of Ancient Egypt and the Holy Land as the cradle of civilization. Richon traces 19th-century obsession with this "paradise lost," the pivotal point at which pre-cultural innocence turned into civilization. He then superimposes another "paradise lost," the pivotal point at which the last moment of illusionistic innocence was transformed by photography. A painting, existing as something unique in itself, marked the loss of the scene it represented. The photograph, available to endless reproduction, marks the loss of the painting's unique aura. The British Museum and the heroic (or anti-heroic) names invoked, conjure up another fantasy world: the means by which a myth of origins is narrated and perpetuated by preserving traces and relics from the past. As Champollion deciphered the hieroglyphics on the Rosetta Stone, and de Lesseps, as engineer, excavated the Suez Canal, Disraeli, the politician, absorbed both into the traditions of Western Civilization so that its descendents could move freely from the Museum into the Mother Country to travel back in time and tour the exotic Orient. There they could enjoy and witness a way of life that belonged to the Bible in all its innocence and beauty, another "paradise lost" to the advanced civilization of the industrial revolution.

Mark Lewis and Geoff Miles are both Canadians and have returned to live and work in their own country. They both use Canadian landscape and mythology as a frame of reference in their work, as a commonly recognized "pool" of aesthetic and theoretical source material for investigation and reverie. "Canada" here can be taken to provide the sphere, or diegetic "world" equivalent to those discussed above. (And, indeed, Miles' *The Trapper's Pleasure of the Text* juxtaposes the photographer's practice with the mythic origins of Canadian national identity, positing, in a manner similar to Richon, that the photograph has a close link with the birth of myth and the myth of birth.) But here the historical and cultural perspective is more immediate. The question of Canadian national identity is political in the most direct sense of the word, and it brings the political together with cultural and ideological issues immediately and inevitably. For the Canada delineated by multinationals, international finance, and US economic and political imperialism, national identity is a point of resistance, defining the border fortifications against exterior colonial penetration. Here nationalism can perform the political function familiar in Third World countries. For the Canada of different cultural groups with a rich range of tradition and diverse, but not necessarily contradictory, aspirations, this constructed national identity poses a threat to interior heterogeneity. Miles' series works as an indictment of the way in which Canadian national identity has actually been constructed as male, Anglo-Saxon, and committed to the principles of "free-trade" and private enterprise. He extends the argument, interweaving image and text, to an indictment of the compromised position of photography itself. Within this exposition of the social, sexual, and economic politics of photography, Miles examines the ancient tradition that once again generates a new mythology and conceals the workings of ideology: the nature/culture opposition. It is here that the Trapper becomes the pivotal point of the narrative and line of argument.

The Trapper image condenses the photographer's activity with that of the original white Canadian adventurer.

Both are out to capture the objects they stalk; both, then, retain remnants of the original, now lost to life; both act as the precursor to a complex system: the colonizing state and its representation of national identity in everyday life. The Trapper as metaphor also illuminates the indexical nature of photography that typically links (fossilized by the mechanical process of light hitting celluloid) the object to image. At the same time the metaphor ironizes and parodies the way that photographic aesthetics have apotheosized the decisive moment (the kill) and consequently the 'Trapper" himself as hero. Miles also comments on the psychoanalytic implications of this power relationship, so that the Trapper's prey is transformed, by the end of the series, into the sexualized image of woman. The quotations from Roland Barthes' *The Pleasure of the Text* (1973) place this work in a particular theoretical frame of reference. For Barthes, "myth" is the false construction of history that conceals contradiction, and photographic images, due to their innate plausibility, are ideally suited means to this end. Miles draws attention to this aspect of photography and ironizes its invisibility by this use of the nature/culture opposition, juxtaposing the theme of nature within culture with the photograph's own construction of nature through a cultural practice.

Mark Lewis uses the landscape and mythology as a terrain on which to project the hero's image and examine the particular construction of masculinity that this image evokes. There is a revealing parallel here with Tabrizian's work on the femme fatale. Just as she sees the masquerade of femininity as an image representing a desire for a strong female sexuality, Lewis sees the masquerade of masculinity as an image that represses the male body and its lived sexuality. The reference to the Amazons in one of the works in the series *Another Love Story* (1984), is an important clue to this perspective on the hero. Greek mythology is the origin of heroic myths and sagas, in which the hero of the myth is himself mythologized. At the same time, the Amazons as strong, wild women, represent what masculinity must repress but men nonetheless desire. Tabrizian conjures up that fantasy woman, using dramatic lighting to create the fictional scene of desire. Lewis, on the other hand, photographs the day-to-day currency of the masculine image, using a variety of models to bring out an emptiness that both evokes the fragility and vulnerability of the masculine masquerade and the hero's vulnerability to his own masochistic desire for death at the hands of, in the arms of, the phallic woman—a point of fantasy rebirth and regeneration for male sexuality. Both Tabrizian and Lewis are working with the sexual politics of representation in a new way, moving beyond a deconstruction of the active/ passive dichotomy, to envisaging a sexuality that is not posited on binary opposition but can risk the desire of androgyny. For Lewis, the hero depends on a certain landscape in which he can travel and adventure freely. The photographs document the persistent representation of the Canadian landscape within the Canadian cityscape, affirming a national heritage that actually lies beyond the reach of ordinary citizens. But the landscape triggers a series of mythological identifications, in which the wilderness comes to personify the feminine—a fantasy territory that the nation explores as hero, as masculine. The Canadian landscape invites reverie and the creation of stories and images in which the gap between ordinary life and adventure may be momentarily forgotten: the daydreamer becomes hero. By placing the hero's masculinity in crisis, Lewis challenges the dreamer's sexual politics and the Canadian's national identity.

Both Mark Lewis and Mitra Tabrizian started off as documentary photographers with a strong political commitment to realism. A shift in concern toward sexual politics, under the influence of feminism and psychoanalysis, has produced an equivalent shift in style and approach to the photographic image; the latter is now freed to convey an invisible reality, dream, myth, and fantasy. But there is an important difference between the two that illustrates the heterogeneity of the work in this group. Lewis, and Miles too, are photographing in their native city, deeply involved with the development and the problems of their own culture. Canadian culture is not yet a closed book. The historical anomalies that Canada has grown from make contradictions visible. Uniform national identity is challenged by a pride in heterogeneity and difference. It is significant that Lewis and Miles have returned to Canada from London. There is a strong contrast here with the other three members of the group, also ex-patriots in London, but still living and working there. Knorr is a US citizen who has never lived in her own country, but was brought up initially in Puerto Rico and then in Britain; Richon is Swiss; Tabrizian is Iranian. All three are in a state of crisis with their own national identity and cultural traditions.

Richon and Tabrizian come from "iconoclast" cultures. For both Calvinism and Islam, the image is a source of deep suspicion and repression. It is then fitting, perhaps, that Richon and Tabrizian represent the "iconophile" extreme of the group. Richon's use of lush color, characters, and sexual drama as an undertow running through images, takes him far from the austerity, ascetism, and commitment to "use value" that is the hallmark of Puritanism. For Tabrizian there is another dimension. Coming from a culture in which women's sexuality is massively repressed, she approaches feminist questions about sexuality and images of women from under the pall of Islam. So the image of female sexuality has strong connotations that are exhilarating and exciting, in contrast to those engendered by Western society in which the sexualized image of woman is the currency of oppression. Once again, there is a lushness and excess in the image itself, the material textures turned into light and shade. Arriving in London during the 1970s she could discover discourses—psychoanalysis and sexual politics of feminism—that made it possible to articulate these issues in a way that was precisely impossible in Iran. For British feminists, the question of women's oppression led straight to the question of representation. But for Tabrizian there is an underlying contradiction: in Iran, women's oppression occupies a different order of reality: "Here I work on the minute nuances of psychoanalytic theory, while in Iran prostitutes are executed."

For Richon, the journey to London was also an escape from his social and cultural origins. Switzerland lacks a coherent national identity, divided, as it is, between three languages and many dialects. Bourgeois life is consequently dedicated particularly to the coherent construction of a class identity through a highly regulated, repressed, and ritualized experience of everyday life. As a Francophone Swiss, Richon felt an enormous attraction to French culture that threatened to sweep up and overwhelm him. Moving to Britain at a point when French theory was at maximum influence, allowed a return to French culture by "a knight's move."

Karen Knorr came to London from the privileged no-man's land of international trade. In the United States, experience of national culture is very much an experience of daily life—the acquisition or rejection of current mythologies. An ex-patriot American may have little sense of "Americanness," but rather an unusual consciousness of hybrid immigrant origins (in Knorr's case: Norwegian, Russian, French, and Polish, in addition to which she grew up speaking German and Spanish rather than English) that are normally buried behind the invisible assumption of national identity. The experience of capitalism at first hand in Latin America and Europe also render American economic imperialism an unusual degree of visibility. Knorr chronicles a world in decay. Its stiffness and rigidity seem to try to hold this inevitable process in check. But it is also a man's world. Behind Knorr's portraits there is an underlying pleasure in role reversal, turning upside down a natural order of things so that the woman outsider acquires, through the act of photography, power over the powerful.

These comments on the cultural origins and national identities of the artists are not intended, by any means, to "explain" their work. There is, however, an important interface, often overlooked in recent art theory, between personal desire, chances or accidents of individual biography, and the forces of history that exert a powerful influence on someone's decision to become an artist and the kind of work that is then produced. There is also an element of curiosity. Why, as Thornton Wilder wondered in *The Bridge of San Luis Rey* (1927), did these five people end up linked together? The final dimension is provided, perhaps, by the aesthetic climate of Britain in the 1970s, in which refusal of cultural and national traditions and a pleasure in heterogeneity were the guiding principles of innovation and experiment. British culture was itself very much in crisis. The 1960s had seen a massive growth of interest in French theory (initiated by *The New Left Review*), both Marxist and psychoanalytic, and also in American popular culture, movies, and music. Both these were essentially antithetical to the "great tradition" of British culture, which was rejected as complacently chauvinistic in both the national and sexual senses of the word. It is to this movement, under the catalyst of feminism, that I owe my own starting point. There is an additional element of personal allegiance in my pleasure in writing about this exhibition. As a Canadian living and working in Britain, it allows me to make links between my two cultures and brings me face to face with my own fantasy of origins in the Canadian wilderness.

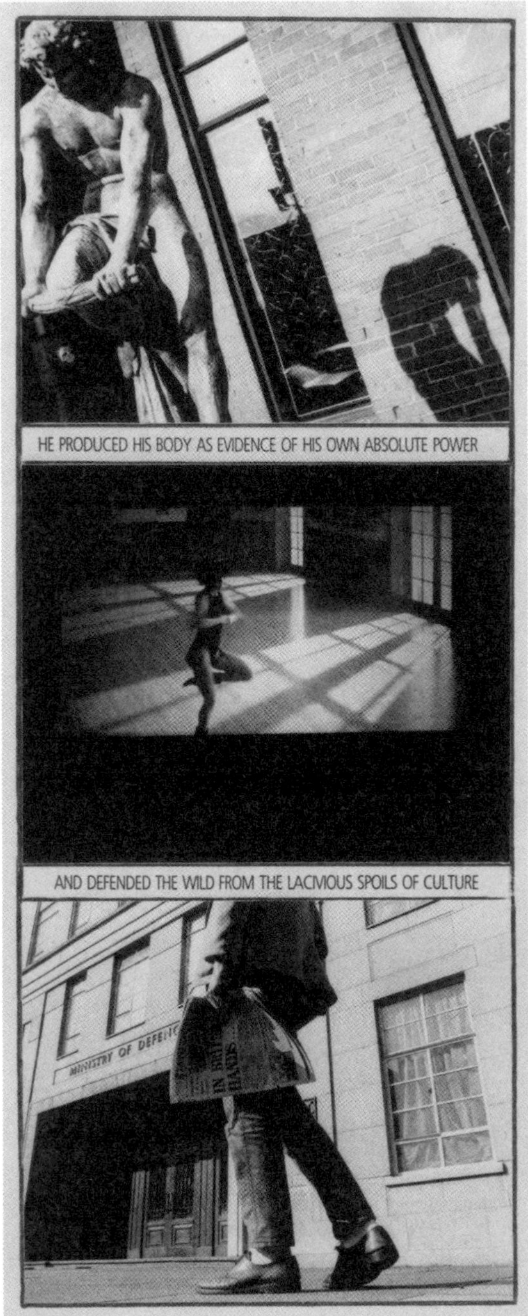

Mark Lewis, *Another Love Story*, 1984 (detail)

The Videos of Bill Viola:
A Space–Time Poetic
Anne-Marie Duguet

Parachute, no. 45, Winter 1986–1987
Translated from the French by Jeffrey Moore

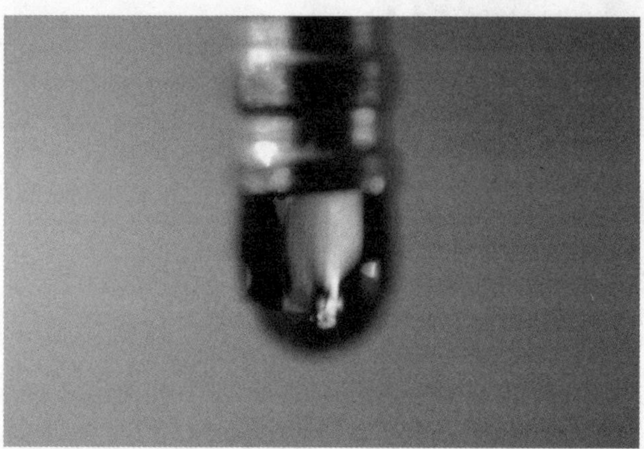

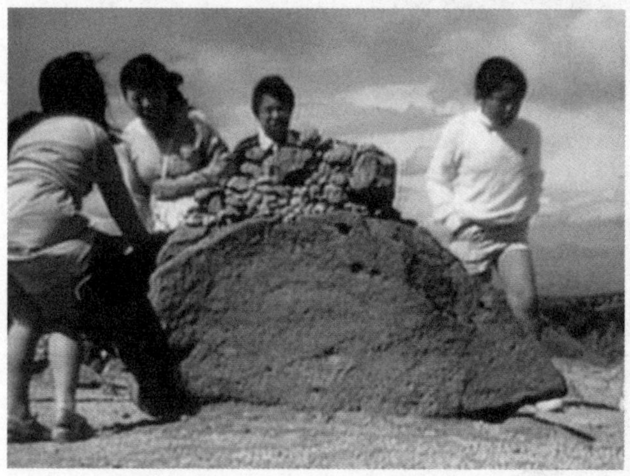

Bill Viola

He Weeps for You, 1976
Installation (detail)

Hatsu Yume (First Dream), 1981
Video, color, sound, 56'

Knowledge of the real is a ray
of light which somewhere always
leaves shadows.
—Gaston Bachelard

It is with the fluidity of water and
the speed of light that Bill Viola
composes his videos, like poetry or
music, but like a scientific experiment as well. A science of mirages
or aberrations of the real. For it
is the familiar world that is made
strange by Viola's electronic opera-
tions, but only marginally so,
forging just enough divergence to
impinge on consciousness and
emotion. Attempting to see a world
in a drop of water, he is experimenting in a realm beyond the
limits of human perception, beyond
the known, beyond appearances.
It is a search for the "implied order"
defined by physicist David Bohm: it
is not "the immediate reality we
are accustomed to studying, but an
order underlying this reality […]
an order that is completely hidden
from the eye of the observer."[1]

Thus, for Bill Viola, video is an instrument in the investigation of the real. He uses it with a systematicness and rigor proper to the scientific spirit, the latter described by Bachelard as the capacity to continually "specify, rectify, diversify."[2] From the beginning, in a series of brief fugues that explore the medium directly, we see the essential themes and concepts; these are later developed by fragments entering into new combinations, subjected to new principles of analysis, like the constant refinement of thought. Viola's works thereby become more complex and more metaphoric. Through such thematic retakes one thus believes he is continually recognizing what is no longer the same.

Experimental psychology and research in neurobiology inform Bill Viola's work, as does his interest in the theory of relativity and quantum physics. Without being a follower of any one school or religion, he also derives a large measure of inspiration from oriental philosophical traditions and various mystical approaches. His work, in fact, reflects the organic, dynamic concept of the universe that, through the opposition of the complementary poles of yin and yang, lies at the base of Chinese thought. It is this principle of contradiction that gives structure to Viola's oeuvre. We see a constant interaction of opposite forces: interior and exterior, physical and mental, movement and immobility, light and darkness, permanence and ephemerality… There is also a principle of circularity, each pole containing its opposite, the principal components of which are birth and death, day and night, along with the constant metamorphoses of things perceived through perpetual flux. Viola, who has also studied meditation in Japan, an exercise in consciousness which involves one's total being, physical and mental, uses his videos for solitary experiments which test his own sensorial limits. While personal experimentation is an integral element of consciousness, it is based essentially on the Taoist principle of observing nature through active contemplation. It is precisely the process of vision that is a recurring theme in Viola's videos.

Viola's conceptual framework is generic, dealing with biological or physical universals, exploring archetypical situations by means of such time-honored symbols as the mountain, the fish, the tree, water, and so on. His work is constructed without anecdotes or psychology, using instead elementary signs, metaphors, and a few enigmas. This is the sort of approach that Antonin Artaud saw and admired in Balinese theater, a kind of "primordial physicality," a "sign-language," "directly communicative."[3] Bill Viola's images have the force of myths. If they are outside verbal expression, it is because he is motivated in particular by an ontological and epistemological investigation of consciousness and the origins of language. "From the beginning I have been preoccupied by the same thing: keeping in touch with that part of me I call the 'part before speech,' that which is pre-discourse. The speech act comes after the thought— I am very much interested in this emergence of thought."[4]

The choice of video as medium is therefore not surprising. It is a system that generates energy more than material, and its operation does not necessarily end up being an inscription. Video can remain pure transmission, as immaterial and ephemeral as thought. Like thought, it exists only in time. So video would seem appropriate to demonstrate origins and mechanisms. "Thought is a process," explains Viola, "it's an energy, not a fixed thing. Thought is like music, it has to be unfolding to be a thought."[5] The term common to music, thought, and video, then, is time, the constituent element of each.

Bill Viola studied electronics, and collaborated on acoustic performances with David Tudor. He has also created acoustic installations. This certainly explains his move to video, and his mastery and understanding of technique. Viola compares learning the techniques of video with that of learning a musical instrument. Music is essential to his video composition. The image is worked out like a sound, particular attention being paid to its texture and various parameters; there are also elements of duration and rhythm, and the overall composition is comparable to a score involving several phonic layers and registers.[6]

Strategies for a Situation
____

Bill Viola's works do not tell a story. While they do involve people, places, and real acts, there is no plot and no causal connections. Very minimal, his works consist of rudimentary gestures: drinking, shouting, sitting, walking forward, waiting, watching… Most often there is nothing but landscapes or, on occasion, beings that mysteriously arise from nowhere. Nothing—or almost nothing—transpires. The "story" is instead composed of a number of perceptual adjustments, of adventures in matter and light, of metamorphoses of space-time. The event is inherent in the makeup of the visible and the audible, in the manifestation of time itself. No longer is it to be considered action, then, but rather situation: "a purely optical and acoustical situation," as Gilles Deleuze describes it in *L'image-Temps* (*The Time-Image*), "which arouses a kind of second sight."[7] The images do not transform into action, but interlock with other potential images, calling up memories or dreams. Viola speaks of landscapes as "the natural raw material of the human psyche."[8] His own landscapes are infinite like the sea or desert; they are horizons or nights from which anything might emerge.

"I install a situation," Viola explains. What he actually creates are the conditions for a particular experience, the system set up allowing the unfolding of the specific process. Here is an important characteristic of Viola's work: as in many experimental videos and films, an essential aim is to invent new uses for machines, new techniques or devices not used—or not exploited—in their normal functioning, and not corresponding to normal modes of reception. With respect to the entire operation of capturing and projecting image and sound, this novel utilization is both the concept and scenography of the works, a strategy as well as a specific ordering element. Everything, or almost everything, stems from this; it provides the particular dynamic of each tape or installation.

Insofar as the landscape itself may be the "subject of a work," the choice of site is crucial. Says Viola, "my travels have taught me that there was always just one 'right place' where an idea can come to life."[9] Likewise, the right moment must be seized, when the sun is rising over oil refineries or when the sea at night makes the red reflection of a boat's lanterns tremble … Viola constructs his images like a painter, arranging the colors within a generally fixed frame, exploring the vibratory quality of the dots, concentrating on contrasts and subtle variations of light.

Viola has formulated various strategies to go beyond the limits of human perception. One method, for example, is to fit the optical system with certain devices normally reserved for science, such as an 800 mm telephoto lens to penetrate the desert of *Chott-el-Djerid* (1979), or a macroscopic lens to frame the drop of water in *He Weeps for You* (1979). Or by exploiting natural phenomena such as the optical properties of water: reflections, refractions, disquieting transparencies… Water thus becomes a pure extension of the camera. "Exploring a situation through video, for a tape or an installation, always involves intervening in the image produced directly by the camera, a kind of preliminary installation."[10]

In every case there is also a very defined placement of the camera. In an image in *Hatsu Yume* (1981), for example, it is placed very close to the ground, taking a close-up of a rock, which looms up like a mountain until passersby are measured against it. The operation of the camera can be unsophisticated: installed at the end of a board suspended on a tree, it captures Bill Viola sitting at the other end. When this axis is made to move, the landscape passes behind the stationary subject, who appears to be rooted there (*The Semi-Circular Canals*, 1975). This movement, like that of the zoom, can also be controlled by a computer, as in *Ancient of Days* (1979). To capture a New York street, the camera has been fitted with a mechanical arm reminiscent of such contrivances as the "camera machine" invented by Michael Snow for *La Région centrale* (1971) and in the tradition of the "customized," often sophisticated, inventions complete with mirrors, motors, and multifarious mechanisms designed by the artists to increase one's perceptive capacities, to widen one's field of vision. Such was the intention of the cine-eye of Dziga Vertov: "I, Machine, show you the world as only I can see it… Henceforth, and forever, I am free of man's immobility."[11]

In this way, the performance can sometimes be that of the mechanism itself. There are no other "special effects" in Viola's videos apart from this basic preparation, the preliminary choices on which the quality of the work depends. The only "treatment" of the image takes place during the editing, through an intervention in time.

Visions

It is not so much a question of seeing more as it is seeing otherwise, showing vision and its complexity. In Viola's works, seeing is never a simple or stationary act. What is aimed at is accessible in the indirect way of the reflection, or subjected to various filters. Often one must look through, not at, plunging into the density of the image. Each time, the density, qualities, and movement of the mediatory elements render vision blurred or delicate. The vibrations of the warm air in the desert of Chott-el-Djerid contort the group of people passing through it like Giacomettian silhouettes, like specters. They also make the dwellings of the distant village tremble strangely, as if suspended in the air, giving them the appearance of a mirage that is precisely not a mirage. Vision here is to be understood as both a perceptual process and hallucination. From the perspective of Deleuze, "it is as if the real and the imaginary were running, one behind the other, each reflecting the other, around a point of indiscernibility,"[12] like the subjective and the objective, the physical and the mental. The effect of abstraction may sometimes prevent the identification of the real, as in the interplay of vivid, vibrant colors that is produced by the close-up of a fish in water (*Hatsu Yume*).

The role of light in the process of constructing and perceiving the image, the role of the persistence of retinal vision and that of memory, are analyzed in the dark room of *Decay Time* (1974). Here the sole source of light is an image projected directly onto a large screen. The video camera situated in the same space obviously cannot record anything in such darkness. At regular intervals, an intense flash illuminates the room, thus providing too much light for the sensitivity of the electronic tube and the proper projection of the image. The viewer is also blinded and, while readapting to the darkness, perceives the image only through his persistence of vision. It is only in progressive stages that he will discern and identify the image he has by memorizing the series of traces, of glimpses. Whatever the process may be, the notion of the subliminal image is very much present in all of Viola's works. One glimpses or half sees, one guesses more than sees, often with the impression of having missed something. Such imperceptible, or barely perceptible, presences are also a function of sound: when a Tokyo night scene fragment of *Haisu Yume* is played at a faster speed, the words and sounds that were inaudible in slow motion can now be heard.

It is the fragility of the image that Viola is illustrating in *Moving Stillness* (1979). A stationary shot of Mount Rainier is projected by three separate tubes of a color video projector onto a sheet of water. Their beams converge to form the image, which is then reflected onto a suspended screen. The existence and sharpness of the image therefore depend on the state of the water, which is easily agitated. A symbol of eternity and stability is thus used to make us feel the transitory. As one of the on-going paradoxes in the works of Bill Viola, the symbol aims at shifting the problematic of the image of the mountain to that of "the mountain as image," a potential image. "When I record a mountain it becomes very fragile as an image; it's like a thought, fragile as thought, but also as powerful."[13]

Seeing is also a question of concentration. In *Migration* and in the installation *He Weeps for You* (both 1976), Viola focuses our attention on a miniscule event. A live, two-fold amplification process is at work here: the sound of a drop of water falling on a tambourine is picked up by a microphone connected to an amplifier; a camera with a macroscopic lens is installed at the level where the drop of water is produced. When the viewer moves in front of the camera, their image is refracted by the drop of water, which acts as an extra lens. Projected onto a large screen, the image is reversed, distorted and transitory. The body is slowly elongated and then suddenly released as the drop falls. Along with the viewer, the surrounding space is captured by this novel "fish-eye" lens. Thus, the whole is present in the minute. It is the "correspondence between the microcosm and the macrocosm," explains Viola, "represented in theories of contemporary physics which describe how each particle of matter in space contains knowledge or information of the state of the entire system."[14]

Migration, through its meticulously constructed time frame, demonstrates the very process of vision adjustment; the amplification here is effected through gradual changes of scale. At the beginning, an abstract image turns out to be a close-up of an electronic screen. But it is not a screen per se; it is an image of a screen on a Trinitron monitor on which another camera is feeding an image of the scene shot from a distance. It is the adjustment of this double shot that allows the image to be focused and reveal a man sitting behind a table. These first few shots test our visual acuity, which is determined by the distance from the object and by the eye's resolving power. We are at once too close to the screen and too far from the scene. When the first camera finally approaches the scene to capture the man's face refracted in a drop of water, the object aimed at escapes. The circular structure here is clearly evident: at one extreme, an electronic problem of resolution, the image being drowned in the screen from which it has been constructed; at the other, an optical problem of reversal and instability.

The focusing device is not a simple forward zoom. The camera is moved forward along an axis; at each prescribed position there is a corresponding shot. The action is produced only by the editing, which connects the shots through dissolves. The discontinuity of each new position is thus bridged by the overlapping of one shot on the next. The transfer time is slow enough to reveal the transition itself.

Once Viola designates the image as surface, the product of a series of layers, he is engaging in perspectivist pursuits. On this trajectory toward the ephemeral vanishing point, namely, the drop of water, the camera shots are like "intersections," to borrow Alberti's term, of a visual pyramid. But although perspective is alluded to, there is no creation of illusionist space. There is no depth of field, but rather a movement of sight, a journey. And the axis of the destination point is a spiral that draws our vision toward the infinite.

Sensitizing Time

All of Bill Viola's works explore, through various images, this four-dimensional continuum that is space-time. Perception is not only a question of distance or visual acuity, it is also a question of speed and scale. Thus duration can be subjected to technical variations of fast and slow motion. The latter can often be extreme to the point of stasis, giving the video image the status of the photograph, or even to the point of total disintegration. At the end of *Vegetable Memory* (1978– 1980), the image of fish is slowed down 16 times. What emerges is the real time of the electronic screen, its continuous vibration as a process of reanimation, an action of life upon death. But a path is always given, not the path of slow motion, but the process thereof. *Science of the Heart* (1983) is composed of auditory and visual variations on a heart projected in close-up on a screen above a bed. From orgastic acceleration to final immobility, from love to death, the cycle repeats endlessly. Most often, these changes of rhythm act specifically upon the immobile. Time "in its pure state" will better manifest itself here since it will not be confused with movement. Viola slows down rocks and speeds up mountains. In that the camera is also stationary most of the time, markers exist within the frame itself, which allow even minute changes to be noticed. And time that escapes our immediate perception is made observable, like a day contracted into a minute. Whatever the timescale may be, Viola also proceeds by fragmenting duration, using a series of shots like chronophotographs. Through editing he restores their continuity in a new and entirely subjective duration. Sometimes it involves a complex procedure based on a concept of multiple and simultaneous time. The selections come from several series, as in the surprising zoom of a Tokyo street in *Ancient of Days*, composed of fragments from a computer-piloted zoom that are repeated six times at various moments, each time shown at a slower speed. From this combination of dual variations (relating to the rhythm and the moment of recording) there results a particularly strange temporal fabric. The structure of *Migration* also evinces this concept of parallel, subjacent times. Alternate selections in two pre-edited sources, composed of every second shot of the video trajectory, run simultaneously and are of the same duration as the tape.

Viola has made frequent use of live action in his early installations by means of electronic surveillance systems. Such works as *Quadrants* (1973) and *Bank Image Bank* (1974) have been conceived as "an extension and manipulation of a conventional closed-circuit video surveillance configuration,"[15] and play on both the architecture and institutional functioning of the site. Other works are more ironic and stigmatize certain stereotypes of live and pseudo-live (delay). *Mock Turtles* (1974), for example, has an eight-second delay in its images of sleeping turtles! In *Peep Hole* and *Trapped Moments* (both 1974) Viola sets a few critical and humorous traps in which the viewer's vision itself is involved. And yet Viola is not so much interested in the viewer's appropriation of his image (as explored systematically by Peter Campus) as in questioning his position in a space where his image is being fragmented or shown elsewhere, and only returns to him in a kind of reversed feedback. The confrontation of the viewer with his live image is the occasion for Viola to involve them not in the dual relationship proposed by the mirror, but rather in a "triangular relationship" into which the point of view of the camera intervenes. In the three installations of the *Olfaction* series (1974), this question is developed through the confrontation of the past with the live present. A performance by Viola has been prerecorded in the very site of the installation, with the same objects in the same place. This image, projected onto a large screen, is then mixed in equal proportions with the live image of the room and visitors, taken by the same camera in the same position. In this way, a disquieting coincidence in two spaces can occur—two different times co-existing. Viola explains: "What I wanted to do in making *Olfaction* was to continue to work with the idea of a reference to space, but to extend the process of reference to time. Making a tape in the same space that the viewer will later enter, establishes a strong reference to a specific location in the past. For the viewer then, your position is not just your physical position, but your physical position as related to time, a spatio-temporal position. That creates a triangle, but a triangle in four dimensions."[16] It is indeed a strange exercise in relativity for the viewer who enters the room and sees his body co-existing with another, of the same size, in a space where the other body is precisely absent. Or, sitting alone in an armchair, he finds himself on the screen keeping himself company. This fusion of present and past, which makes their temporal categories inascertainable, can only occur through a density reduction in each image. The ambiguity of co-existence is derived only from loss, and the present must be reduced to the spectral for the past to appear as present. It is this overlapping, this action of the two separate times on each other, that constitutes memory. The *Olfaction* series proceeds from an analysis of smell as an element of memory, and bases itself on the persistence and density of traces. Viola attempts here "a work that visually functioned the same way the sense of smell does … like a translation from smell to image."[17]

Journeys Through Black Rooms

Contemporary physics has demonstrated that no observation is objective, that the observer is inevitably involved in the observed object. In all of Viola's creations, the viewer is an essential element of the strategy employed. They are included directly in it, not so much when their own image is projected on the screen, as in the more subtle way they are summoned by the work, their activity solicited or their attention focused, the way they are invited not simply to enjoy an image, but to participate as well in its genesis and metamorphoses. The methods used in this involvement process are not the same for tapes and for installations, the latter existing in a three-dimensional space. Viola's installations not only offer the spectator a particular sensorial experience, they also involve them in an activity that is both physical and mental and that requires a certain availability. Invited to move about the room, devise their own itinerary and pace, the viewer builds their perception in progressive stages through a constant interplay of associations and references; it is like a personal edit based on elements proposed by the particular apparatus involved. With no imposed duration or point of view, the installation can only be grasped when the following conditions prevail: a multiplicity of positions, a mobility not only of vision but of the entire body, the freedom to come and go, adjustments in purely subjective temporality … It is generally an overlapping of bi-polar structures that the viewer must apprehend: when two sources of sound compete with each other or when two totally contradictory spaces are joined, it is impossible to grasp one without the other. The cell in the middle of the gallery in *Room for St. John of the Cross* (1983), for example, interferes constantly with the vast image of the mountain. In the two rooms of *Heaven and Hell* (1985), on the other hand, the contrasting spaces are completely separated

and take on meaning only in relation to each other, only in
their opposition.

Certain installations, however, establish special zones
of perception; not a point of view, but a position in which
the apparatus is clearly manifest. That is to say, a position
which allows one to experience most clearly the system's
opposition, or simply to participate more directly in the
apparatus force, feeding it with one's own image or synchronizing oneself with the other elements at play. It is situating
oneself along the axis of the camera and the drop of water
in *He Weeps for You* (1976) or sitting in the chair of *Reasons for
Knocking at an Empty House* (1983).

The basic materials of these projects are simple
and few: a dark room, a monitor or projected image, sound,
light, sometimes an architectural structure, objects, a
few elements of a symbolic nature or necessary for erecting
the system.

Since 1973 Viola has been working with large-scale
images using a video projector. This allows him to exploit
the relationships of contiguity or coincidence between
the body of the viewer and the body of the image, to amplify
a movement or show a minute detail. The large chaotic
image of the mountain in *Room for St. John of the Cross* thus
acquires a surprising destabilizing power. Moreover,
the projected image is free of the limitations of the framed
monitor; often suspended, it seems to float immaterially
like an idea. What is involved here very often are veritable
images/environments.

The auditory element has an essential role in the
production of such "psychoplastic" spaces in which all of
the viewer's senses are summoned. Sound is employed here
for its specific expressive qualities and explored in all its
registers: the vibration of a pure sound, the resonance of a
drop of water on a tambourine, a voice reading poetry,
the sound of breathing, the howling of the wind… Live or
prerecorded, these functions are similar to those of the
image: the amplification of sounds scarcely audible under
normal conditions, but especially the creation of distinct
acoustic spaces, or spaces that melt into a complex fabric
of sounds of different origins.

Since 1975, all of these installations have been dark
rooms in which the light from the electronic image is often

the only guide. Such a choice is no doubt partly technical, necessary for the projection of the image. But at the same time it conveys a break, a privileged place. Viola explains how gradually he "developed a desire to create a space that is separate from our normal situation."[18] The darkness obviously facilitates this by absorbing the architectural elements, by masking our familiar landmarks. At the same time, darkness is a powerful mythic element, whether it is associated with oblivion, death, or the unconscious. One speaks of the "night of time." "Night takes one back to the foundation, to the origin,"[19] says poet Henri Michaux. For Viola, it is an essential metaphor: "The rooms in the installations are black because this is the color of the inside of your head. So the real location of all my installations is the mind, it's not really the landscape, the physical land-scape."[20] Viola is not simply referring to the apparatus of camera obscura from which Leonardo da Vinci constructed a model of the eye. The camera obscura no longer enables us to comprehend the more complex process of vision relating to the brain's processing of information transmitted by the retina. The model employed will rather be the "black box" of cybernetics or the computer. Viola's black room is becoming more and more a mental space, where metaphors of memory, of the nervous system, of thought, are deployed…

Reasons for Knocking at an Empty House

Themes common to installations and tapes are often at play, as in *Reasons for Knocking at an Empty House*. This is suggested by the choice of the same title for the installation (1982) as for the tape (1983); it does not suggest that the tape is a comment on the installation.

Although Viola has not used the live concept since 1976, he produces in this installation a strange effect of live. In a vast black room, a wooden chair is placed before a monitor showing the image of a man, the artist, sitting motionless. Despite obvious fatigue, he strives to keep his eyes trained on the viewer. The scale is carefully calculated to correspond to the normal size of a man. Approximately every ten minutes, another person calls him to order by hitting him on the head with a magazine. This is what any visitor can observe on the screen; but if the visitor sits down and puts on the headphones suspended above the back of the chair, the face-to-face becomes a body-to-body. What is heard is a mixture of whispers and organic sounds (swallowing, breathing, yawning) picked up by tiny microphones placed in Viola's ears during the video recording. Each time he is hit by the magazine, the intimate sound continuity is abruptly interrupted. The sound of the slap triggers another recorded segment of very loud exterior sounds, which last a few seconds. The little shock sets off a loud clamor, in keeping with one of Viola's familiar paradoxical devices. This brief and violent sound is the only one heard by viewers not wearing headphones. The division between interior and exterior is thus accomplished by a strategy of sound; contrary to the other installations, the exclusion here is radical. But it is also through the intermediary of sound that the viewer enters into a more direct relationship with the video figure. This identification may go so far as an attempt to synchronize breathing with that of the artist or to check to see whether someone is sneaking up from behind with a magazine! The ambiguity of live action is maintained, since the recorded action is continuous and there is no editing. Thus Viola could perform the same experiment in an adjacent space.

Here the strategy is that of the inquisition. In the cave of the Chartreuse of Villeneuve-lès-Avignon, a light from high above as in a medieval dungeon illuminates a wooden chair, solid and coarse like a seat of torture. Putting on the headphones, moreover, practically immobilizes the head, as an orthopedic device would to ensure proper television consumption. Viola returns to the use of the monitor in this installation, for it is the elementary working of televisual control that is presented in this theater of persuasion, through the fixed hypnotic gaze. The viewer is also directed back toward his own gaze in a loop that connects two enclosures, one by sound, the other by images. Two solitudes confront each other in a mode that is often used in this work. "I'm making tapes for one person, not a person. There is no specific age group or country. It's the idea that each individual person contains a complete perception of reality, a personal world that I want to connect with directly."[21]

Such a desire can be understood by bearing in mind that at the base of all Viola's works is experience of an extremely personal kind. His performance in the tape is realized by remaining alone in an empty room for three days and three nights without sleeping, in the presence of a video camera. The work, Viola explains, is born "of the need I had to confront certain vital forces. This piece speaks of solitude, isolation, endurance, duration, life, and death."[22] A performance leading to total exhaustion, it is also rooted in mystical experience. (It was created in the same time period as *Room for St. John of the Cross.*) Shot in black and white with a video surveillance camera, these 20 minutes of extremely minimal action shot with a stationary camera call to mind the early video performances of Bruce Nauman or Vito Acconci. At first glance, this work may appear surprising inasmuch as Viola has now worked with color and sophisticated apparatus for a long time. It may appear as a kind of critical provocation, pointing to the abuse of special effects and syncopated editing in commercial videos. But it is also to provoke questions on the complexity of his apparatus. Far from being a simple return to the style of the 1970s, this tape demonstrates Viola's major issues and working principles. The duration is reconstructed in the editing into three cycles of days and nights in which time is manifested in this contraction itself. What is shown is the work of time on the wearying body, the variations of light, density, and direction in the shadows on the floor and walls, the contrasts between the shadow of the room and the lightness outside, or between the electric lighting inside and the nocturnal darkness outside… There are variations of sound as well: different traffic noises according to the hour, which contrast with the intimate sound of the room and Bill Viola (breathing, swallowing, etc.). The interior/exterior relationship here is not one of exclusion but one of overlaps, tensions.

Thus, the space is not totally closed nor the perfect isolation deliberate, like the choice of the hermit. The essential elements of the scenography are the signs of entry and exit: a door and two windows more or less open. The effect of enclosure is here more subtle, or at least more contemporary, than in the installation connoting mediaeval processes. We have moved to the model of the modern penitentiary inspired by Bentham's 18th-century Panopticon.

Michel Foucault describes how the essential element here is the fact that the prisoner knows he is being continually observed. The power resides with the observer. "The Panopticon serves to dissociate the see/seen dichotomy: in the outer ring, one is totally seen without ever seeing; in the central tower one sees everything without ever being seen."[23] This is the principle of today's video control. Through the surveillance devices installed in this work the camera is stationary and somewhat elevated and covers a large portion of the room and in particular the exits. The viewer is first of all called upon as an observer, whether they are voyeur, policeman, laboratory technician…

Viola's works are deeply rooted in experience, but only insofar as that experience allows the unfolding of metaphors. These metaphors—of the individual struggling against the social and political order, of tensions between interior vision and environment—demonstrate the essential role of thought in the construction of the real. It is the process by which the mind is continually building this universe it perceives and in which it is physically limited. The space of Viola's work is a mental one, conceptual, and it naturally leads him to the computer. A computer's memory does not record definite images, but rather data, which allows the creation of a multitude of images, of possible viewpoints on the same stage. The digital three-dimensional image is a potential image, but it is especially a stage. It takes on the status of an architectural structure that the viewer/visitor is invited to wander through, cross over, explore like a labyrinth. Through the experience of space-time that they propose, through the conception of representation that they signify, Viola's tapes and installations would seem to lay the foundations for a transition from the optical to the digital.

[1] David Bohm, "Physique et Philosophie," *Sciences et Symboles*, Colloque de Tsukuba, Albin Michel/France Culture, Paris 1986, p. 253 and 257.

[2] Gaston Bachelard, *The Formation of the Scientific Mind* (1938), Clinamen Press Ltd., Manchester 2002.

[3] Antonin Artaud, *The Theater and its Double* (1938), trans. Mary Caroline Richards, Grove Press, New York 1994.

[4] Bill Viola, interview with Eric de Moffarts, "La vidéo et l'image-temps," *Arte Factum*, November 1985/January 1986.

[5] Bill Viola, interview with Anne-Marie Duguet, April 27, 1986, unpublished.

[6] See Bill Viola, interview with Raymond Bellour, "La sculpture du temps," *Cahiers du Cinéma*, no. 379, January, 1986.

[7] Gilles Deleuze, *The Time-Image* (1985), University of Minnesota Press, Minneapolis 1989.

[8] *Bill Viola*, exh. cat., ARC Musée d'Art moderne de la Ville de Paris, Paris 1983, p. 26.

[9] Ibid.

[10] Bill Viola, interview with Dany Bloch, "Les vidéos paysages de Bill Viola," *Art Press*, no. 80, April 1984.

[11] Dziga Vertov, *Kino-Eye: The Writings of Dziga Vertov*, University of California Press, Berkeley, 1985.

[12] Gilles Deleuze, *The Time Image*.

[13] Bill Viola, interview with Anne-Marie Duguet.

[14] Quote from Bill Viola.

[15] Ibid.

[16] Interview with Anne-Marie Duguet.

[17] Ibid.

[18] Ibid.

[19] Henri Michaux, *Emergences/Resurgences* (1972), Skira, Geneva 2001.

[20] Interview with Anne-Marie Duguet.

[21] Ibid.

[22] Interview by Dany Bloch, "Les videos paysages de Bill Viola."

[23] Michel Foucault, *Discipline and Punish* (1975), trans. Alan Sheridan, Vintage Books, New York 1995.

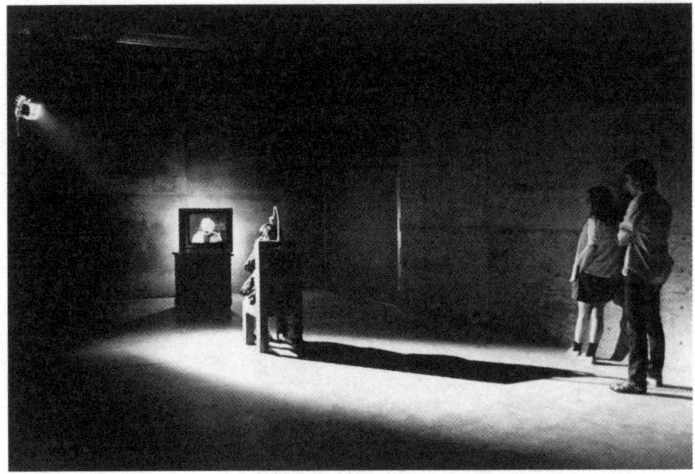

Bill Viola, *Reasons for Knocking at an Empty House*, 1982
Installation

Photopolis, Photo-Police:
Photography and the City
Guy Bellavance

Parachute, no. 68, Fall 1992
Translated from the French by Donald McGrath

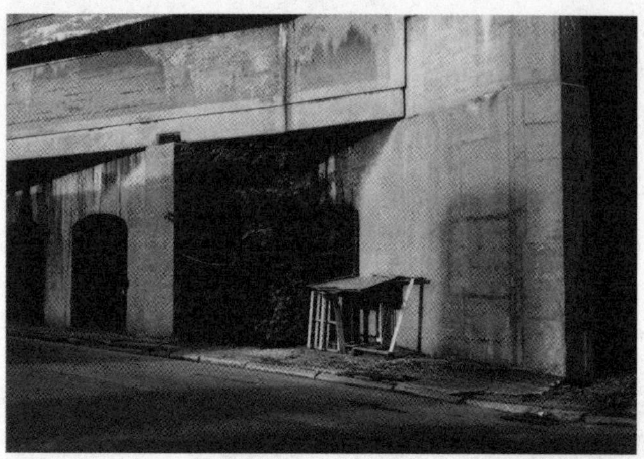

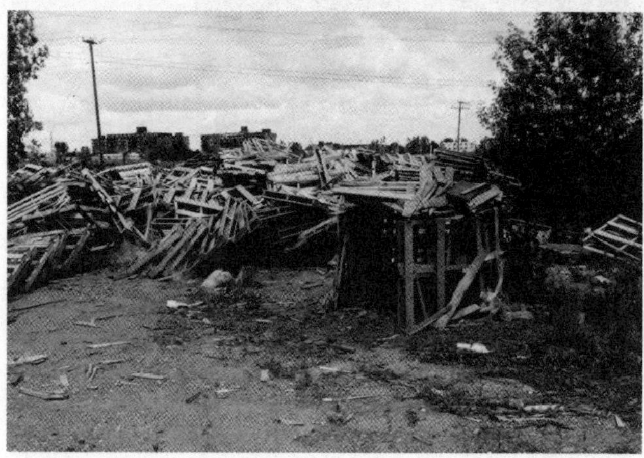

Tadashi Kawamata

Field Work in Montreal #11 (rue Smith, Vieux-Montréal), 1991
Black and white silver print, 71 × 100 cm

Field Work in Montreal #5 (boulevard Des Grandes-Prairies, Saint-Léonard), 1991
Black and white silver print, 71 × 100 cm

[I]n such a community it is easy for foreigners and resident aliens to usurp the rights of citizenship, for the excessive number of the population makes it not difficult to escape detection. It is clear therefore that the best limiting principle for a state is the largest expansion of the population, with a view to self-sufficiency that can well be taken in at one view.
—Aristotle, *Politics*, Book 7, 1326b, in *Aristotle in 23 Volumes, Vol. 21*, trans. H. Rackham, Harvard University Press, Cambridge, Massachusetts/William Heinemann Ltd., London 1944.

The city is first and foremost a place where something is happening. But what, exactly? It little matters, but whatever it is, is happening on many fronts at the same time. Here, the demographic factor takes precedence over all others, whether industrial, economic, political, or cultural. A "city" exists wherever an "agglomeration" can be said to be

populous, dense, and *heterogeneous* at one and the same time
(Louis Wirth). The more pronounced these characteristics
are, the larger the city will be said to be, and the more
accentuated will be the characteristics associated with urban
life. The demographic factor explains a good many attitudes
toward the city, particularly the mix of attraction and
repulsion it generates within the city itself: people seek out
crowds, desirous of gathering together in great numbers
within a relatively confined space (density); but these
gatherings also lead those who make up the crowd to
experience and accentuate their differences (heterogeneity).
The tendency toward standardization is thereby immediately countered by a more "eccentric" movement toward
individuation, distinction, and differentiation. In such a
context, the possibilities for encounters between strangers
are multiplied, with each individual potentially intruding
on some other. Large modern cities respond to this unique
situation by making "strangers" coexist daily within a
relatively limited territory (Georg Simmel). By doing so,
they give rise to specific forms of interaction, and
generalize a mentality that can be grasped in the figure
of the *stranger*.

Citizens, City Dwellers

The contemporary city dweller has little in common with
the classic citizen. From our current standpoint, the great
cities of antiquity were tiny towns. From the Greek era to
the dawn of modernity, the right to citizenship, which was
primarily the much sought-after freedom of the city, was
granted quite sparingly because, according to Aristotle, an
overly large population makes it "not difficult to escape
detection," and strangers could easily "usurp the rights of
citizenship." Their fraud, he says, would easily go unnoticed.
The main difference between today's cities and those of the
past resides in this new possibility offered to the individual
to easily avoid detection by the close-surveillance apparatus
of the *government or police*, this novel capacity to blend in with
the crowd, to disappear into its multifariousness. The new
modern city is no longer the Acropolis, Citadel, Enceinte, or
Fort that could be taken in with a single sweep of the gaze.
It is a sponge afloat in the national or global ocean: our

municipal governments have nothing in common with the Greek city-state or with any other *conspiracy* of citizens. The only power left to them consists in the management of social problems that essentially stem from supra-municipal, national, or transnational factors. These changes necessarily involve the establishment of very different surveillance systems. Professional police and volunteer detectives have replaced the citizen's army. The new police forces, which are far less political than that of the ancient *polis*, are more concerned with common criminality, ordinary deviance, and strangers within the city than they are with outside enemies. The current urban mentality corresponds less to that of the "good citizen" (in the Greek sense) than it does to the more eccentric, mobile, and destabilizing mentality of the stranger/urban dweller. Simmel's stranger is a synthetic figure: someone from the outside, hence distant, but located inside and thereby proximate, combining restless wandering with *the fact of being nonetheless established at a fixed point*. From his *proximity* and *distance*, he watches us, is watched and watches himself. The "city of strangers" is one where those who *arrived today will remain tomorrow*, but also one where those who have established themselves at fixed points *have not completely given up the freedom to come and go*. In this respect, the stranger is not so much a tourist passing through as a "potential traveler" and, also, a subject/object of surveil-lance. The "city of strangers" is an agglomeration of these "potential travelers," *fundamentally mobile* beings who must be prevented from colliding with one another. If the nerve center of the Greek city was the *agora*, the site of political debate, that of the large modern city is the intersection dominated by the traffic light, that main monument of the new fragmented public square. The main task of urban police forces will be, therefore, to ensure the smooth flow of traffic, a task distinguished once again from the more political and military function formerly exercised by a police intimately bound up with the State.

The more or less conscious sharing of this pervasive condition of being strangers to one another gives rise not so much to an "urban culture" as to a "mentality." Indeed, there remain very few organic, ancestral, or territorial links on the basis of which a common cultural content could be maintained; the strictly formal and profoundly disrupting knowledge of the initial situation is, on the contrary, what gets shared in the city, which itself results from this knowledge. This is what unites city dwellers: proximity within distance and distance within proximity constitute the mobile background of their social relationships. One result of this is the anonymity, impersonality, and superficiality of social relationships (urbanity): city dwellers are endowed with a capacity for reserve (or tact) stemming from a sort of right to mistrust (Simmel). But this is also the outcome of an *intensification of nervous stimulation*, a form of resistance specific to that continual erosion of convictions in which the ceaseless confrontations of strangers (with and among themselves) takes place. In such circumstances, one of the city dweller's main activities is to manage these spatial, social, and symbolic *proximities and distances*. Visual reference points and appeals take precedence over every other form of signal. And a city will be said to be that much bigger, and its situation that much more urban, insofar as the spatial proximity of symbolic distances is accentuated and the opportunities for *distancing* are *close*.

Urban Mentality, Photographic Mentality

There is a deep-seated affinity between the "city dweller mentality" and the "photographic mentality," if only because, here again, the term "mentality" must be preferred to that of "culture," and for the same reasons: the diversity and great number of uses of photography confer on it a unity of form rather than of content, a systemic unity. The emergence of this photographic mentality points, moreover, to a rupture in art history as brutal as that represented by the mentality of the city dweller in the political history of cities. The history of the photograph, a *fixed explosion* according to the Surrealists, is in more than one way in sync with that of the modern city, that "confused explosion," in the words of Robert Ezra Park, the founder of urban sociology—an explosion of events [*faits divers*], we might add. The photograph was not so much born in large modern cities as it was brought about by an even more profound affinity of mentalities.

As we know, Walter Benjamin made this *dialectic of proximity and distance* the basis of an analysis of photography that often sounds like an analysis of the city. Less is known, however, about what this same author owes (often *contra* Adorno) to Simmel's analyses of the metropolitan mentality: photography makes what is nearby distant, and what is distant closer. This corresponds word for word to Simmel's definition of the formal position of the stranger as a synthesis of distance and proximity. Atget's photographs, which guide Benjamin's analysis, are perceived as a compound of exotic gratuitousness and the tension of criminal inquiry, with the picturesque view tending continually toward the sites or scenes of crimes. And the "urban landscape" genre that developed out of photography is largely inscribed between these two reference points: the "sensationalist press" (as represented by *Photo-police*, a popular local weekly) and the tourist brochure or booklet (*photopolis*, to describe the Stendhalian vertigo, the exotic or cosmopolitan aspect of the city). These two markers represent the locus of professional photographic activity focused on the city, as well as the reading conventions that become unavoidable when it comes to interpreting "city photos": *photopolis*, *photo-police*; the photograph and the city thereby form a sort of narrative pact that cannot be broken at will.

Photography typifies the surveillance systems of the large modern city. A miniaturized and portable *panopticon*, it automatically becomes a form of police technology. Its first steps are indistinguishable from the birth of the crime novel: "the original social content of the detective story was the obliteration of the individual's traces in the big-city crowd," wrote Benjamin, who, in the same breath, read Atget's "crime scenes" as an invitation to gather clues to this obliteration. Emerging from this *jumble of virtual clues* represented by the large modern city, it is in phase with that other instance of effacement—that of the classic citizen, political in the full sense of the term, who has been superseded by the contemporary city dweller, a cross between a police officer and a delinquent. The contemporary city dweller is a stranger, hence a potential deviant, eccentric, or unstable character who is forced, nonetheless—given the customary proximity of other eccentrics and forms of eccentricity different from his own—to distance himself or, on the other hand, to abolish distance (social, cultural, etc.) using techniques of *rapprochement*.

If the figure of Atget is part of the legend, then the later figure of Usher Fellig, aka Weegee, also plays a role in the plot. A specialist of bloody *faits divers* (over 5,000 murders over the course of his career), but also a detective and a publicist of urban eccentricity and its polymorphous deviants, he is thereby at the source of works like those of Arbus. Between Atget, the primitive, documentary-making *paysan de Paris*, and Weegee, the immigrant *become* professional photojournalist, the distance can initially seem impassable. It is as if the figure who used to blend in slowly with the late-19th-century crowd had since picked up speed. While Atget recorded exclusively a sort of urban flora in architecture, Weegee studied the fauna, i.e. the inhabitants. The old deserted Paris of the naturalist/landscapist Atget forms a sharp contrast with Weegee's city of characters and actors, one in which Usher himself, having become Weegee, plays a role that takes him center stage. His trajectory, unlike Atget's, describes, therefore, a form of social climbing, that of the immigrant nonentity who becomes someone—but remains, nonetheless, too suspect to be a truly eminent figure, a "personality" in the full sense of the term. His legend reads in fact like a series of changes of identity, or a path among multiple identities. Usher Fellig (Zellig?) becomes first of all Alfred, thanks to the ministrations of an immigration officer, then Weegee (this time owing to the police). He lives permanently in his car, scooting from one tragic turn to another, and for some indeterminate time his only known address is at police headquarters, in the missing persons section. Both Atget and Weegee match the description of the man of the crowd, a mix of cop and criminal, a tourist from within who has haunted the city since the days (or nights) of Edgar Allan Poe. Both strangers, one expelled from his city and the other thrown into a city of strangers, they use their photographs for the same destabilizing purpose, injecting an element of the strange and the asocial into group life.

The three photographic experiments that constitute the subject of this article, which are undoubtedly more contemporary and very different from one another, nonetheless share the quality of being drawn to, or attracted by, the city. Each in its own way updates what we have just said. One, which is strictly speaking documentary in form, refers explicitly to Atget. Another incorporates the photograph into a very subtle installation process, in tandem with ironic commentary on public sculpture in urban space. Meanwhile the third, produced in color, is akin to a work of scholarly reconstruction, referring in more than one respect to the tradition of photojournalism. All three pick up the thread of that same narrative pact that drives individuals to make photographs and makes room for their utterances. And each in its own way records things that are generally *seen but unnoticed*, as a detective might put it—or an ethnomethodologist like [Harold] Garfinkel, in relation to social norms of interaction.

Agglomeration, Depopulation

Atget's images pave the way for that movement (salutary according to Benjamin) *in which human beings and the world around them become strangers to one other*. Thomas Struth's photographs inevitably remind us of this lesson. From this perspective they evoke the same sites and scenes of crime. Some of them, moreover, deliberately repeat Atget's point of view—but with a greater degree of abstraction, as it were, and less of the "picturesque"—as if Atget's images were to become more abstract. As we know, Atget stated that he wanted to document "*everything* in Paris that presented a *picturesque* and *artistic* side." This was undoubtedly only a final invocation to ward off the moment of separation/effacement that was really at work in his images. It also marked the involuntary feature of an undertaking whose chief advantage or flaw (depending on who you spoke to) resided precisely in the ability to bypass reality, however picturesque it might be. In Struth's work the collection of evidence is certainly less involuntary and more acknowledged and informed, with all things picturesque set aside. We are dealing here with the standard type of the city, a pure artefact perceived unlovingly by the (almost inhuman) gaze of the average man, with cities that are neither very rich nor very poor, run-down in places but mainly out of touch, given the general absence of inhabitants. And we are dealing, too, with a general figure of agglomeration, one both architectural and universal, involving repeated aggregates of intersections, city blocks, and windows, a sort of inert body on which certain inhabitants move about by accident, but only in order, it seems, to indicate the scale. Thus we are led initially, as in Atget's work, to seek in the image not what is there, but what is not… to have the true experience of the city in the full sense of the term. First we notice the lack of inhabitants, then the absence of events: Who lives here? How do they function? The "they" here refers inexorably to the native "us," yet each building appears as a more general figure of the city itself. Seeking the form of the city as an "agglomeration," each image manages to represent that universal movement of agglutination through which cities are constituted, short of their inhabitants. Pursuing a singular and strictly architectural totality, the only part of Atget's approach that Struth retains is the desire for a *total record*, without any promise of an additional hedonist bonus. From this angle, his images are more like those of August Sander or, more recently, the Bechers. Typological to the core, clinical, with a focal width that allows us to search out the tiniest detail in the inmost depths of the image, they have a utopic and literally *panoptical* quality that was foreign, or dimly present and latent, in Atget. Utopic in nature, the panoptical dimension involves, among other things, a view of the city that is less strictly "circumstantial"—by a long shot—than that of a crime scene. The city is then no longer simply a backdrop, for it too seems to be under close surveillance. Whose fault is this? Can we attribute it only to architects and architecture? Is it not also to some small extent that of the photographer and photography? As used by Struth, the photograph questions the place of the observer and the absence of the photographer as much as it does a type of architecture. Where then do we find that central tower from which Bentham's observer could keep watch over his captives? Stationary in Bentham, but made mobile by photography, it advances here toward other towers, maintaining, at the same time, that other panoptical property of transforming the surrounding environment into an enclosure complete with the foliage of facades, and hemming in the watcher as much as it exhibits the captive.

For Struth, each new image is undoubtedly another opportunity to repeat a largely universal type of functional differentiation of the city, with deliberate depopulation leading to a view of the city as more of a natural than a social phenomenon. Instead of the regularity of architects' drawings, we see functional clusters and knots of intersections proceeding, like certain crystals, from impersonal processes that form rather singular constellations, which are disordered and never identical. The process of functional differentiation to which cities have been submitted is therefore not consistent with strict standardization, but with continually repeated and always partially overflowing movement. One can henceforth be amazed at the fundamentally serial character of urban differentiation—just as, despite everything perhaps, we can also be struck by diversity's resistance to serialization: the serial is the road on which diversity now travels.

Refuse, Projectiles, Statues

Would [Tadashi] Kawamata's *Field Works* exist without the photographs that record, commemorate, and thereby publicize them? In any case, they highlight an act that might otherwise have gone unnoticed due to the secrecy required by the miniaturist urban guerrilla warfare recorded here, and to these unexpected assemblages' relative lack of distinctiveness when set against the backdrop of their environments. In short, they remain an integral part of a highly personal and almost intimate act performed by the artist on the city, on the body "peculiar to" the city, its "foreign" bodies," "warts and all," i.e. its refuse, garbage. Attesting to a repeat offence, where curiosity always wins out over culpability, they are undoubtedly the only proof that the act was indeed committed, and committed repeatedly. But they steer or conduct us in a more playful manner from one city to another, and into various corners of the same city, making use of a sort of puzzling invocation of the "shabbiness" and the "cleanliness." Quite often these assemblages evoke someone's passage, an arrival or departure, recalling that figure of the *potential traveler* without any fixed address. The act of assembling diverse materials in the city, and of verifying their precarious and transitory result, lends itself to multiple readings. A highly specific field of constraints and associations appears, one in which the various prohibitions regarding cleanliness combine with those targeting property—just as the condemnation of the poor blends in with the condemnation of immaturity, instability, and vulnerability. For the *Field Works* are primarily a successful experiment about tolerance of, and in, the urban environment.

Punctuating the periodic completion of works officially commissioned or, in any case, asked for, and introducing a figurative element (the temporary shelter) generally absent from more abstract pieces in the same series, the *Field Works* are also more dispersed. The difference does not stem, however, from the *more* temporary nature of the construction or from the inevitably *more* explicit nature of the figurative element, or the dispersal involved. Rather, it derives primarily from the fact of authorizing oneself to intervene "without waiting for an invitation." The fleeting nature of the act, with its explicitly figurative element and scattered quality, does not mark a break with the other type of intervention; it represents, rather, a difference of degree—of tolerance that is, which affects that of the materials as well as that of the meaning that can be applied to them. On the one hand, the great public commissions are hardly more precarious and temporary: from this perspective, the *field works* appear finally to be only more clearly subject to the vagaries of the environment, barely surviving there for a shorter period. On the other hand, the irruption of a figurative element, although more legible, remains barely explicit and is more likely to mislead: depending on the mood, opinion, and context, one sees by turns the shack of the homeless person or one built by children, a more stupidly haphazard pile of rubbish. The object appears to attract rather than give off meaning. It is cluttering up the eyes. And it is the type of congestion that calls upon the police to clear the streets and get people moving. By acting in this way, Kawamata pushes a little further ahead, or shifts by a hair's breath, that which is also at work in the great public commissions. From this standpoint, *Field Works* partakes of the same associative process, one whose main terms and phases proceed by way of the three successive states of *rubbish*, *projectiles*, and *statues*: scrap converted to a projectile, temporarily stabilized in the form of a shack; a haphazard assembly subjected to the urban field; a spit sent flying against a wall; material collected in a crack; an act/statue invoking by turns the dignity of the poor, the vulnerability of child's play in big cities, and that permanent movement of assembly and disassembly that constitutes cities from one day to the next. Depending on one's mood, social position, and time or place in life, one will be attentive to one or more of these phases. The duration of the work will depend entirely on the natural and social reactions coming from the urban surroundings, as will its meaning. In this sense, the *Field Works* not only punctuate more serious works, but explain their approach. And they can even have a pedagogical function.

To ask oneself, in such a context, whether such images (or actions) are offensive or inoffensive would be to make something of the same mistake. For the artist's motivations are not very clear in themselves: "What on earth is this will of mine that wants to make such *lumps* every-where in towns?" The allusion to eyesores, to warts, those more or less intimate excrescences on the body, does provide a clue however. Depending on one's attitude, one will put up with them, expect them to disappear, or have them removed. In this respect, interventions directed at the city proceed by way of the greatest intimacy, and the feeling of cleanliness [*propreté*] will likewise appear hopelessly bound up with that of property [*propriété*]: the very body of the city. The work associates and blends together, in one and same movement, poverty (that of materials and of the homeless) and vulnerability (of childhood, communication, art, and the statue). The most troubling element in the evocation of the *very poor*, particularly those with no fixed address, is first and foremost that same state of vulnerability/immaturity that makes them akin to the *very little*: poor people are little, immature, vulnerable; the city has grown up around them; each of their little shacks, appearing here and there, create so many fragile intersections where, like two unstable people, the "very poor" and the "very little" encounter one another; the deliberate multiplication of these "downfalls" can even resonate like an appeal (one that is, at times, "Christlike") to the *dignity of the poor*, an invocation that simultaneously relies on the vitality of the child and the unpredictability of the cyst's appearance on the body.

Eviction

Most of Jeff Wall's works, and maybe everything he has made so far, draw deliberately on an experience of the city as a place policed. They are also carefully planned and erudite, simultaneously incorporating elements of scholarly and popular culture, art, photography, film (or telefilms), and even advertising. "Scripted" and even cast, they oscillate between documentary fiction and dramatic documentary. They also speak to us of a selective memory, whether modern or postmodern. From all these angles, *Eviction Struggle* (1988) is a particularly strong image, a postmodern icon. Eviction is certainly a very hot topic in day-to-day policing, one parceled out here among the interlocking gazes of the neighbors/watchers in attendance. Wall has always paid attention to the direction of the gaze. His image compresses, in a highly synthetic and dramatic manner, various forms of representation. Is what we are seeing an overhead shot taken from a police helicopter (Weegee), or a subtle reference to Bruegel's *Landscape with the Fall of Icarus* (c. 1560s)? Also mixed in are a suburban version of Manet's *Déjeuner sur l'herbe* (1862–1863) and an *execution of a Maximilian* kicked out of his *bungalow*—in short, the nightmare of the indebted suburbanite evoking the compositions of Manet, that painter of modern life, as much as it does the pictures of suburbs formerly explored by [William] Eggleston and [Lewis] Baltz (Maryland), Garry Winogrand's public interactions in airports, and the New York intersections of Joel Meyerowitz's first pieces. The series of images that Wall has produced in recent years are, in effect, synthetic products by virtue of their polychrome raw material and their polysemic references.

The city is presented as an event, a *fait divers* or micro-event set in motion by the encounters of people and objects, buildings and furniture, architectural elements and urban segments. Photographers tend to treat such animate and inanimate aspects separately, as any survey of "urban landscape" photographs will attest. It is technically very difficult indeed to capture, at one and the same time, the city as monument and the city as event, its architecture and its inhabitants. Another of Wall's concerns consists in compressing these two types of views into the same image.

He achieves this through staging that blends these two orientations between which photographers have generally had to choose. The interactions, or better still, the intersections of his characters and objects, can then lend themselves more readily to an "interactionist" type of analysis than to (let's say) a Marxist one: very quickly then, this last interpretation can be valid only for the specifically institutional aspect of the works, where it is a question of knowing, for example, what happens when the photograph enters a museum, or when painting goes into the photograph; it applies only in a secondary manner to the images themselves, to what the positioning of objects and the staging of subjects generates.

What happens when this or that object encounters this or that subject or character? How do these encounters of objects and subjects produce *events*? Most of the pictures, or at any rate the most interesting ones, are first and foremost photographs of events, turning points in a story. The meaning of such events is not always so clear, since the situation is always on the point of spilling over, like the drop that causes the vase to overflow. "Strangers"—animate creatures, but also sometimes inanimate things as well (a glass of milk that breaks, for example)—are about to collide. These images experiment with the dramatic workings that tend to accompany modes of vision and communication in an "urban framework," in a sort of Goffmanian "frame" where the positions of objects are just as important as those of subjects, and where strangers continue to intersect— checking out ways of moving about, of encountering, avoiding, ignoring, and confronting one another, of managing the proximities as much as the distances brought about by city life. Confrontation is not more current than avoidance. The intersection is the dominant feature and, at it, one sometimes sees expressions of violence or despair, but they are merely figures among other figures, like passers-by. Light is shed at this point on another aspect of urban life, namely, that it leads not so much to individual anonymity as it does to a heightened sense of the self, which is not the ego. So we are dealing, then, more with characters than with persons, although in Wall's work the person is often on the point of being extracted or expelled from the character through the interplay of differences between self and self.

Stan Douglas: *Evening* and Others
Peggy Gale

Parachute, no. 79, Summer 1995

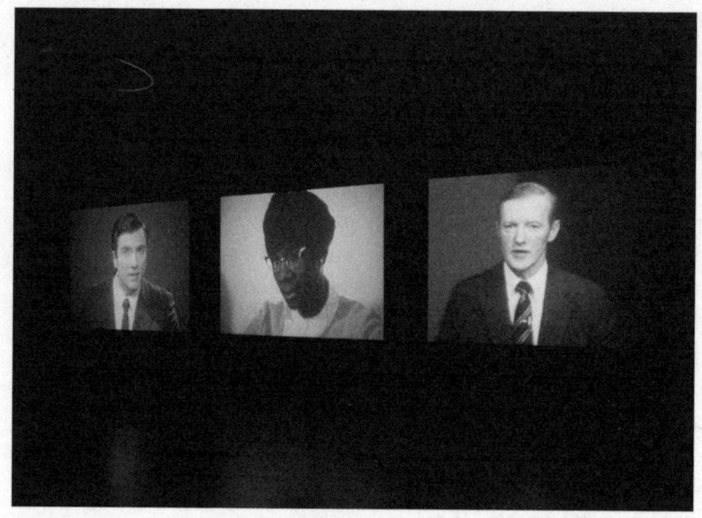

Stan Douglas, *Evening*, 1994
Installation view

Stan Douglas works on a public
stage, tuned to the world he sees:
political, historical, intellectual.
There is work to be done with the
out there.

Evening, of 1994, is a three-
channel video installation work, a
fiction aimed at fact for a moment
of change in contemporary history.
Just like television news, its
apparent referent, the subtexts are
numerous and complex. For what
is more contentious than the fact
quotient of television news today?
At best, those few minutes allotted
to a nightly overview of world
developments are fragmentary and
the choices subjective, a brief
installment assuming or counting
on supplementary (unspoken)
previous information for filling
in the larger issues. Viewers
have become cynical these days,
conscious of the slide toward
infotainment and stations' reliance
on simply *believable* news-anchor
personalities.

It used to seem that The News was just a matter of information, a public service, the newscaster's formal reading manner denoting dispassionate, balanced consideration on the part of someone who had access to the whole story. Listening to the news was presumed to be a duty rather than a pleasure. Is this opinion today simply naive? We are now more often aware of formula in both form and content for news presentations. As in the newspapers, there are a few striking headlines with the important facts bunched together in the opening paragraphs, with a seemingly random collection of filler stories and notes further along, leading to sections devoted to sports, weather, market reports, advertisement. It all feels far more like business than any sort of public service. Different television stations—like different newspaper chains—are known for their greater interest in violence, their more generous use of photographs, or their preference for the local rather than a larger arena. But all are selling their newscasts, aiming to appeal to a public with choices to make.

In 1993 The Renaissance Society at the University of Chicago invited Douglas to create a new piece for his upcoming solo exhibition. Ideal. It was an opportunity to relate to events specific to Chicago and to media issues and history. In a preliminary visit for researching recent broadcast vernaculars and editorial policies in Chicago, Douglas came to focus on a unique moment which he saw as two "related crises in the legitimation of television news"[1]: the controversies surrounding the Democratic National Convention in August 1968, and the killing of local Black Panther Party leader Fred Hampton in December the following year. While up until this time newscasters had been considered objective "readers" or "reporters," now they were accused of (and even rather proud of) actually making the news, through their choice of events for highlighting and through (biased) construction, explanation, and presentation. Immediate viewer perception and response as well as the development of subsequent "newsworthy" events were all being influenced. The Convention, demonstrators, and the police, Mayor Daley, Abbie Hoffman, and the Yippies, Students for a Democratic Society (sDs), the Black Panthers —along with May 1968 in Paris, the first manned Moon landing of 1969—there was plenty of "news" at the time.

Television news is rightly seen as a portrait in miniature of contemporary social and political concerns, a checklist of influences and changes in an anxious environment. Printed newspapers—the major information vehicles from the 19th century through the 1940s—have tended since World War II to be supplanted by spoken news reports: hourly radio updates and, more recently, "all-news" stations on both radio and TV. Nevertheless, an evening news wrap-up retains its appeal as predictable, familiar, comfortable: an overview made by experts of what is "important," all you need to know. So the news mirrors a larger social reality.

All of this had been noticed by others, previously. Compare *The Last 10 Minutes* by Antonio Muntadas, premiered at documenta 6 (Kassel, 1977) where taped recordings of the final minutes of one day's television broadcast and sign-off in Moscow, Kassel, and Washington were screened simultaneously on three adjacent TV sets. Taking place in the post-Nixon period, and with Kassel (so near the DDR border) as a geographic bridge, *The Last 10 Minutes* offered both comparison and classic confrontation of capitalist and Communist, West and East. Muntadas presented the off-air footage with no further comment, confident that the difference between the three was evident, and its significance understood: a direct relationship and interplay between art and life, art and politics, and of psychology, sociology, and anthropology.[2]

For Stan Douglas' *Evening*, selections of actual news items from 1968 and 1969 in Chicago were compiled and rewritten for three invented broadcasts of 15 minutes each, as if presented on the local feeds of NBC, ABC, and CBS respectively. As significant as the content—still important today—is the presentation. To a notable degree and despite the intervening generation, its style seems familiar, and totally convincing.

A condensed and instructive comparison of changing television styles may be found in *Political Advertisements* (1988), a videotape by Muntadas in collaboration with Marshall Reese, in which actual promotional spots were collected from campaigns for the American Presidency from 1956 to 1988 and simply presented without comment, in chronological order. While Eisenhower in the mid-1950s seems predictably stiff and earnest in the still-new medium, one is surprised that John F. Kennedy's ads from 1960 also seem old-fashioned from today's vantage point. It is obvious that the poised speakers are often reading from cue cards just off camera, with only a few campaign-trail inserts giving a flavor of excitement. By 1968, already, many more changes are evident, with man-in-the-street opinions incorporated into testimonials for Hubert Humphrey, and reference to violent crime for women walking alone at night turning up in slogans for Richard Nixon. Just a few years earlier such "news" references would have been considered inappropriate, irrelevant to the high politics of a presidential campaign. By 1976 we find such euphoria as, "There's a change that's come over America" with Gerald Ford, "America is smiling again!" And in 1988 George Bush talks of "a thousand points of light" and "a kinder, gentler nation" to swelling music, while fireworks explode spectacularly over the convention center. By the late 1980s, *selling* was the only plan: a visible and significant shift over 25 years. Muntadas and Douglas are both active observers. An important difference is that Muntadas, dealing with the literal and the *present* tense in his news/information interventions, shows a certain didactic quality in his comments. Douglas, looking to the past, makes use of hindsight in his reconstructions. Bracketed by acting and script development, the issues become "storied" no matter how relevant to the present moment. His view is more constructed and dynamic, and more distanced.

In retrospect we can see 1968 as a watershed for television news. Color was being established as the new broadcast norm, and there was a new colloquialism in manner, a personalizing of appeal to viewers. Vocabulary and phrasing still followed the print media's somewhat formalized usage, but more than one race and sex appeared (were represented) on screen, and newly-introduced "human-interest" stories were calculated into the equation. What are these still-awkward diversions, and what is their purpose? What's the relationship of on-site reporter and desk-bound announcer, the banter between double-anchors appearing at this point for the first time?

In a project for "Local television news program analysis for public access cable television" proposed to the Nova Scotia College of Art and Design in 1978, Dan Graham isolated this "happy talk" as a fictional matrix in which "the 'news team' is like a family at ease in a domestic setting." As he pointed out:

> The time at which the "happy news" is scheduled, corresponds to the time between work and relaxation in the family house before dinner; it is a transition between the outside world and the "inner" world of private self-indulgence. As it is when the workers in the family come home from work, it serves as a transition period from the frame of public to that of domestic space. Like the cocktail "happy hour," it has the socially important function of ritualizing the passage from public sphere to private sphere.[3]

Graham's proposal for this analysis of television news is overtly instructional. On a cable channel for the four following days, Monday's newscast would be examined during the time slot of the regular broadcast news; the programs would be divided into sections dealing with home reception, studio production, and formal elements of the program itself, achieved through replay and verbal/visual comparison of behind-the-scenes or invisible-to-camera sources.

Graham and Douglas are both concerned with the forces of social intervention and manipulation as revealed by television news formats. But Stan Douglas has employed a *quasi-fictional reconstruction* of reality; content is as important as form. Evening is an active statement and implied commentary, a bringing into focus and study in comprehension, rather than an actual intervention or quotation. It evokes and reveals, rather than shows or tells.

Evening was completed in 1994, a work written by Douglas for performance by actors playing five reporters and six anchors (one of whom had once been an actual newscaster) for three television stations. In *Evening*, the three stations begin simultaneously with "Good evening," then launch their shows in counterpoint; each presents the news for January 1, 1969, then, beginning simultaneously again, the first broadcast for January 1970. One is slightly shocked to see the card insert, "PLACE AD HERE:" appear during each presentation—a blunt reminder that The News sells products (delivers an audience) as much as hockey games and movies.

The personality of the three stations is revealed in their choice of news items and style of presentation; Douglas has differentiated them with background studio colors of blue, red, or green. The blue ABC station, "WCSL" is "Your Good News Station" with James Devereli and Dennis Cameron; by the following year, Cameron had been replaced by James Mooney. The green CBS begins simply with "This is Channel 6, WBMB Evening News," and the following year a title card spelling out the top stories precedes this curt opener; announcer Finton O'Neil is solo anchor and, unlike the others, never mentions his own name on camera. As the red NBC, "WAMQ" is hosted by Bill Loudon and Ed Hughes for 1969; in the following year Hughes is replaced by Dennis Cameron, brought in from the blue ABC, and now red says they have "News That Matters" along with a self-consciously chattier style. Evidently, there had been some behind-the-scenes ratings discussions in the interim. The green CBS, one notes, maintaining its more reserved manner and its acknowledgment of the complexity of issues, is the only station this second year with just one ad in its roster; the others have achieved two sponsors per broadcast as their reward for viewer appeal. News was no longer just information, it was also a matter of intrigue, excitement, and the almost conspiratorial pleasure of an announcer's comments and asides, of little jokes with a co-anchor.

Close attention reveals many small differences between the three stations, in their choice of language, their ordering of stories—but the similarities are also revealing. Slides, film clips, quotes, and comments are often identical on all three stations, presumably due to identical sources for news releases. In 1969, out of five to seven stories presented, all stations noted the release of three prisoners of war by the Viet Cong, and the fact that they wore open-toed sandals and carried their personal effects in a rice bag, though two also referred to another American officer who had escaped the day before. Only two discuss Adam Clayton Powell reclaiming his seat in Congress after being cleared of charges of misuse of Congressional funds. A different two talk about J. Edgar Hoover's FBI report and the FLQ bombs found in Montreal and Ottawa. In 1970, all three stations mention the delays in Mayor Daley's appearance at the trial of Abbie Hoffman, and to different degrees discuss Hoover's warnings about the threat of Communism, but only two report on developments in the My Lai trials, and just one, the traditionally serious (green) CBS, says that Hampton's death is now seen as murder, and notes a resulting sway in public sympathy in favor of the Blacks for their treatment by police.

The conflicting representation of issues surrounding the deaths of Black Panthers Fred Hampton and Mark Clark, the role of State Attorney Ed Hanrahan, and the question of police as murderers in the case are jumbled together, scattered around in many different references; no casual listener could make an informed judgment. Hypotheses, opinions, deductions, and plain propaganda are all presented interchangeably, piled up together indiscriminately. The news, authority or not, is finally just presenting tonight's list; it is virtually impossible in such an arrangement to understand and judge layers of information or comparative values at work. One gets an impression, remembers in retrospect the slide of the Minutemen's "arsenals" of confiscated weapons or images of single faces as they are flashed on the screen behind a speaker, notices that a commuter train is delayed by fire. But paranoia is hardly mentioned, fear is never shown, though none of this news is "good" news after all. A detailed listing of the program contents suggests that the real attention is being paid to visual appeal on the part of the stations, to available background slides and film clips, to the single (pointless) sentence that sounds "right," to the variety of speakers on location. It is all in the interest of "interest."

Five years earlier, Douglas had worked on a film-loop installation titled *Anchor*, with its "preoccupation with the forms of coercion and deferral found in television," as he wrote in June 1990, that largely prefigures *Evening*. *Anchor* was composed entirely of footage taped off air from American and Canadian television in late 1989, another high-energy moment of international crisis and change involving Romania, Czechoslovakia, Panama, East Germany, and the fall of the Berlin Wall:

A rapid montage of different announcers is seen, and then ends with a momentary dissolve to black. Groups

> of these monologues are broken into four sections by
> brief slow-motion glimpses of an elsewhere: Russian
> women talking at a table, an airlift in Azerbaijan,
> a stormy sea and the ship upon which Bush and
> Gorbachev met, and fireworks over the Brandenburg
> Gate. A blur of fragmentary but authoritative
> remarks.[4]

Though *Anchor* was completed and transferred to film,
Douglas now considers it "an abandoned work." Perhaps the
use of actual footage kept its effect too discrete, and did not
provide the internal contradiction and implied commentary
that informs *Evening*. Perhaps the film-loop format proved
less immediate than the three video projections side-by-
side, their comparison inevitable and their verisimilitude so
nearly right that one feels, first, only a suspicion that the
clues there have an intended revelation. *Anchor* seems more
like a framed picture, a "presentation" with the sensibility
of the luminous *Overture*, while *Evening* is subtly a gauntlet
thrown down. Douglas' politics are more exacting now.
The more recent work selects a moment of racial tension
and public unrest, with harassment and confrontation
shown as pivotal factors in the development of contemporary history and media. Within the normal variety of the
evening news, threads of Black history are drawn judiciously
together as quiet evidence and unspoken challenge.

Douglas had intended *Anchor* as the last in a trilogy
of film loops on the history of the cinematographic media,
all designed to play without apparent beginning or end,
in which the continuous mechanical repetition would lend
emphasis to the intended focus of each piece. They were
thus views of a media history, rather than concerned with
an immediate present. *Overture* (1986), the first of that
group, had used materials from earliest cinema: a sequence
of clips filmed by Edison a century before the Canadian
Pacific Railway lines, seen from the front of a train as it
hurtled along tracks and through tunnels in the Rocky
Mountains. Overlaid with a reading of passages from Proust's
Remembrance of Things Past, the work evokes the uncertain
state between waking and sleeping, of consciousness itself.
Next, *Subject to a Film: Marnie* (1988) repeated brief cycles
of Hitchcock's *Marnie* (1964) to highlight an aspect of classic

Hollywood cinema—the dwelling on obsessive fantasy.
In his structure here, Douglas also links the body with the
mechanical as imposed by the routine of office work, in
keeping with reproduction and the character of the machine
age. In *Anchor*, finally, "the heterogeneous but closed
continuum of 'television flow'"[5] was foregrounded. With the
completion of *Evening*, however, Douglas speaks of far more
than the flow of television, showing also its stresses and
manipulations. At a moment when American social tensions
were particularly acute, and the role—and power—of the
media in flux, history seemed more visible. The 1960s were
conscious of self and image to an unusual degree, and
with the assassinations of the Kennedys and Martin Luther
King paired off against the "peace and love" of popular
culture, who could presume any social vision to be clear
or accurate?

Anchor, one guesses, was too formal, too reserved, too
self-contained for a meaningful comment on television
news. With the opportunity to work in and with the Chicago
context, *Evening* is more aggressive intellectually, more
conflicted. As a work in situ, developed in response to the
impact of actual local events, its message is all the more
pointed, whatever its location for eventual exhibition.[6]

Douglas has used time-related and photo-based
media since the early 1980s, black-and-white and color
photography, slide sequences with dissolve units and
voice-over audio text or music, in works reflecting his
environment and cultural experience. But consistently, he
has tended to move from formal concerns to more charged
political ones. His recent use of video and television imply a
growing need for immediacy, a direct reference to popular
experience. *Hors-champs*, for example, is a work referenced to
its site of production, a double-sided video projection
produced at the Centre Georges Pompidou in 1992. Though
conceived as a study of the developing jazz idiom of Black
American musicians in Paris (expatriates not necessarily by
preference) during the late 1960s and early 1970s, and its
translation for the classic French national television station
ORTF (a demonstration of multi-camera studio shooting),
one's personal experience of the piece is undiluted aural and
intellectual pleasure. Stan Douglas is not preceptive or
pedantic. He located the right musicians—George Lewis/

trombone, Douglas Ewart/saxophone, Kent Carter/bass, Oliver Johnson/drums—all based then or now in Paris, and found the right music, a 1965 composition by Albert Ayler. He based his television shooting/editing style on that of Jean-Christophe Averty, a figure as noted in France as Norman McLaren or John Grierson in Canada. The recto image is a fine two-camera TV documentary on contemporary jazz—while the verso contains all the other material, seen by the "other" camera. It would have been edited out as irrelevant to a good television program, but typically shows the other musicians while they are not being featured in their solos, and reveals the intimacy of their collaboration and cooperation, their participation and pleasure in each other's music. The verso, then, shows the musicians rather than the "performers," person rather than persona. These are the extranea that delight an on-the-spot audience; it is the irrelevant that makes the real. Seeing the two sides of this story (pace Michael Snow, whose double-sided film of 1976 bears that name) reveals to us and underlines the customary, usually ignored limitations, and highly fabricated nature of the television mode, whether in the Paris of the 1960s or in our living rooms now. The wonderful music invites us to linger again for the replay, and one sees and revalues that verso image: the unnecessary, the deleted, the essential.

By continuing to review media images and forms from the past—photographs, films, video/television, recorded music—Stan Douglas reminds us, returns to us, the foundations of our present and of our cultural history. His themes return as variations, always with an underlying consciousness of the political sub-strata of the everyday. History by example. Yet as he considers the outside world he addresses also his own knowledge and experience. Douglas speaks of his sense of the marginal, of "absence" and doubt as his constant concerns. Yet the richness and physicality of Douglas' visual constructs and his evident pleasure in music, in the rhythms of gesture and speech, belie (or disguise) the potential for existential doubt in his work. That consciousness of the void, however, may be a source of the resonance to be found there.

The newest work is a complex film loop installation titled *Der Sandmann*, shot in Berlin for presentation at the

1995 Whitney Biennial in New York. Responding to the charged atmosphere of present-day Germany, Douglas collapses the history of the small garden plots established for the poor in the early 19th century, with intricately cross-referenced writings of E.T.A. Hoffmann and Sigmund Freud. The gardens, now being replaced in Potsdam (a Berlin suburb) with hotels and luxury housing, form a backdrop for comparison of the "old" Berlin and the newly united present one. The gardens are linked historically with Moritz Schreber, whose son Paul published *Memorabilia of a Neurotic*, which inspired Freud to develop his theory of paranoia. Hoffmann's gothic tale in turn suggested themes to Freud for his essay "Der Unheimlich" ("The Uncanny").

The film installation juxtaposes two time frames, each projected as abutting half-views that show a Potsdam garden site in the early 1960s and at the present time. This offers, then, a recollection of geographical and political change within the span of Stan Douglas' own lifetime, the crossings of Berlin/Vienna and literature/psychology over a century, the interplay of present realities with childish memories (and fears for nighttime bogeymen and the loss of a father in the Sandman story). There is more than one golem. The Gothic elements signal a return to and of the repressed, a factor Douglas indicates is of crucial import to the German psyche now. One is tempted to see Douglas' own experiences over 1994–1995 in Berlin on a DAAD fellowship as relevant as well. Berlin is full of foreigners, but being visibly non-Aryan surely remains an issue.

Increasingly, Stan Douglas' work evidences a social commitment, and one infused with political consciousness. But it is an ambiguous statement, more commentary than prescription. Its message is there by example and implica-tion, a demonstration of themes and issues without recourse to direct propagandizing. The "art" takes precedence over any "teaching" aspect, and the work is the stronger for that set of decisions. Machines and the mechanical are visibly central to his constructions; the ideas as well as the engines presenting them are manmade, products of the past hun-dred years. We are meant to see these mechanical processes as progressive, linked to labor, and consuming energy, space, and time. Despite clear evidence of the research, even scholarship, underlying his productions, an adamant physicality infuses Stan Douglas' constructions of experience. His works, even as ephemeral television broadcasts or published texts, are *made* things.

Their "sources" are mere speculation, their relationship to others' works tangential. Perhaps "correspondences" is the more apt term. Stan Douglas graduated from Emily Carr College of Art and Design in 1982, and has information and interests in common with other Vancouver artists: Rodney Graham especially, and to a lesser extent with Jeff Wall and Ian Wallace, perhaps Ken Lum as well. Douglas has continued to show a respect for the arcane, for intensive research, and his use of existing texts and musical scores holds much in common with the sensibility of Rodney Graham, who would seem to have a like appreciation for musical history and its uses. All these artists show an aptitude for synthesis and cross-reference between media and periods, an ability to apply research tools yet benefit from chance discoveries and intuitions. Douglas, like Rodney Graham in particular, shows a love of literature and a fascination with Time as form and content of artworks in four dimensions. Even Douglas' rediscovery of the player piano (for *Onomatopoeia*, 1986, and *Pursuit, Fear Catastrophe: Ruskin B.C.*, 1993) is prescient. As a machine replacing the live performer while reclaiming or insisting upon the present-tense of performing a musical work, its modern presence/absence is allied also with the quaintly historical made new, and is echoed in Rodney Graham's use of a similar piano for *School of Velocity* (1993) or, for that matter, Vera Frenkel's piano in … *from the Transit Bar* (1992) and *Raincoats, Suitcases, Palms* (1994).

Like the others, Douglas shows respect for research and authority. Technology and media retain their stature. Like Rodney Graham, Stan Douglas works "logically" from a premise developed and expanded in research. The 19th century as an underpinning to present day knowledge—inventions and assumptions—was an early fascination, and the writings of such authors as Sigmund Freud, Herman Melville, Edgar Allen Poe appear alongside music by Johann Sebastian Bach, Richard Wagner (for Graham), and more contemporary masters. Neither vast scale nor impeccable detail seems to daunt—analogous, perhaps to the obsessive "staged" aesthetic of Jeff Wall's photographs, which have

often been built on references to 19th-century works by
Manet or Delacroix, or bloody contemporary battlefields.
Elaborate constructions recreate the past for a present eye
(or ear), precise in every detail.

These "correspondences" are by no means presumed
to be Stan Douglas' conscious intention, though they
indicate something of his place in the ambitious and fertile
Vancouver milieu, important as both margin and intellectual
hub. Douglas works in the present, but his position grows
out of and is informed by a past rich with associations and
meaning, a living history. It is his study of Others that
counts.

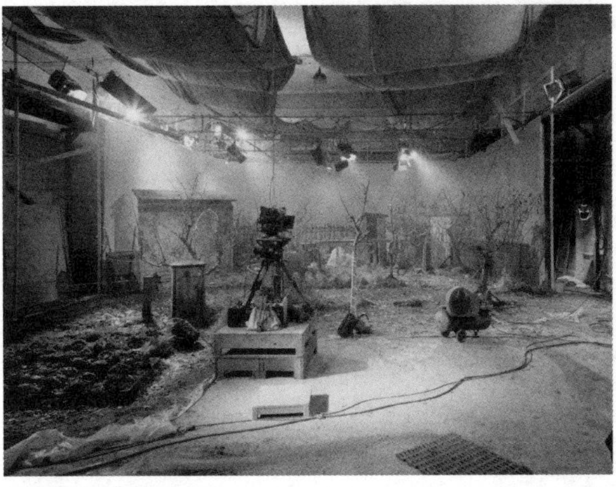

Stan Douglas
"Contemporary" set for *Der Sandman* at Dokfilm Studios, Potsdam Babelsberg, 1994

[1] Correspondence with the author, September 1993.
[2] Two years later Muntadas pursued his interest in news-
gathering with the half-hour documentary *Between the Lines*,
a study of the preparation of an actual item for broadcast
news, where it is made clear how the reporter/editor's
"take" on a story's significance will necessarily shape the
final item. But as Muntadas points out in a statement of
1979 for *Between the Lines*, "we are completing information
from the text with our own process of thinking, knowledge,
information, subtlety. We are looking deeper than the
printed words … [W]ith television there is no time to stop
and think while we absorb information from a moving
image." The TV form has a particular kind of influence.
[3] Dan Graham, *Video Architecture Television/Writings on Video
and Video Works 1970–1978*, The Press of the Nova Scoria
College of Art & Design/New York University Press,
Halifax/New York 1979, p. 60.
[4] Correspondence with the author, June 1990.
[5] Ibid.
[6] *Evening* was premiered at the Institute of Contemporary
Arts, London, England, September 1994, in *Stan Douglas:
Television Works* and in May 1995 with The Renaissance
Society at the University of Chicago, which had originally
commissioned the work. *Evening* was also included in the
exhibition *Public Information* at the San Francisco Museum
of Modern Art in January 1995.

Transnational Objects: Commodities in Postcolonial Displacement
Laura U. Marks

Parachute, no. 81, Winter 1996

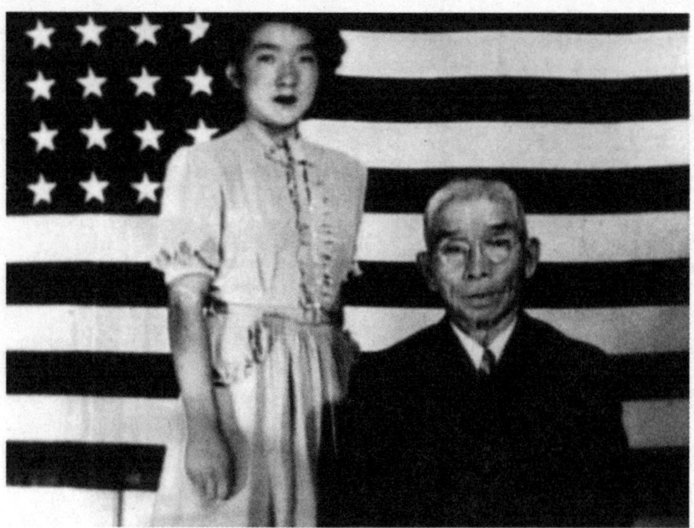

Rea Tajiri, *History and Memory: For Akiko and Takashige*, 1991
Film still, film duration: 32'

Films that are produced in contexts that breach the boundaries of nation and question nationalist narratives can be called transnationalist documentaries.[1] They neither describe international trajectories that leave national boundaries intact, nor remain within the leveling and totalizing narratives of multi-national capital. Transnational documentary, then, traces the effects of cultural and national intermixing at a scale that is smaller than the nation but also crosses among nations.

Documentary film then can be transnational even when its subjects are stationary. Objects that travel along paths of human diaspora and international trade encode post-colonial cultural displacement. Commodities, though subject to the deracinating flow of the transna-tional economy and the censoring process of official history, nevertheless retain the power to tell stories of where they have been. Films can document this process by decoding the displacements, and social relations, that objects carry. These films might constitute a subgenre of the transnational independent genre discussed by Hamid Naficy.[2] If that genre focuses on the diasporic movements of immigrants and exiles, these films excavate the traces left by things that "emigrate" due to similar global flows of capital, power, and desire.

By following the movements of objects, these films describe a transnationalism that intersects the unifying movements of globalization. Globalization occurred during a period of colonial and postcolonial unification: of markets, of the nation-state, of time, and of a notion of the individual.[3] As such, is a trend that is already beginning to unravel, as attested by increasing polyethnicicy in nations, factional civil wars, and disputes over the definition of the individual in terms of human rights and citizenship. This new uncertainty about the status of global interconnections signifies not a retrenchment, but the limits of the usefulness of the Western category of the nation-state. If globalization is a movement of unification, then transnationalism is a tendency that follows many of the same movements, but often to contradict or complicate them. For example, if the establishment of nation-states around the globe has facilitated the dominance of multinational capitalism, then transnationalism would describe both the movements of capital among nation-states and the subversion of capitalist flows, such as barter or the diversion of commodities into unique objects.

The use of film to trace the movements of objects is not incidental. Meaning is embodied and communicated materially, both by objects and by film. The films here trace the transnational and intercultural movement that produces transnational objects. Film's ability to animate objects makes it a suitable medium to follow their transformations. Film is capable not only of following this process chronologically, but also of discovering the value that inheres in objects: the discursive layers that take material form in them, the unresolved traumas that become embedded in their flesh, and the history of the material interactions that they encode. Film has an archival quality that allows unresolved pasts to surface in the present of the image. For Gilles Deleuze,

> It is as if the past surfaces in itself but in the shape of personalities which are independent, alienated, off-balance, in some sense embryonic, strangely active fossils, radioactive, inexplicable in the present where they surface, and all the more harmful and autonomous.[4]

Deleuze's terminology graphically evokes the way in which elements from the past may disrupt the present signified in an image. A recollection image is an image that exists on the plane of the present, but has the power to evoke a plane of the past. If an event is represented as a smooth, consistent plane of meaning, a recollection image is a sharp point that punctures it with a chronological or discursive presence at odds with the present. In the cases below, the disjunction is not necessarily temporal as much as spatial. The movement among cultures creates the same sort of discursive disjunctions that the passage of time within a culture does. So when an image surfaces from another place, another culture, it disrupts the coherence of the plane of the present culture.

It is useful to bring anthropological approaches into the discussion of fetishism and representation that Marxist cultural critics have fostered. The generations following Marcel Mauss' germinal study of gift economies have tended to focus on the process of exchange itself. Lately, however, anthropologists have also been returning to the question of particular objects of exchange, and describing how they move within and between cultures as not only a market exchange, but also a cultural one. Their approach permits a certain obduracy of the object to remain, so that we can pay attention to its fetishistic quality, in contrast to other efforts to reduce transnational flows to simply the flows of capital or of signs.

There is no doubt that our world system is interconnected by the flows of capital and power. Similarly, there is no doubt that the postcolonial condition describes not only "third world" situations, but a space we all inhabit, interconnected as we are by global flows. Nevertheless, this process of worldwide interconnection is more complex than an inevitable process of capitalist reification; it is incorrect, as well as Orientalist, to understand only "third-world" cultures to operate on gift-type economies, while "first-world" economies are commodity-based through and through. Even objects that move in the apparently sanitized flows of transnational capital encode movements of cultural translation and mistranslation. Arjun Appadurai looks at these translation processes in the social life of an object in terms of knowledge: the continuities and discontinuities in knowledge between the producer and the consumer.[5] There may be no knowledge gap in the local movement of a quart of peaches or the transnational movement of a car, both cases in which the producer and consumer share knowledge about a commodity thanks to proximity or standardization. And large knowledge gaps mark the movement among cultures of objects that encode personal or ritual meaning. Film can follow an object as it embodies and communicates, or refuses to communicate, knowledge.

Appadurai complicates the Marxist notion of the commodity by understanding objects to move in and out of commodity status in the course of their lifetimes. In cross-cultural movement, an object's "commodity status" is highly mobile; for example, a thing that is sacred in one society may be a commodity in another, and intercultural relations heighten the likelihood that an object may enter the commodity context of another society.[6] Objects may pass in and out of identities as commodity, gift, ritual object, or trash.

The films I will discuss begin with the relatively simple transnational conversions of labor to capital, and move to more idiosyncratic and intimate travels of transnational objects. First are those films that trace the movement of an object as it shakes the traces of local cultures to become a deracinated, transnational commodity. The transnational object in Amos Gitai's *Ananas* (1983) is a can of pineapple. Its contents are produced in Hawaii, label printed in China, can assembled in the US, and so on. The traces of humans who smelted the steel, cut down the fruit, and ran the printing press would be utterly lost, as in most commodities, were it not for Gitai's excavation, which de-alienates their labor.

In Marta Rodriguez's *Love, Women and Flowers* (1989/1990) the transnational object is a carnation that travels from a Colombian hothouse to KLM jet to European florist. The film takes a highly cultivated flower—it seems to grow right in the refrigerator—and endows it with the haunting histories of women's labor. The flower's low cost in Amsterdam reflects union-busting in Bogota; its conventional length is the product of women who mechanically lop off extra buds; its unblemished uniformity results from toxic fungicides that cause workers to sicken and die. In Deleuze's terms, the carnation is a recollection-image of women's work, pain, and solidarity. In Appadurai's terms, the film fills in a knowledge gap about the conditions in which Colombian women labor, a gap that makes it easier for Northerners to buy the flowers. These films undertake the Marxist work of reconstituting human labor to powerful effect. Nevertheless, it is hard to see the traces of human presence in these objects as any sort of communication: mass-produced commodities are absolutely deracinated by transnational capital.

More complex intercultural movements endow objects with greater powers of memory and transformation. Jean Rouch has long exploited the transformations that people and objects experience as they cross between cultures, in films like *Jaguar* (1971), *Petit à petit* (1969), and recently *Madame L'Eau* (1993). Here what moves is windmills, from Holland to Nigeria, supposedly at the inspiration of Rouch's Nigerian friends to relieve the drought in their region. Rather than being a miniature model of World Bank-style development, the importation of windmills is marked by magic and the mutual contamination of cultures. After the Dutch government has agreed to donate three windmills, the three Nigerians perform a divination sacrifice on the Dutch seacoast. Perhaps it is this ritual of translation that invests the windmill with non-Dutch powers, so that it causes a field of tulips to spring up overnight on the banks of the Niger.

Another sort of film that traces the movement of commodities transnationally, gathering and erasing meanings as they go, is that which reconstitutes the path of an object as it becomes commoditized. Dennis O'Rourke's *Cannibal Tours* (1988) and Ilsa Barbach and Lucien Taylor's *In and Out of Africa* (1992), for example, trace the process of cultural translation that makes local African objects into artifacts for export. However, films like these follow not simply the process of commodification of indigenous use-values into exchange-values, but the willful creation of fetishes in transcultural translation. The latter especially, which follows the traffic of the Muslim merchant Gabai Baare between West Africa and New York City, shows how Westerners desperately desire to import not just commodities but histories, and how go-betweens pander to that desire. Baare hires African workers to carve massive numbers of traditional ritual objects and then age them with root-based dyes and mud. Again, the fake antiques prove to be recollection-images that put the lie to some of the collectors' lofty notions of the universal beauty of African sculpture. When the American collectors buy these objects, they are buying, simply, aura: the encoding of human history in an object.

Other films trace the movement of objects whose meaning resides least in their identity as commodities and most as personal fetishes with the power to release memories. These processes are not "merely" personal, but rather suggest how the personal and idiosyncratic may be the only visible aspect of widespread cultural flows.[7] The significance of this transnational movement cannot be underestimated. How often have memories that were seen as "only" private proved to be the sole repositories of diasporic cultures? It is important to take seriously what seem to be isolated and idiosyncratic phenomena, because they may prove to be the only level at which widespread cultural movements are able to speak.

The transnational object in Rea Tajiri's *History and Memory: For Akiko and Takashige* (1991) is a wooden bird her mother carved in the Japanese-American detention camp. It comes to resonate on another historical level when Tajiri finds a photograph of the bird carving class in the National Archives. One day, going through a box of documents from the internment camps, Tajiri comes across a photograph of a roomful of people working at long tables, labeled "Bird-carving class, August 1941." The archive—in this case, the literal archive—is as ignorant of Mrs Tajiri's private history as she is willfully amnesiac of it. The bird, traveling from the prison camp to the family home, embodies a recollection that is now lost. The carved figure that now resides in Mrs. Tajiri's jewelry box is material evidence of a trauma she has almost wholly forgotten.

In Shauna Beharry's *Seeing Is Believing* (1991), it is the sari of her deceased mother that works like a fetish. The artist, mourning, is unable to remember her mother by looking at photographs of her. It is only when she puts on her mother's sari that she feels she has "climbed into her skin." The feel of the fabric awakens a flood of memories lost in the family's movement from India to Europe to Canada. Both *History and Memory* and *Seeing Is Believing* restore the history that has become fossilized in an object. Ultimately they de-fetishize the object, by teasing out the narrative it contains.

As these examples demonstrate, some objects embody memory as well as labor. Theories of fetishism describe how a value that is not reducible to commodification comes to inhere in objects. Of the many theories of the fetish that operate in anthropology, psychoanalysis, and Marxist analysis, I focus on those that explicitly attend to it in terms of a series of historical, intercultural displacements. Objects can encode cultural knowledges that become buried in the process of temporal or geographic displacement, but are volatile when reactivated by memory—like fossils, or what C. Nadia Seremetakis calls "the stratigraphic witness of the artifact."[8] Fetishes get their power not by representing that which is powerful, but through *contact* with it, a contact whose materiality has been repressed. As such, they have an indexical relation to an original scene like that of a photograph. The objects I discuss here encode material conditions of displacement as well as discursive ruptures.

I attempt to build here a recuperative notion of fetishism, but certainly the critical notion of fetishism is still at play in the transnational movement of objects. Fetishism aptly describes the violent colonialist impulse to metonymize living cultures and suspend them outside of time. Critics such as Edward Saïd, Johannes Fabian, Trinh T. Minh-ha, and Homi Bhabha have skewered this fetishistic quality of colonialism with finality. I want to claim other meanings of fetishism in order to describe other aspects of transnational movement. For example, *In and Out of Africa* follows a trade route built precisely to materialize fetishistic colonial desires for a primitive authenticity. Yet in following this route, the film not only deconstructs the collectors' desire, but also reveals that the African sculptures are precisely *intercultural* products. Commissioned by the trader Baare, they are the result of their African producers' reasoned second-guessing of Western collectors' fantasies. This precisely meets the definition of the fetish proposed by William Pietz.

Pietz describes the fetish as a historical nexus of different material discourses, a node of meaning that is not proper to a single culture, but produced in the abrasive contact between two. "In Marxist terms, one might say that the fetish is situated in the space of cultural revolution."[9] Colonial power relations in particular, with their propensity for cross-breeding indigenous and imported meanings, are prime sites for the production of fetishes—which often turn out to be commodities as well. Pietz's etymology of the word "fetish" uncovers a long and complex history of colonization, appropriation, and translation. Significantly, the notion of the fetish was mobilized during an imperial expansion predicated upon Enlightenment dichotomies. European intellectuals such as Marx borrowed the idea of the fetish from the written travelogues of European merchants, who portrayed African fetish worship as the perversion of rational self-interest.

If we understand fetishes as properly the product not of a single culture, but of the encounter between two, then we see how fetishes are produced not only in the course of built-up time, but also in the disjunctive movement through space. Postcolonial life is producing these lateral fetishes at record speed as people become displaced, especially as they immigrate to their former colonizers' lands. Hence the proliferation of auratic objects in the gray areas of the global economy.

This fragmentary survey of the way film excavates the traces left by transnational objects has moved from films about the most abstract, highly commoditized of objects to films about the most personal. While the former are richest as records of the global movements of capital, the latter are best able to expose the cultural differences in which fetishes are produced. Let me end by demonstrating how films draw on the memory of the senses in order to draw out these cultural differences. As a record of sense memory, film is a medium for diasporan experience and other experiences of suppressed histories.

Both *History and Memory* and *Seeing Is Believing* draw on the ability of transnational objects to awaken sense memories (and of tactile memory to create a communication between daughters and mothers that words, and audiovisual images, could not). Non-visual sensory information is a casualty of commodification, and of the extraction of objects from their cultural contexts, as curator Laura Trippi points out. Discussing an installation by artist Sowon Kwon about the traffic in Asian porcelains, she notes that the work "calls attention to the way that conventions of fine art display, taking objects out of context, stimulate a tendency to experience vision as if it operated objectively, independently of the other senses, and even outside the contingencies of history."[10]

The memory of the senses can be enlisted to discover the cultural histories of auratic objects lost to the flattening effect of cultural appropriation. Or, conversely, such objects may call forth buried cultural memories by eliciting the memory of the senses. In cultural transformation, and especially in the diasporic movement to the modernized West or from rural areas to metropolitan centers, where certain senses are devalued, information about specific cultural histories seems to get lost.

But perhaps it is not lost, so much as encoded in ways it takes special skills to decode. Hamid Naficy writes that it is especially important to consider the non-audiovisual ways that exiles experience film and television:

> The exiles produce their difference not just through what they see and hear, but through their senses of smell, taste, and touch. Indeed, these aspects of the sensorium often provide, more than sight and hearing, poignant reminders of difference and of separation from homeland.[11]

What is left out of expression registers somatically, in pain, nausea, memories of smells and caresses. How can knowledge be embodied in senses other than the visual? How can one form of sense knowledge embody another?

Vivian Sobchack has provided some important answers to how film evokes sense experience by examining the relation between the film viewer and the film as a relation between two sensing bodies.[12] The film viewing experience sets up relays between the audiovisual image and the viewer's own circuits of memory, enriching the image with associations that are not simply semiotic but occur at the level of sense perception. I want to propose that an audiovisual medium can *remember* the experiences of other senses. Vision can evoke touch or smell, for example; sound can evoke the kinaesthetic. But it is not simply a matter of association; senses can translate the experience of other senses. "Sensory memory is a form of storage. Storage is always the embodiment and conservation of experiences, persons, and matter in form of alterity."[13] Hence film itself can function like a fetish: it can encode a given material experience in altered form.

I do not want to speak of touch, smell and other senses as individual. They encode collective, cultural experiences. The senses, however, are educated differently in different cultures and classes; sense memory is also inflected by gender. The primal scene in *History and Memory* is, significantly, one of touch. The single recollection image Tajiri attributes to her mother is of gurgling water that overflows her canteen. Its cool wetness as she splashes her face is a moment of relief on a hot, dusty day. A tiny puncture of pleasure in the eternal vigilance the woman must hold in order to survive the concentration camp, it will be the only image to remain years later, when that other narrative of deprivation has been put away.

Seeing Is Believing, as mentioned earlier, is a mourning piece. The tape evokes the closeness of daughter to mother expressed not in terms of vision, which would imply distance, but of touch. While Beharry tells her story, the camera looks closely at the silk fabric of a sari in a photo. When the tape superimposes a smaller image of the portrait on the folds of the sari, it emphasizes the startling difference between two ways of seeing. I realized that the tape had been using my vision as a sense of touch; I had not been looking at the image of the fabric so much as brushing it with the skin of my eyes. Beharry has said she wanted to "squeeze the touchability out of the photo."[14] It makes us realize that memory may be encoded in touch, smell, or kinaesthesia, more than vision. Between two cultures' regimes of sense knowledge, she suggests, memory can be lost in translation.

It is important not to overvalorize the theme of Western capitalist commodification versus non-Western integrity, but rather to see the dynamics by which objects change in cultural translation as a complex intercultural and interclass movement. Similarly, Beharry's excavations are not just about finding an Indian "voice" silenced by generations of life in the West. They are excavations of histories that were repressed at home as well. Fetishism as an intercultural relation involves a tremendous amount of translation, decipherment, and excavation. And ultimately there is no question of getting to a truth about either culture, for the fetish is produced only in their power-mediated difference.

[1] Patricia Zimmermann and John Hess, "Notes Toward a Definition of a Transnational Documentary Practice," paper presented at "Visible Evidence," Duke University, September 12, 1993. My title for this article alludes to D. W. Winnicott's theory of "transitional objects," which help subjects to reorganize and make themselves anew. They might also describe fetish objects created in transcultural movement. D. W. Winnicott, "Transitional Objects and Transitional Phenomena," in *Essential Papers on Object Relations*, ed. Peter Buckley, New York University Press, New York 1986.

[2] Hamid Naficy, "Phobic Spaces and Liminal Panics," *East West Film Journal*, vol. 8, no. 2, 1994.

[3] Roland Robertson, "Mapping the Global Condition," in *Global Culture*, ed. Mike Featherstone, Sage, London 1990, p. 27.

[4] Gilles Deleuze, *Cinema 2*, trans. Hugh Tomlinson and Robert Galeta, University of Minnesota Press, Minneapolis 1989, p. 112–113.

[5] Arjun Appadurai, "Commodities and the Politics of Value," in *The Social Life s/ Things*, ed. Appadurai, Cambridge University Press, Cambridge, Massachusetts 1986, p. 42–44.

[6] Ibid., p. 14–17.

[7] C. Nadia Seremecakis (ed.), *The Senses Still*, Weatview, Boulder, Colorado 1994, p. 135.

[8] Ibid.

[9] William Pietz, "The Problem of the Fetish, II," *Res 13* (Spring 1987), p. 10.

[10] Laura Trippi, "Globalization," in *Trade Routes*, New Museum of Contemporary Art, New York 1993.

[11] Hamid Naficy, *The Making of Exile Cultures*, University of Minnesota Press, Minneapolis 1993, p. 152–153.

[12] Vivian Sobchack, *The Address of the Eye*, Princeton University Press, Princeton, New Jersey 1992.

[13] C. Nadia Seremetakis, "The Memory of the Senses," in *Visualizing Theory*, ed. Lucien Taylor, Routledge, New York 1994, p. 216.

[14] Shauna Beharry, interview with the author, May 1, 1993.

What Is a New Technology?
Machine Drawings, Sentience, Intercultural Contact
David Tomas

Parachute, no. 84, Fall 1996

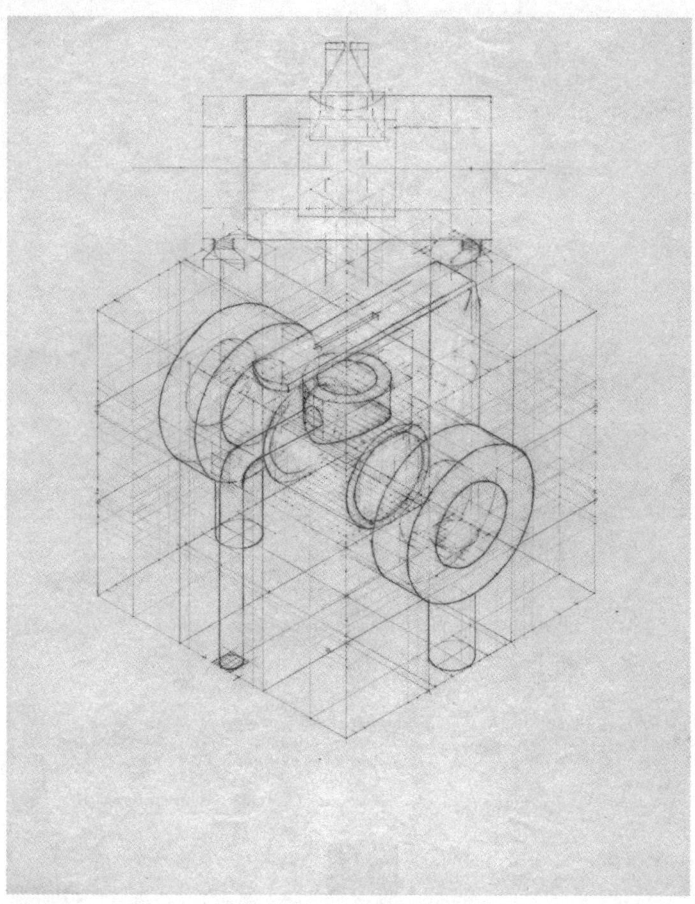

Projection view of a graphite oven used for measuring the yields of indium and gallium in the proton-induced fission of natural uranium. The oven (which contains the target material) is surrounded by a tantalum heat shield connected to a "chimney" in which ionization takes place. The chimney terminates in a slit facing the optics of a mass spectrometer. The drawing was commissioned for a scientific publication in 1977.

The traces of an intimate zone of imaginative activity and an obscure world of sentience await discovery in the archival sediments of the technological foundations of our modern industrial world. Like ancient fossils, their outlines are preserved in layers of documents that record the construction of machines, machine systems, large-scale machine ensembles, as well as the systems and intersystems of transportation and communication that have dominated our landscapes since the early 19th century. Some of their outlines are clear and polished, others are raw and barely recognizable. However, whether polished or raw, clear or obscure, they have one common characteristic: they take the form of graphic representations. These representations of machines or mechanized processes are commonly known as engineering drawings, and they include initial or preliminary sketches, designer's drawings, project drawings, production drawings, presentation drawings, maintenance drawings, and technical illustrations.

The distinct novelty of these and similar kinds of representations is to be found in their relationships to the objects and processes they depict. Instead of functioning as illustrations of preexisting things and processes, these drawings represent a zone of emergent possibilities. It has been noted, for example, that engineering drawings "are about what might be," that they wrestle "with future possibilities," and that they attempt to "give form to uncertainties."[1] In addition to these characteristics, they function as extended perceptual frames in their capacities to shape a mechanism not only as a function of space and time, but also *through* space and time: from the first register of an idea, through production drawings, to technical illustration. Whether considered as a medium for design or an autonomous language, engineering drawing, produced by the human hand or by machine proxy, is still a primary mode of design today, insofar as it allows us to "foresee how things might perform, to imagine how they might appear, to control their production, and to look after them when they have been made" (p. 202).

Historians have argued that the Industrial Revolution promoted a distinctively modern form of engineering or mechanical drawing insofar as it evolved in tandem with "new forms of manufacture and organization" and was dependent on their "success and consolidation" (p. 11). Indeed, in their estimation, it was precisely the distinctive form of production associated with the new manufacturing processes and organizational forms—the division of labor—that rendered this type of drawing essential. It did so because it "made possible a new relationship between management and manufacture and separated the process of design from the process of construction" (p. 11). These historians have pointed out, moreover, that this relationship set engineering drawing apart from earlier forms of technical representations that were also coupled to design and production, like those produced in the context of ship building and architectural construction, or other forms of technical illustration such as scientific illustrations. Inasmuch as these observations are correct, it can be said that this category of drawing is at the foundation of our modern industrial world. One might suggest, moreover, that machine drawings are privileged entry points to complex machine spaces and machine cultures, spaces with their own geographies, cultures with their own system of beliefs and language.[2]

The space and history of engineering drawings is intimately coupled to a space and history of the contact between the most unobtrusive and ubiquitous of marking instruments: the pencil. It is worth noting that the common Western pencil has a history that coincides with the history of Western modernity. This history's significance, its pivotal role in the development of modernity, has been eclipsed by technology's more spectacular history. The most visible history is that of machine artifacts, since this is the one that we are most familiar with. The other history exists in surrogate form in archives, and has seen the light of day only occasionally. The elements of this latter history—engineering drawings—are, in fact, for the most part, the products of the meetings of the pencil and another menial technology: paper. It is to the possibility of an anthropology and of an aesthetics of contact between these primitive technologies as displayed in the service of machines and similar artifacts that I now turn. For this contact, I will suggest, has generated something that exists in excess of a history of the representation of machines. It has spawned a shadow—a kind of graphite-based alter ego, or a form of consciousness—which is co-extensive with each engineering drawing or scientific representation.

What Is a New Technology?

We are often tempted to talk about the representations produced by leading Western imaging systems such as photography and cinematography as if they were autonomous entities. We talk about a history of photographic images or a history of moving pictures as if they existed independently from their modes of production, or even their modes of apprehension. This is perhaps not surprising, nor is it entirely illegitimate, since it is in the nature of these kinds of images, and of the culture in which they circulate, that they should be conceived to function as independent entities subject to their own physical and disciplinary attributes. Each photograph, each film, and, now, each computer image can be presented and treated as if it were a system unto itself.

The abyss that separates imaging technology and image seems to be as absolute and as magical as the abyss that appears to separate mind and body; we live in a culture where representations are collected, classified, and archived in isolation from their modes of production. The how and the where of production rarely enters into the debate about the nature of modern representations. Rarely, if ever, are we confronted with an imaging system's inner spaces, its culture. And we are almost never confronted with this culture's representational shadow.

There are, however, more evocative ways of apprehending these images and their unique cultural characteristics. Other types of insights about the nature of these imaging systems, their historical and perceptual impacts on the human imagination, can sometimes unlock surprising viewpoints, or unforeseen vistas. An opportunity to experience, in one's lifetime, four impossibilities—"the ocean-steamer, the railway, the electric telegraph, and the Daguerreotype"[3]—can point to the existence of a relational viewpoint, a relational history, which could suggest that it might not be possible to separate such technologies and histories, except through an act of intellectual violence.

Other observations can open the way to new forms of history that begin not with the mind conceived as a synthetic or analytic tool, but with the body treated as a primary sensory organ, and with sensual histories that might cascade from particular organs. The proposition that there exists "a sort of umbilical cord" that "links the body of the photographed thing to my gaze: light, though impalpable is here a carnal medium, a skin I share with anyone who has been photographed,"[4] highlights private histories of the senses and of particular sensibilities rooted in individual bodies. When conceived in these terms it is not hard to endorse viewpoints that begin with these other kinds of histories and other bodily sites, especially if they lead to strange ways of apprehending both old and new technologies and one's relationship to them. "Why mightn't there be, somehow, a new science for each object?" Roland Barthes asks in *Camera Lucida*, his remarkable meditation on photography's capacity to prompt a radically different History: a History of the Look (p. 8). New histories of technology and novel ways of conceiving of these histories as the generative sites of new experiences can be conjured up in the wake of these and similar "eccentric" speculations on the nature of a technology and its products. The world of technology can suddenly mutate and take on interstitial characteristics as one's experience with them is refracted through the optic of unconventional observations like "cameras … were clocks for seeing" (p. 15). Remarks like this one, made in connection with sounds associated with the use of early cameras, transform archaic mechanisms into fantastic hybrids that can even "infect" the most recent imaging technologies with the evocative power of their poetic spaces and imaginative potential.

A first contact with a new, but also with an old technology. This is the profound intuition contained in *Camera Lucida*. The lesson is simple, yet profound: every encounter with a new and old technology holds the possibility of a first contact, if one's habitual frames of reference are for some reason or another shattered by the appearance of an anomalous, punctorial detail. Indeed, a precise balance between the old and new technologies, an individual consciousness and a collective existence, transform *Camera Lucida* into a strange narrative of first contact:

> The first photographs a man contemplated (Niépce in front of the *dinner table*, for instance) must have seemed to him to resemble exactly certain paintings (still the *camera obscura*); he knew, however, that he was nose-to-nose with a mutant (a Martian can resemble a man): his consciousness posited the object encountered outside of any analogy, like the ectoplasm of "what-had-been": neither image nor reality, a new being, really: a reality one can no longer touch. (p. 87)

In contrast to a history which begins at the threshold of a look, we are sometimes prompted to think of new technologies as potent collective thresholds. Studies such as Wolfgang Schivelbusch's *The Railway Journey* are important references for further exploration of the aesthetic, social, and political parameters of both old and new technologies and their familiar or extraordinary languages.[5] Indeed, the critical power of these studies, in contrast with those that treat images as autonomous entities, lies in their range of disclosures. Explorers are able to systemically sound out a technology's unknown perceptual spaces, its strange culture, mode of social organization, its political structure and economy.

Finally, there is the distinct if little-known world of engineering drawings and the more remote and enigmatic world of preliminary sketches. These worlds point to a zone of ongoing activity that suggests that modern existence does not unfold according to a materialized logic whose cutting edge is a succession of "new" technologies (camera obscura, the railway ensemble, photography, cinematography, television, or virtual reality), or new types of scientific and technological practices. On the contrary, this world floats on a sea of obscure, often esoteric representations that fan out in a complex array through different spaces and times.

One could choose to explore the spatial and representational characteristics of this array, and its possibilities (including its aesthetic possibilities), instead of investigating the characteristics of a given technology's primary communications channel. What impact would such a choice have on the conventional idea of a new technology, on the fact that the evolution of new technological forms creates privileged sites for new kinds of previously unexperienced sensory activity? Where, for example, would any given new technology *begin* and where would it *end*?

Herbert Simon has suggested that "an artifact can be thought of as a meeting point—an 'interface' in today's terms—between an 'inner' environment, the substance and organization of the artifact itself, and an 'outer' environment, the surroundings in which it operates."[6] According to this model, the "new" is an effect of the interface (p. 131–132). However, insofar as each artifact can also be thought of as an intersystem of artifacts, a matrix of emergent possibilities, an array of engineering drawings, or the product of a series of tactile traces that spread out in space and time, there is a sense in which artifacts cannot be encapsulated by the vision of an ultimate and totalizing interface.

Extended Instrumental Contexts

Bruno Latour has warned, in the case of scientific representation, that

> There are two ways in which visualization processes
> may be ignored; one is to grant to the scientific mind
> that which should be granted to the hands, to the
> eyes, and to the signs; the other is to focus exclusively
> on the signs qua signs, without considering the
> mobilization of which they are but the fine edge.[7]

For Latour, "realms of reality that seem far-apart (mechanics, economics, marketing, scientific organization of work) are inches apart, once flattened out onto the same surface" (p. 54). However, Latour cautions, it is "possible to overestimate the inscription, but not the setting in which the cascade of ever more written and numbered inscriptions is produced"; and he suggests that

> what we are really dealing with is the *staging* of a
> scenography in which attention is focused on one set
> of dramatized inscriptions. The setting works like
> a giant optical device that creates a new laboratory, a
> new type of vision, and a new phenomenon to look
> at. (p. 42, emphasis in original)

Michael Lynch has proposed, in a similar vein, that a scientific image can be thought of as being "impressed and circulated" by way of "graphic and instrumental fields," and that the latter are equivalent to "externalized retinas."[8]

While sociologists of science like Latour or Lynch are sensitive to the complex procedures involved in the creation of scientific representations, they stop short of treating the generative sites of such representations as special kinds of technological and sensory interfaces. One can, however, adopt a point of view that transforms these sites into complex sensory transducers with interesting consequences not only for the way we habitually conceptualize scientific representations, new technologies, a mechanics of sentience, or what qualifies as an instance of intercultural contact, but also with regard to the possibility of generating new aesthetic practices.

Recent models of scientific visualization bring to mind Gregory Bateson's descriptions of a cybernetic ecology of "mind." One of the metaphors Bateson uses to synthesize previously distinct questions about the boundaries of the self, the nature of information, technology, and "mind" is the image of a blind man. "Suppose," he asks, "I am a blind man, and I use a stick. I go tap, tap, tap. Where do I start? Is my mental system bounded at the handle of the stick? Is it bounded by my skin? Does it start halfway up the stick? Does it start at the tip of the stick?"[9] Bateson's answer dissolves the optic that brings such questions into focus by redefining the existential boundaries that previously governed the separation of human bodies and technologies:

> The stick is a pathway along which transforms of difference are being transmitted. The way to delineate the system is to draw the limiting line in such a way that you do not cut any of these pathways in ways which leave things inexplicable. If what you are trying to explain is a given piece of behavior, such as the locomotion of the blind man, then, for this purpose, you will need the street, the stick, the man; the street, the stick, and so on, round and round. (p. 459)

The extraordinary simplicity and analytic power of the blind man metaphor resides in its ability to succinctly present an ecological model of the interaction between human organisms, technologies, and the environments in which they operate at any given time. More important, however, is the way that it draws our attention to the point of contact that brings systems, circuits, and "mind" into existence, a point of contact—or interface—that can be recognized by *the sounds it produces*.

The tap, tap, tap of the blind man's stick produces acoustic differences that travel in a circuit. A different set of parameters, a different environmental context, a different goal or set of goals would produce a different configuration of "mind."

Hyperphysicality

The domain of engineering drawings can be treated in a similar fashion. Let us imagine that these drawings are the products of a linked, yet often interrupted and sometimes recontextualized movement of an interface: an engineer uses a pencil (to pick the simplest and most convenient of drawing tools) to trace the outlines of an idea, of a machine, on a piece of paper. Let us imagine that this process continues on other pieces of paper, as this or other pencils engage or are disengaged from the task of transforming this idea into an artifact, a machine.

The obscure "magic" of a point of contact—the meeting of two technologies cast in terms of an eccentric erotics of touch—an interface where "mind" first becomes tangible as trace. The circuit of mind and image that is closed through the actions of the hand, a probe (whether pencil, pen, or computer keyboard) at the service of an idea, and paper (or screen in the case of a computer-based imaging system) that registers this idea, is best described in terms of a *tactilo-ecolographic-logic* because of the way that this logic foregrounds the relationship between touch, an inscriptive ecology, representation, and consciousness.[10]

Let us note that this point of contact is also a breeding ground for inconspicuous sounds, acoustic slithers, the latent sonic images of the friction of contact between pencil and paper. For it is the contact between a pencil and paper that produces friction and a mark that is accompanied by the unobtrusive acoustic echoes of this contact. What are the first sounds of an idea? What would a history of "ideas" be like if it were registered in terms of an array of sonic images? Can the traces of an idea be mirrored as a cascade of sonic debris? What kind of apparatus would be needed to transform latent sonic images into tangible acoustic signifiers? What other ways are there of conceiving of new technologies which might lie beyond this parallel sonic world, but which are nevertheless linked to the meeting of a pencil and piece of paper?

Let us return to a nest of questions. What is a "new" technology? Where are its conceptual, sensual, or erotic limits, as opposed to its more obvious material limits, to be found? Indeed, where are its boundaries to be drawn?

What kind of complex sensory world is generated by the genesis of an idea as it unfolds in space and time, from two to three dimensions, and from three to four dimensions? Where is or are the points of contact that bring into being the circuits and systems of information that generate "machine" as a particular manifestation of "mind?" Where are the limits of the draughtsperson or draughtspersons to the drawn in relation to these circuits and systems? Are there other vistas to be discovered that might harbor unforeseen peculiarities inhering in the obscure confines of a technology's extended instrumental context?

What about the existence of earlier engineering drawings: can they be treated as if they harbored traces of a type of sentience? Are they perhaps in some *hyperphysical* sense "alive" insofar as they too are the products of similar tactilo-ecolographic activity and exist in a state of suspended animation? Can one detect a sort of "mind" that is hibernating in the stillness of their archival sites? If so, how does one go about reanimating and communicating with it? Can we speak of an extended instrumental context, of an externalized retina, or of "the staging of a scenography" that "works like a giant optical device that creates a new laboratory, a new type of vision, and a new phenomenon to look at" in relation to its process of reanimation?

A "new" technology can no longer solely be defined in terms of the new perceptual spaces that it might inaugurate. Its "newness" must be treated as a function of its evolution as an idea and is thus amplified over space and time.

In the context of an extended instrumental context, the imagination will engage with a series of perceptual thresholds as it is caught in-between past and future, but outside of the present. Multiple entrances will be revealed at the various sites of this dislocation. These entrances lead into a subterranean world where the imagination might make contact with hyperphysical configurations of information, with strange cybernetic patterns of sentience that have been fossilized at a zero degree of existence.

The mirage of the new, its ability to marshal thresholds of perception, under the sign of progress, tends to evaporate when one treats machine systems as matrices of different spaces and times, as agents in one's personal sensory and sensual articulation, or as immanent,

hyperphysical traces of previous tactilo-ecolographic
activity.

While acknowledging the necessity of formulating
questions about the composition of newness and cultural
function of original and unfamiliar boundaries, one must
also cultivate approaches to machine systems that acknowl-
edge their identity-generating capacities, or their abilities
to serve as laboratories for conceiving of different configurations or patterns of human consciousness. Other ways of
blurring and even erasing the boundaries between machine
systems and the human body must be explored than those
that have already been proposed in connection with the
future of the human/machine interface.[11]

Engineering drawings point to a world that exists
independently of machine systems and independently
of their representational products. And yet, of course, these
drawings are of the machines themselves. Thus, insofar as
an engineering drawing or initial sketch is at the foundation
of each prototype, or each final product, that might
eventually enter into mass production, the representations
that I am talking about are more than the simple products
of the initial meeting(s) of two technologies: a pencil
and piece of paper. For it is the contingent contact between
these technologies, an initial point of contiguity, that closes
a circuit and creates a living image of a "mind." In addition
to serving as a point of genesis, contact marks a vanishing
point for the kind of world we live in. In order to access
this vanishing point, we need more subtle instruments, tools
that are not necessarily crafted or drafted for service under
the sovereignty of progress. These tools could be used to
construct new types of imaging technologies and aesthetic
practices. Finally, what we need today is a new type of
anthropology to deal with this zone of human/machine
activity. This anthropology must not only be directed
toward a given machine culture, or the senses that are
erotically engaged in its genesis, but it must also address
the traces of different forms of sentience that have been and
are continuing to be recorded as echoes of "mind."

[1] Ken Baynes and Francis Pugh, *The Art of the Engineer*, Lutterworth Press, Guildford 1981, p. 13. Further references are noted in the text.

[2] Besides *The Art of the Engineer*, the other principal English-language book dealing specifically with engineering drawing is Peter J. Booker, *A History of Engineering Drawing*, Chatus & Windus, London 1963.

[3] Henry Adams, "A Law of Acceleration" (1904), in *The Education of Henry Adams: An Autobiography*, Houghton Mifflin, Boston and New York 1927, p. 494.

[4] Roland Barthes, *Camera Lucida*, trans. Richard Howard, Flamingo, London 1984, p. 81. Further references are noted in the text.

[5] Wolfgang Schivelbusch, *The Railway Journey: Trains and Travel in the 19ᵗʰ Century*, trans. Anselm Hollo, Urizen Books, New York 1980.

[6] Herbert A. Simon, *The Sciences of the Artificial*, MIT Press, Cambridge, Massachusetts 1981, p. 9. Further references are noted in the text.

[7] Bruno Latour, "Drawing Things Together," in Michael Lynch and Steve Woolgar (eds.), *Representation in Scientific Practice*, MIT Press, Cambridge, Massachusetts 1990, p. 52. Further references are noted in the text.

[8] Michael Lynch, "The Externalized Retina: Selection and Mathematization in the Visual Documentation of Objects in the Life Sciences," in *Representation in Scientific Practice*, p. 154.

[9] Gregory Bateson, "Form, Substance, and Difference," in *Steps to an Ecology of Mind*, Ballantine Books, New York 1972, p. 459. Further references are noted in the text.

[10] For a more detailed discussion of this tactilo-ecolographic-logic, see David Tomas, "Echoes of Touch and the Temptations of Scientific Representations," *Public #13* (1996), p. 104–117.

[11] See, for example, Donna Haraway's classic cyborg text "A Cyborg Manifesto: Science, Technology, and Socialist-Feminism in the Late Twentieth Century," in *Simians, Cyborgs, and Women: The Reinvention of Nature*, Routledge, New York 1991, p. 149–181.

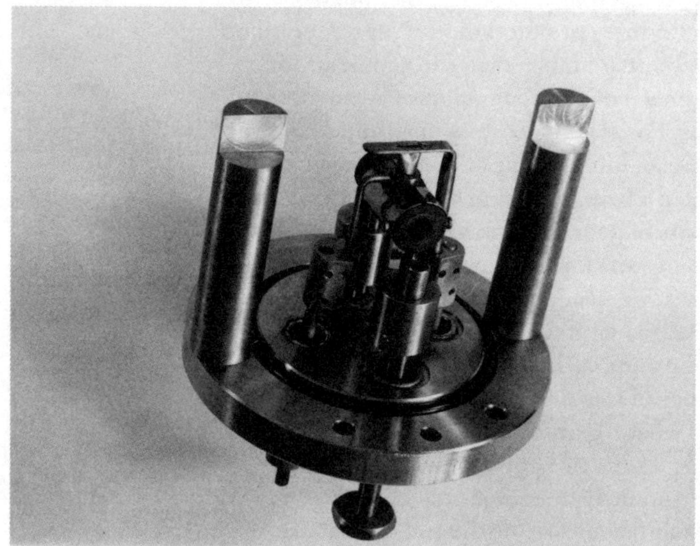

Photograph of an actual graphite oven used in experiments at the Foster Radiation laboratory, McGill University, c. 1977

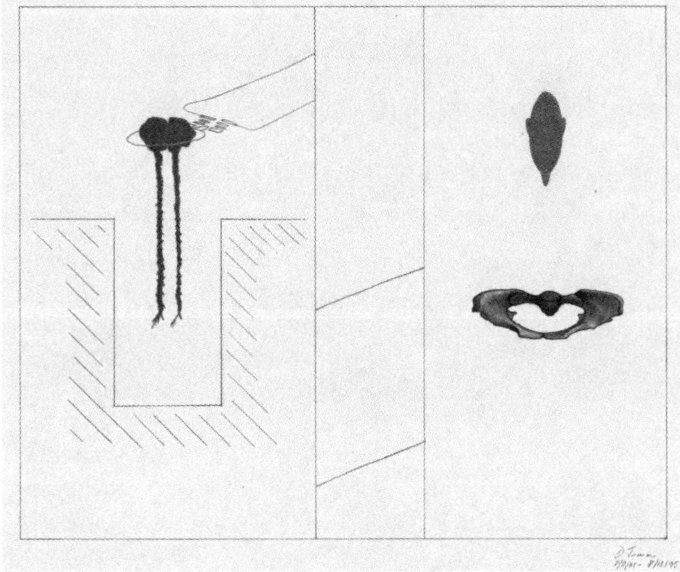

David Tomas, *Untitled*, 1995
Lead and colored pencil, 25.4 × 30.5 cm

A hybrid sketch/presentation-type drawing for an experimental situation that unfolds in a virtual environment. The drawing functions as an investigative tool for exploring the anthropological and aesthetic possibilities that are generated in the interfaces between imaging systems and between these systems and different kinds of scientific and technical representations.

The Data Dandy and Sovereign Media: An Introduction to the Media Theory of ADILKNO*
Geert Lovink

Parachute, no. 85, Winter 1997

The data dandy does not bring about any partial media connections, but dedicates himself to an aesthetic attitude toward the phenomenon of information. The motto of the "User as Artist" is, "La toilette digitale est l'expression de la société." A dandy always figures in an ambiguous social situation, and in this fin de siècle that is the state of profound confusion and boredom. In the face of an overwhelming assortment of identities, the data dandy concerns himself with the depth of devotion to computerized elegance. Like the splendid heroes of the 19th century, he is solely dedicated to his own perfection. Beyond hype or lifestyle, beyond criticizing the corporate character of technoculture, the dandy tries on programs one after the other, with Oscar Wilde's line, "The first duty of life is to be as artificial as possible," as a guideline.

The data dandy collects information to show off and not to transmit it. He is well, too well, or even exaggeratedly well-informed. Pointed questions are met with unwanted answers. He always comes up with something different. The phenotype of the data dandy is as feared as his historical predecessor, whose playground was the street and the salon. The elegant extravagance with which he displays the most detailed trivia shocks the practical media user. The data dandy makes fun of the gauged consumption and the measured intake of current news and amusement, and doesn't worry about an excess or overload of specialized knowledge. His carefully assembled information portfolio bespeaks no constructive motive. He goes to the greatest effort to appear as arbitrary as possible. One wonders: Why did the data-head want to know all that stuff? He zaps not out of boredom, but out of unwillingness to keep abreast of current events and everyone else's latest worries.

The data dandy considers his avatar in cyberspace the center of the digital universe. He knows he can only assume this position through the grace of the open structure of the network. His irksome interventions are preconditioned by public access, which he does not view as a means of changing the nonvirtual world. He recognizes the Net as a space to display oneself, not to communicate. Simulation is the fundament of his "General Principles of Digital Elegance," which is dismissed by essentialists, who still believe in the real/unreal binary, as "Lust am Untergang" or "Reinen Hedonismus." The data dandy is a secret democrat waging a relaxed battle for the unbounded expansion of digital human rights. Because if the plug is pulled on the Net, his personality will evaporate.

The data dandy displays a disquieting kinship with the politician, who also forces himself upon us with empty phrases and won't go away. Now that the political classes in their death-struggle have discovered the media, they are impossible to get away from, and their fanatical attempts to solicit support are taking on dandyish traits. The data dandy surfaces in the vacuum of politics, which was left behind once the oppositional culture neutralized itself in a dialectical synthesis with the system. There he reveals himself as a lovable as well as false opponent, to the great rage of politicians, who consider their young pragmatic dandyism as a publicity tool and not necessarily as a personal goal. They vent their rage on the journalists, experts, and personalities who make up the chance cast on the studio floor, where who controls the direction is the only topic of conversation. Yet they find the data dandy hopelessly difficult, since he doesn't want to play the sporting opponent and neglects to ask politely critical questions. Our bon vivant enjoys all displays of banality and takes absolutely no offense at pointless dedication. It would have been useful to be malicious, but the imperfect subversive shows precisely his engaging side. His charm is deadly.

The Net is for the electronic dandy what the metropolitan street was for the historical dandy. Strolling along the data boulevards cannot be prohibited and ultimately jams the entire bandwidth. The all-too-civilized conversation during a rendezvous turns up a few misplaced and objectionable data, but never results in dissidence. The point of willfully wrong navigation and elegant joyriding inside someone else's electro-environment is admiration, envy, and confusion, and consciously aims for stylized incomprehension. The dandy measures the beauty of his virtual appearance by the moral indignation and laughter of the plugged-in civilians. It is a natural character of the parlor aristocrat to enjoy the shock of the artificial. This is why he feels so at home in cyberspace with all its attributes. Cologne and pink stockings have been replaced by precious Intel; delicate data gloves and ruby-encrusted butterfly goggles and sensors are attached to his brows and nostrils. Away with the crude NASA-aesthetics of cybernauts! The data dandy has moved well beyond the pioneer stage; the issue now is the grace of the medial gesture.

*   ADILKNO is an abbreviation for Society for the Advancement of Illegal Knowledge.

The Photography of Nan Goldin
Is Touching
Larys Frogier

Parachute, no. 86, Spring 1997
Translated from the French by Donald McGrath

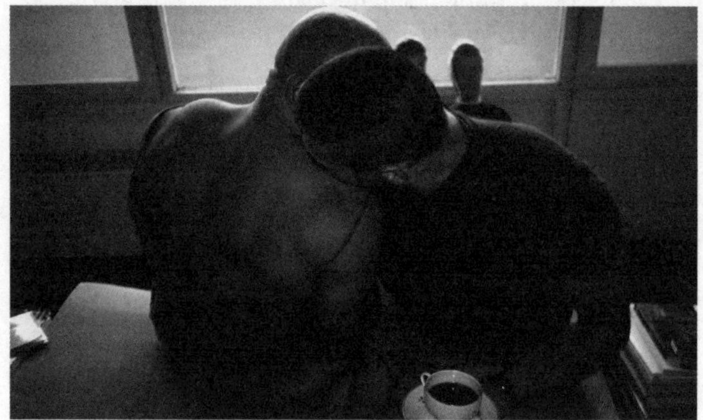

Nan Goldin, *Gilles and Gotscho Embracing*, Paris, 1992

Nan Goldin experiences, memorializes, and exhibits emotional and physical states that she shares with those close to her, whom she describes as her "extended family." These include, among others, David, Cookie, Bruce, Greer, Siobhan, Joey, Gilles, and Gotscho… She has photographed them in the privacy of their apartments, on the street, and in bars and discotheques, in what are moments and places of communal life, time/spaces that extend beyond the studio and the practice of journalistic realism. Her works feature bodies apparently devoid of any desire for aesthetic originality and, taken together, display affinities with the private photographic journal. Her taking of photographs produces images and compels the gaze, which becomes suffused with streams of affective and corporeal intensity. However "informal" it may seem, Goldin's work stems from a complex and carefully worked out photographic act that first and foremost targets the visual sense. Her charged photography requires that we reconsider how the body has been represented in this medium, as well as the photographic process of memorialization, the visual display parameters of the private journal, and the critique of the concepts of *punctum* and documentary. In Goldin's work there is something like an ardent desire to put to the test how what really and truly "figures" in a photograph is represented and how it determines the processes whereby images acquire meaning.

Contacts

On a ferry en route to Mykonos, Rebecca looks straight into Nan's eyes and camera (*Rebecca on the Ferry to Mykonos*, 1995). In Paris, Gilles and Gotscho embrace while Nan tenderly enfolds their bodies within the orbit of her lens (*Gilles and Gotscho Embracing, Paris*, 1992). In Provincetown, Bruce, his upper body bare, stretches out on a bed and casts a tender look at Nan, who is looking down from above (*Bruce on a Motel Bed, Provincetown*, 1994). In Goldin's photographs, the body is constantly leaving its mark or imprint; even her pictures of empty rooms show the traces of the bodies that have lived in them, as well as those of her deceased friends.[1] This extreme contiguity of the body/referent to the indexical character of the photograph must be emphasized; for Goldin, the act of photographing is initially less concerned with representation than it is with making contact with the bodies she photographs. "To photograph someone," she says, "is to touch them, a caress."[2] This contact is actualized in the act of taking the photograph, is materialized in the (im)print, and endures in the act of looking at the photograph.

When she takes photographs, Nan Goldin does not create a distance between the "photographer" and the "model." She is not after a quick slice of reality, but seeks instead the haptic dimension, the tactile energy between two bodies.*

Likewise, the print must not be understood only as stasis, as a fixing of the image. An examination of Goldin's photographs tells us that the bodies in them do not *expose* themselves to the camera, but *impose* themselves upon it in an ongoing quest for their own carnal and affective sensations. The bodies represented do not cease being bodies of desire, desires for bodies.

The aspect of Goldin's approach to photography that truly grasps our attention is its fundamental experience of touch through sight. Her eye is far from being a disembodied, rational, conceptual, informative, or documentary one; it confirms Merleau-Ponty's idea that "every experience of the visible has always been given to me within the context of the movements of the look, the visible spectacle belongs to the touch neither more nor less than do the 'tactile qualities.'"[3] More than a phenomenological touching of the gaze, Goldin's touch is both carnal and affective:

> The instant of photographing, instead of creating distance, is a moment of clarity and emotional connection for me. There is a popular notion that the photographer is by nature a voyeur, the last one invited to the party. But I'm not crashing; this is my party. This is my family, my history.
>
> My desire is to preserve the sense of people's lives, to endow them with the strength and beauty I see in them. I want the people in my pictures to stare back.[4]

The visual means of such "affective contact" are those of a photographic act designed to set in motion processes in which bodies continue to touch one another, where looks cross in mirrors or stare boldly at the lens. Goldin's framing does not select the aesthetic pose most appropriate for a "model"; on the contrary, it reveals the way in which her body collapses into other bodies, circles around them, and encounters them head-on or from behind. Framing does not, in this case, cut up or fragment the body, but shows the tension and motion, the physical and emotional energy that impels the photographer toward other bodies; it comes from an impulse that precedes the taking of the photograph.

Something like an unceasing stream of gazes circulates between the photographed body and the body of the viewer. Or, to put it somewhat differently, the photograph actualizes a body-to-body relationship between the photographed subject and the viewing subject. Between these two, the image is no longer meant to expound

exclusively upon its status as a realistic or codified signifier.
A Nan Goldin photograph authenticates the existence of
someone dear to her, someone who has survived the proof**
of the shoot to in turn authenticate the existence of the
viewing subject. This brings to mind Roland Barthes at the
moment at which he attempts to give an account of his gaze
as it comes to rest on a photograph of his mother:

> The photograph is literally an emanation of the
> referent. From a real body, which was there, proceed
> radiations which ultimately touch me, who am here;
> the duration of the transmission is insignificant; the
> photograph of the missing being, as Sontag says, will
> touch me like the delayed rays of a star. A sort of
> umbilical cord links the body of the photographed
> thing to my gaze: light, though impalpable, is here a
> carnal medium, a skin I share with anyone who has
> been photographed.[5]

Memorizing by Heart

At the same time as Goldin's photographs trigger a carnal
relationship with their figures, they develop a double
temporality that takes the photographed body out of its
day-to-day temporality. This double temporality comprises,
on the one hand, the time of the shoot, of photographic
framing, and, on the other hand, a time of duration consisting
of the accumulation, arrangement, and narrative recasting
of images.

Philippe Dubois has clearly articulated the distinctive
feature of the photographic image in the act of shooting:
this is a matter of *"cutting into the flesh to perpetuate death*—of
decapitating time with one stroke of the scalpel, cutting
away the moment and embalming it flatly and clearly under
(on) strips of transparent film, so as to conserve it and
preserve it from *its own loss*."[6] For Goldin, photographing
comes down to blending, at one and the same time, amorous
contact and potential separation from the other body. For a
better understanding of her approach, we have to go to her
own autobiographical narrative, which explicitly ties the start
of her photographic career to her family history and, more
specifically, to the suicide of her sister at the age of eighteen:

I realized that in many ways, I was like my sister. I saw
history repeating itself. Her psychiatrist predicted
that I would end up like her. I lived in fear that
I would die at 18. I knew it was necessary for me to
leave home, so at 14 I ran away. Leaving enabled
me to transform, to recreate myself without losing
myself. When I was 18 I started to photograph.
I became social and started drinking and wanted to
remember the details of what happened. For years
I thought I was obsessed with the record-keeping of
my day-to-day life. But recently I've realized my
motivation has deeper roots: I don't really remember
my sister. In the process of leaving my family, in
recreating myself, I lost the real memory of my sister.
I remember my version of her, of the things she said,
of the things she meant to me. But I don't remember
the tangible sense of who she was, her presence, what
her eyes looked like, what her voice sounded like.
I don't ever want to be susceptible to anyone else's
version of my history. I don't ever want to lose the
real memory of anyone again.[7]

"To perpetuate death"—in Goldin's work the expression is
heavy with meaning. The memory of her sister's body
persists, of course, but this mental image is not enough.
What Goldin needs is a "tangible perception," and photography is what enables her to accomplish the actual act of
remembering and mourning the beloved body. Goldin
responds to the trauma of definitive separation, of arrested
temporality, with a photographic act that takes the affirmation of life and the return of death upon itself. Goldin's
shoots always exist, then, on the edge between bodily
pleasure and physical disappearance. There is nothing
morbid about this; it has to do, on the contrary, with the
desire to take the photographic image to the full range of its
existential or auratic status: although it can be reproduced
ad infinitum, the photographic image attests to and authenticates the existence of a body within a given time that will
never be repeated. It is here, perhaps, that we can locate
the shift that Goldin brings about in the concept of the
figure of the body. The indexical nature of the photograph is
no longer enough for her; no longer can she say simply

"there" in the way that Pierce might have. What she does say is this: "There, that existed, there it lived and moved!" The photograph does not simply attest to something, it radiates. "Such is the *metonymic* and literally *mobilizing* drive of photography, which starts from almost nothing, from a simple point (*punctum*) or unique singularity and spreads, invading the entire field and imbuing it with affective life."[8] The maturity of Goldin's work resides in the difficult task of memorializing the figure of the body.

This work with temporality within the photographic act acquires a precise meaning once we know that most of the friends, lovers, or acquaintances whom Goldin has photographed have died prematurely from AIDS-related infections. We just said that the miracle of photography consists in reproducing *ad infinitum* what takes place only once, of regenerating unique life moments frozen by the photographic lens. But a closer examination of Goldin's work reveals that things are not so simple. Let us listen to what she has to say.

> I used to think that I couldn't lose anyone if I photographed them enough. I look at my photographs of all my friends who've died from AIDS in the last years, hoping to keep them with me. In fact, these pictures show me how much I've lost. There were the people who carried my history, they were my past and my plans for the future. We were meant to get old together.[9]

Goldin is clear on this point: the technique of photography is not in itself capable of assuming the task of mourning and remembering. This act depends, rather, on the social context in which the temporality of a life can or cannot come into its own. Those not directly concerned by the impact of the AIDS crisis may have a hard time imagining the very real and radical extent to which individual tempo-rality has been turned upside down. It is always painful to mourn and remember the loss of someone dear; but it becomes literally unmanageable when, at the height of the AIDS crisis, your friends' names are repeatedly crossed off in your address book over weeks and months. Goldin's photographs visualize the shattered temporality of an

individual striving to carry on her own life and keep her
social life going within a drastically reduced circle of friends.
They also constitute an act of resistance against a "public
discourse" that refuses to mourn many of those dear to one.
For numerous, indeed, are the situations in which families
openly accept the death of a child yet forbid all mention
of the supposedly shameful fact that the person "died of
AIDS-related illnesses." It is as if the "victim" were guilty
of his own death and should just make a silent exit. This
kind of collective mind-set leave those who were truly close
to the deceased without any way of articulating, visualizing,
or commemorating their deaths. In this respect, Nan
Goldin's photographs are active memories of her extended
family, of the lives that were part of it, and the love that
was part of them.

In an essay entitled "Death and the Marketplace,"[10]
David Deitcher conducts a critical analysis of the plethora
of contemporary artworks that deal with death and mourning
related to the AIDS crisis. He cautions us against allowing
these works to serve an art market bent on concealing
the political contexts out of which they emerged, a market
set on stressing and capitalizing on a universal and nostalgic
idea of death, mourning and sadness. The author quite
rightly says that today "activism continues, but in different
and less visible ways." It is imperative that we recognize,
along with Deitcher, that the need to "maintain critical
consciousness about art that testifies to contemporary
struggles with sickness, death, and loss. Contrary to what
some have said, there is no conflict between being humane
and being critical of all aspects of the culture we inhabit.
In times of crisis, such as ours, being critical isn't just
possible, it's a moral responsibility."[11] Deitcher is, however,
too quick to contrast Goldin's works with those of Felix
Gonzalez-Torres. He reproaches Goldin for supposedly
taking a too literal and sensationalist approach to death,
one that, in his view, lends credence to the ideology of
bohemian artistic life. The works of Gonzales-Torres, on the
other hand, purportedly give viewers a historical and critical
awareness. This opposition between two different—
though not incompatible—visual strategies appears reduc-
tive. To label Goldin's work as simply a strategic exercise
coming out of bohemian art circles is, on the one hand,

to miss the complexity of her photographic ruminations on sexuality, memory, and death. On the other hand, it is to forget her involvement in the key contexts of the sexual-identity politics of the 1970s, 1980s, and 1990s. The subjective, literal, and affective dimensions of Goldin's photographs in no way exclude critique.

Exhibiting as Keeping a Journal

The writing of a private journal does not stem from confessional, exhibitionist, or voyeuristic impulses. It is at the opposite pole from journalism, from the mythologizing of events. The private journal is characterized by the quest for the instability of the event, for the survival of contact with daily life and emotions. It is not a matter of uncovering a reality, but of speaking one's truth, of saying what it is one experiences as real. Maurice Blanchot has the following to say with regard to the journal that grows out of this endeavor:

> The journal is not essentially confessional; it is not one's own story. It is a memorial. What must the writer remember? Himself: who he is when he isn't writing, when he lives daily life, when he is alive and true, not dying and bereft of truth [...] It is a route that remains viable; it is something like a watchman's walkway upon ramparts: parallel to, overlooking, and sometimes skirting around the other path—the one where to stray is the endless task. Here true things are still spoken of. Here, whoever speaks retains his name and speaks in this name, and the dates he notes down belong in a shared time where what happens really happens.[12]

It is in this sense, of course, that Nan Goldin's photographic journal escapes being voyeuristic, something it achieves through its ability to bring to life, in their brutal rawness, daily emotional dramas that individuals simply cannot escape.

Goldin's work of memorializing by means of a journal proceeds through two phases: accumulation and exhibition. "If each picture is a story, then the accumulation of these pictures comes closer to the experience of a memory, a story without end."[13] The temporality of the figures that Goldin has accumulated is not that of a logical sequence closed upon itself. Rather, the time of the accumulated photographs has nothing realistic about it; it is already integrated into an individualized story.

With accumulating, however, there is always the risk of losing oneself in overabundant memories. To activate memory, one must go beyond simple accumulation to formulate and visualize recollections. The practice of exhibiting is what enables Goldin to cast raw memories into narrative form. Exhibiting, publishing, and grouping images together, arranging them in series, writing texts to accompany exhibitions—all of these together constitute the act of "preserving memory." Visitors to Goldin's exhibitions are struck first by the display of the artist's personal history. But this is a history devoid of any didactic or documentary narration of facts. This is what Goldin means when she speaks of photography as a way of "taking notes on my life." The form of her exhibitions parallels that of the private journal, which is noticeably different from that of the (self-) portrait in the strict sense of the term, and from that of the (auto)biographical narrative.[14]

The gaze that takes in the so-called "private" photographs of Nan Goldin also scans a "public" space, namely, that of the exhibition space or publication. The pictures of the bodies of Goldin and her friends are intended not only for those close to her, but also for the anonymous gazes of strangers who have never shared in their lives. Indeed, the various ways in which she exhibits her photographs are very carefully calculated to ensure that I as a viewer am tempted to give up my pure viewing space for that of a subject momentarily sharing a few snippets of life. To visit an exhibition by Nan Goldin is to enter into various constructed yet unstable spaces constituted at those points where gazes meet. Exhibition space is used to subvert the concepts and ideological boundaries between public and private space. The exhibition operates by circulating and shifting affective and corporal intensities back and forth among the gazes of the photographer, the photographed subject(s), and viewers.

First viewing: photographic negatives are printed on medium-size paper (generally 50.8 × 61 cm) before being framed and hung on gallery or museum walls. These photographs are arranged in horizontal or vertical viewing patterns determined by their embedding narrative structures. We might have, for example, a self-portrait series, a trip-to-Japan series, a series devoted to the lives of Gilles and Gotscho, or a series on the life of Cookie Mueller. But the photographs can also be hung in accordance with the narrative shapes of certain corporal intensities, such as those of bodies touching, hugging, kissing; or bodies in drag, bruised bodies, stretched-out bodies. In the *Tokyo Love* series, shown at the Galerie Yvon Lambert in 1995, a large section of wall was painted red; on it, unframed photographs were mounted edge to edge to form a large panel recounting various romantic and sexual adventures that occurred in Japan. In this way, the wall became the support for a compact photographic series, with the wall color serving as a frame.

Second viewing: slides are projected continuously in a dark room, forming narrative series like those of *Self-Portrait* and *Tokyo Love*. The rate at which the slides are shown takes over from the movement of the viewers' bodies in the exhibition space, in the process setting up specific temporalities. That of *Self-Portrait* is chronological, while that of the *Tokyo Love* series is more like the time of a compact group of snapshots. The projection is accompanied by one of the artist's favorite songs; "All By Myself," sung marvelously by Eartha Kitt, lends rhythm and meaning to the successive images of *Self-Portrait*. Remember that this way of showing slides was practiced in the spaces that Goldin shared with her friends from the 1970s, when she organized slide-show parties using photographs developed by commercial laboratories.

Third viewing: the photographs are intended for publication, and the book becomes an album. A narrative series can be a book in itself—this is the case with the extraordinary series dedicated to Goldin's best friend, Cookie Mueller.[15] Or a book can provide the occasion for an ongoing dialogue with a close friend who is also a photographer: *Double Life*, made with Goldin's friend David Armstrong, covers the private lives of two individuals within a community of friends and lovers during the years from 1970 to 1993.[16] Goldin's books often include a preface relating an encounter with one of her subjects; this forms, in fact, an autobiographical narrative in which the photographic act and happenings within her community of friends are intricately entwined.

These different exhibition modes constitute forms of private journal keeping that are specific to Nan Goldin. Her varied exhibition strategies cast in visual form that particular act of the diarist which consists in *taking notes* on one's life. The private journal does not contain writing that could be called unique and stable; rather, journal note-taking tends toward the fragmentary, ephemeral, and discrete. Its author comes to exist through events, moments, memories, and associations. The resulting self and others present in the private journal attempt to constitute and represent a unity, but always within the mode of spatio-temporal discontinuity: each day and place are different; I'm not the same person each day, yet I'm unique—and so are you, the person I love. In the private journal, the fragmentary coexists with the unitary, the discrete with the continuous, the momentary with the ongoing. In the specific case of Nan Goldin's photographic journal, the various books and exhibitions constitute new temporalities, in other words, additional opportunities to recreate this journal by recombining old photographs, repeating series of photographs, or juxtaposing them with recent images. One could say, therefore, that the visitors to Goldin's exhibitions and the readers of her books constitute the nodal points of this unity of the gaze. The viewer who looks at what is strange or foreign to him or her has the task of reconstructing the unity of the private narrative—a task that is, of course, impossible in reality, yet incredibly moving within the different temporalities of visits to exhibitions and readings of books.

Index, Code, Punctum

Since its invention, photography has overturned the concept of the figure in the order of representation. As early as 1895, Charles Sanders Pierce showed how photography inaugurated a new relationship with representation, its images being traces of the real or "indexical" signs:

> Photographs, especially instantaneous photographs,
> are very instructive, because we know that they are in
> certain respects exactly like the objects they repre-
> sent. But this is due to the photographs having been
> produced under such circumstances that they were
> physically forced to correspond point by point
> to nature. In that aspect, then, they belong to the
> second class of signs, those by physical connection.[17]

The history of photography is based on the exploitation
of this indexical character of the image. Nan Goldin's
photographic work developed within the critical context
that established and critiqued the power of the index.

In numerous texts on photography, Rosalind Krauss
has repeatedly stressed the indexical nature of the photograph. For her, the art of the 1970s was marked by artists'
tendency to use the photographic index to short-circuit
questions of style, and cancel out formal artistic intervention. Photography became the operative model of indexical
practice: in the 1970s artists stripped artworks of all the
coded messages specific to artistic disciplines and replaced
them with uncoded messages that fall outside all cultural
systems and do nothing more than present us with the mute
presence of the real.[18] It is interesting, then, to observe how
Krauss makes use of a technical property, the photographic
index, to set up a new postmodernist aesthetic of abstraction: in opposition to modernist pictorical abstraction,
which effects a reduction of painting to its zero degree,
she posits a postmodernist photographic abstraction that
brings about a reduction to the zero panorama of the real.
We come back here to the properly modernist notion of
presence: Krauss replaces the pure transcendental presence
of the work with the pure physical presence of an uncoded
event within the real.[19]

Craig Owens, for his part, refuses to accept the use of
photography as proof of the work's transparency to the real,
to the index. For him, photography is concerned first and
foremost with the notion of mise en abyme[20]: the photograph describes itself, not the reality represented; it does
not make reality present to us, but plunges us into the abyss
[*abîme*] of representation—that is, a structure of unlimited
duplications of the image, a ceaseless deconstruction of

the idea of representation of reality. The notions of pure visual presence and pure physical presence are obliterated on behalf of others: absence, contingency, arbitrariness, entropy. With reference to the emergence of artists like Sherrie Levine and Cindy Sherman, Douglas Crimp has tried to articulate how the photographic practice of the 1980s no longer refers to the notions of index or physical presence, but revives the *praxis* of reproduction and copy to undermine the modernist ideas of "pure presence to the work" and "photography as art." He writes: "The desire of representation exists only insofar as it never be fulfilled, insofar as the original always be deferred. It is only in the absence of the original that representation may take place."[21]

Nan Goldin's work, which spans the time of this debate, is guided neither by the desire for a pure aesthetic of the index nor by the practice of the photograph as simulacrum. Here we must go by the artist's own statement: "I feel a bit like a dinosaur because I still believe that photography is true, or can be true. I think I'm the only person in America who still believes this."[22] The truth that Goldin has sought over the past 20 years is not the truth of a social reality, a goal espoused by the New Objectivity. Nor has she set out to establish a new aesthetics of the index. Her truth resides, rather, in what binds the index and the code to the *punctum* articulated by Roland Barthes:

> The *punctum*, then, is a kind of subtle *beyond*—as if the image launched desire beyond what it permits us to see: not only toward "the rest" of the nakedness, not only toward the fantasy of a *praxis*, but toward the absolute excellence of a being, body and soul together.[23]

Many historians and theorists of photography have vehemently critiqued Barthes' concept of the *punctum*. For John Tagg, this idea is dangerous because it would have us believe in the evidentiary value of photographs, whereas the latter are actually constructed within the framework of specific institutional practices, and rely on a social and semiotic process that we cannot ignore.

> For this, however, we must look not to some "magic"
> of the medium, but to the conscious and unconscious
> processes, the practices and institutions through
> which the photograph can incite a phantasy, take on
> meaning, and exercise an effect. What is real is not
> just the material item but also the discursive system
> of which the image it bears is part.[24]

If Tagg's argument is fundamental and compelling, it is
important to point out, however, that Barthes had already
embarked upon such a semiotic critique of the image in his
first texts on photography. The issue is more one of determining whether there is a radical incompatibility between
the recognition of the *punctum* and the critique of the code.
This question is already built into Goldin's work, which
seems to assume this apparent opposition in order to link
the existential and the auratic to language and critique.
Goldin is fully aware that her photographs are made up of
both uncontrollable emotions and external rhetoric. The
image she produces constitutes her truth with respect to her
existence in a given community and specific context. It does
not claim to speak on behalf of others, or in favor of any
artistic style, but asks itself how it is that a body becomes a
subject, and how individuals represent themselves within
complex signifying systems (gender, sexuality, illness,
community, etc.). Goldin has no desire to engage in a
critique of representation as simulacrum from the outside;
she wants, on the contrary, to critique it from inside—in
other words, to show how it is possible to work out representations of the self, and relationships to the body and the
image, from within a contemporary context. This is what
leads her to say:

> My work deals with the difficulty of being human and
> with the fact of making the most personal things public
> so that others will dare to do likewise. I think that we
> have made secrets of things that have no reason to be
> concealed. Now we have to open the windows.[25]

The journal narrative, and the figures of her own body and
proper name and her friends do not, therefore, exclude the
capacity to engage in a critique of representation. In other

words, the truth of the photographic *punctum* does not block access either to rhetoric or to the critique of rhetoric.

Resisting Documentary

> On August 18, I came back to Berlin from Salzburg because I'd been told Alf was doing badly. He was the first person who ever invited me to Berlin in 1983 and he became my closest friend here. Since I moved to Berlin in 1991 he's been in and out of the hospital with AIDS-related illnesses. I went to the August-Victoria-Krakenhaus early that day—he was breathing with difficulty, I heard his Death Rattle. He could no longer speak, but he heard me read letters from his friends and talk about our love for him. In the mid-afternoon, I went to see my book designer and to meet his five-day-old son, Fritz, who had just arrived home from the hospital. When I got back to the hospital, Alf was dead. The nurses had laid him out and covered him with yellow roses. There was a trace of a smile on his face. My friend Darryl called that day my "existential wallop." In one day, my perspective of the world had been stripped down to the essential. Berlin has lost its center for me with Alf's absence. The death of so many has devastated my community—the babies are a faint hope for some kind of continuity.[26]

Nan Goldin assumes the right to transpose to the public sphere emotions between individuals who are most often considered marginal. This mixing of public and private might be put down to gratuitous voyeurism—were it not for the fact that Goldin's photographs invite viewers to question the meaning of these two concepts in our contemporary culture. The strategies used by communications networks to give a public face to homosexuals, prostitutes, drug addicts, and transvestites consist in stripping them of all existential bonds of friendship, all ties to lovers and family members. While Goldin does not hesitate to show us bodies sexualized, dead, suffering from physical and psychic ailments, or surrounded by friends, these are first and foremost bodies that never lose their proper name. In other words, they are continually in the process of becoming subjects.

Goldin's critique of documentary photography has acquired its effectiveness in the history of representations of AIDS. Her photographs surreptitiously alter the usual reading of the "public image of the pathological and deviant body" being addressed to the so-called "general population." She overturns the ideological codes of the family and the concept of love. As she never ceases to remind us, "these images are of my tribe, my friends, our family."

One should know that, starting in 1983–1984, the print media took over the task of disseminating images of "the public face of AIDS." Scientifically inaccurate yet deliberately sensationalist expressions like "the AIDS illness," "the AIDS virus," "carriers of the virus," "to catch AIDS," "risk groups," and "the gay plague" accompanied visuals that would eventually establish the stereotypes of the body and person living with AIDS. The way was thus paved for the elaboration and dissemination of the *image* of AIDS, namely, that of the *victim*. The first press photographs of AIDS "victims" typically showed a haggard-looking solitary figure—a man, of course—stretched out on his hospital bed with the stigmata of the disease plainly visible on his body and his face masked or wracked by suffering. Simon Watney has made it crystal clear why such journalistic and documentary photographs are ideologically harmful:

> The person with AIDS is invariably imprisoned within the demeaning category of the "victim," in which he or she is stripped of all power and control over the actual complex meaning and dignity of an individual's life. In this manner the entire experience of living with AIDS is censored, and the diseased body is transformed into a signifying husk which is only there before our eyes to evidence the "knowledge" of AIDS commentary which both precedes and exceeds the life of the person in the photograph, whose living being is ruthlessly obliterated.[27]

Thus the stigmatized body of the AIDS sufferer, visualized with impunity by the apparatus of photography, has facilitated the establishment of the AIDS myth—in the sense of the term understood by Roland Barthes:

> Myth [...] abolishes the complexity of human acts, it
> gives them the simplicity of essences, it does away
> with all dialectics, with any going back beyond what is
> immediately visible, it organizes a world which is
> without contradictions because it is without depth, a
> world wide open and wallowing in the evident, it
> establishes a blissful clarity: things appear to mean
> something by themselves.[28]

Nan Goldin's photographs demythologize the concepts of
"private" and "public" within the context of the AIDS crisis.
This process of demythologizing operates by repeatedly
transposing material from the private sphere into the public.
To quote Barthes once again: "The best weapon against
myth is perhaps to mythify it in its turn, and to produce an
artificial myth [...] Since myth robs language of something,
why not rob myth?"[29] Goldin's photographs do more,
however, than engage in a pure process constituted by the
repetition and deconstruction of the myth of AIDS; they
also remind viewers that, from the start of the crisis, there
existed—and indeed still do exist—manifold representations of AIDS to which the majority of newspaper readers
and television viewers do not have access. These include, for
example, photographs of people living with AIDS taken by
their friends, lovers, and family, photographic and video
archives maintained by organizations devoted to the fight
against AIDS and by associations for drug addicts, homosexuals, and prostitutes. Images like Goldin's are produced
not because someone is diagnosed with HIV/AIDS,
but because they create continuity in the private lives of
such people and attest to their activities within various
organizations or communities. The body of the person living
with AIDS is shown as that of someone who is indeed a
person in the full sense of the term.

[*]   Translator's note: In the French text, the next sentence, deleted here, is an untranslatable pun. The *prise de vue*, which means the actual shooting of the photograph, is likened to a *prise de corps*, which literally means an "arrest" but, in the present context, suggests something more like a grasp of, or hold upon, the body.

[**] Translator's note: The French word *épreuve* can mean "proof" or "trial," in the sense of something to be endured. This secondary sense does seem to be intended as well.

[1]   See Nan Goldin, with poems by Joachim Sartorius, *Vakat*, Walter König, Cologne 1993.

[2]   Nan Goldin in *Über-Leben*, exh. cat., Bonner Kunstverein, Bonn 1993, p. 79.

[3]   Maurice Merleau-Ponty, *The Visible and the Invisible*, trans. Alphonso Lingis, Northwestern University Press, Evanston, Illinois 1968, p. 134.

[4]   Nan Goldin, *The Ballad of Sexual Dependency*, ed. Martin Heiferman, Mark Holborn, and Suzanne Fletcher, Aperture Foundation, New York 1986, p. 6.

[5]   Roland Barthes, *Camera Lucida: Reflections on Photography*, trans. Richard Howard, Hill & Wang, New York 1981, p. 80–81.

[6]   Philippe Dubois, *L'Acte photographique et autres essays*, Nathan, Paris 1990, p. 161.

[7]   Goldin, *The Ballad of Sexual Dependency*, p. 9.

[8]   Dubois, *L'Acte photographique*, p.75.

[9]   Nan Goldin in *Über-Leben*.

[10] David Deitcher, "Death and the Marketplace," *Frieze* (July 1995), p. 41–45.

[11] Ibid., p. 44–45.

[12] Maurice Blanchot, *The Space of Literature*, trans. Ann Smock, University of Nebraska Press, Lincoln 1982, p. 29.

[13] Goldin, *The Ballad of Sexual Dependency*, p. 6.

[14] See Philippe Lejeune, *Le Pacte autobiographique*, Seuil, Paris 1996.

[15] Nan Goldin, *Cookie Mueller*, Pace/MacGill Gallery, New York 1991.

[16] David Armstrong and Nan Goldin, *A Double Life*, Scalo, Zurich 1994.

[17] Charles Sanders Pierce, "Logic as Semiotic: The Theory of Signs," *Philosophical Writings of Pierce*, Dover Publications, New York 1955, p. 106.

[18] See Rosalind Krauss, "Notes on the Index: Part II," *The Originality of the Avant-Garde and Other Modernist Myths*, MIT Press, Cambridge, Massachusetts 1985, p. 210–219.

[19] To escape falling into such essentialism, Krauss points out that "the reduction of the conventional sign to a trace [...] produces the need for a supplemental discourse:" photographs are subtitled with captions, i.e. explanatory text. The uncoded message is, therefore, doubled by a text that "repeats the message of pure presence in an articulated language" (ibid., p. 211). But are we not dealing here with a Greenbergian mode of looking at artworks, one that, for its part, envisions abstract painting's need to preserve a minimum of spatial illusion to enable viewers to have access to pure visual flatness? Krauss's historical interpretation of the indexical practice of the photography of the 1970s seems to be a misplaced repeat of a modernist point of view, and this in a context where she trying to characterize this practice as marking a rupture with the modernist conventions of the medium.

[20] See Craig Owens, "Photography en abyme," *October*, no. 5 (Summer 1978), p. 73–88.

[21] Douglas Crimp, "The Photographic Activity of Postmodernism," *October*, no. 15 (Winter 1980), p. 98. Reprinted in Douglas Crimp, *On the Museum's Ruins*, MIT Press, Cambridge, Massachusetts 1993, p. 119.

[22] In a televised interview (*Métropolis*, Arte, February 10, 1996.

[23] Barthes, *Camera Lucida*, p. 59.

[24] John Tagg, *The Burden of Representation: Essays on Photographies and Histories*, The University of Massachusetts Press, Amherst 1988, p. 4.

[25] *Métropolis*.

[26] Nan Goldin in *Über-Leben*.

[27] Simon Watney, "Photography and Aids," *The Critical Image: Essays on Contemporary Photography*, ed. Carol Squiers, Bay Press, Seattle, Washington 1990, p. 183. Revised and reprinted in Simon Watney, *Practices of Freedom: Selected Writings on HIV/AIDS*, Duke University Press, Durham, North Carolina 1994, p. 60–75.

[28] Roland Barthes, *Mythologies*, trans. Annette Lavers, Jonathan Cape, London 1972, p. 143.

[29] Ibid., p. 135.

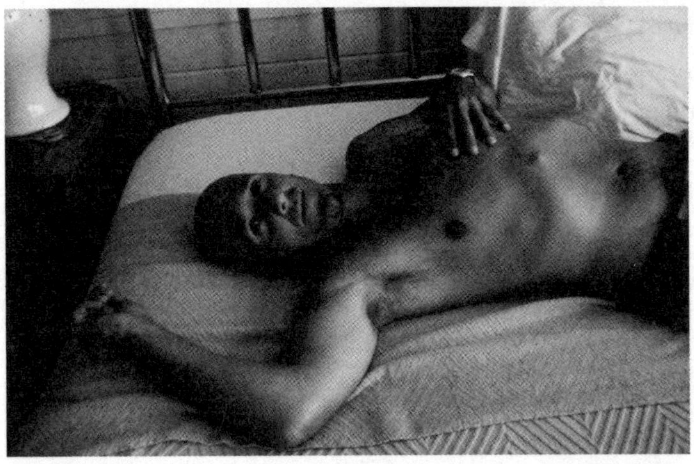

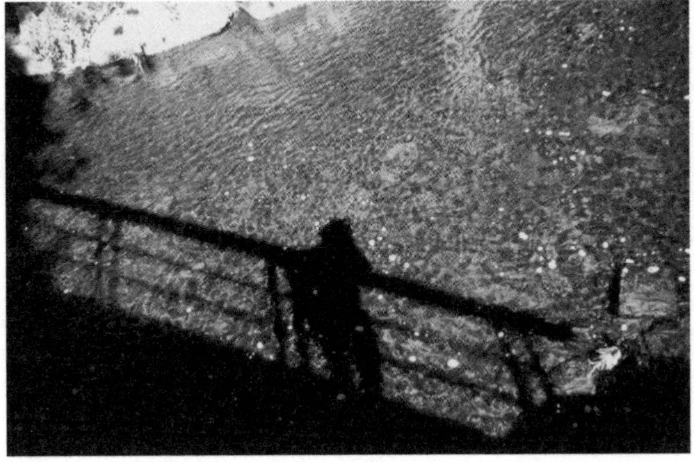

Nan Goldin, *Bruce on a Motel Bed*, Provincetown, 1994

Nan Goldin, *Self-Portrait on Bridge, Golden River, Silver Hill Hospital, Connecticut*, 1998

Intimacy, Greenery, and Dazzling Whiteness. Representations of Family Life in Eija-Liisa Ahtila's Video Works
Jean-Charles Massera

Parachute, no. 94, Spring 1999
Translated from the French by Gila Walker

Between fiction and documentary, between the *détournement* of the commercial break and the talk show, the videos of Eija-Liisa Ahtila seem to question the way in which mass culture, class, family relationships, and relationships between couples inform and structure our private behavior. Exhibited as films or slides, these works assign to the spectator a position that oscillates between that of consumer, voyeur, and confidant. They are an exploration of the use of the image, and of the possibilities of the reappropriation of the forms of representation that speak to (and for) us, and that form us.

<u>Waiting for Supper (A Nondescript Family)</u>

1997. *Today*: In an exhibition space, one projection screen facing the viewer; to the viewer's right and left, two more screens facing each other. Consider a video projection composed of three distinct monologues. Three stories generated by a single event: one night, somewhere in Finland, a man is hit by a car and dies instantly. One after another, his granddaughter, a woman named Vera (his son's companion?) and his son appear on the screen. Outside the house, the granddaughter, a teenager in a red tennis shirt and a blue skirt, bounces a ball off a wall. Close-ups of her staring at the camera. Her grandfather's death does not affect her. She describes her father's despondency, dwelling on the physical signs of a pain she doesn't feel. ("Today my dad's crying […] His shirt and pants are all soaked […] Two vertebrae were sticking out of his back"). The over-the-shoulder shots adopting the girl's viewpoint standing at some distance from her father and looking at his back as articulating a distance that cannot be overcome. A distance between the girl and her father that he puts into words when he says "When I ask her 'How do I look?' she says 'You look like a dad.'" Whereupon we see an over-the-shoulder shot of the girl watching her father standing on a bridge below, his back turned to us, looking out over the water… "Standing at the quay, I felt in my back a feeling as if my braces would have snapped and my pants dropped to my ankles." And when the teenager talks about herself, she again adopts an exclusively external, factual point of view ("I'm in an armchair, I have a boyfriend. I have something on my lap"). A point of view stated in a tone and rhythm that makes everything she says sound like a statement of fact emptied of content, and that places everything on the same plane of reality. Boredom, absence of intensity, and lack of connection between three pieces of information that don't belong to the same reality. What is the relationship between sitting in an armchair and having a boyfriend? Why does the information about the girl's affective situation come between—and interrupt the continuity of—two pieces of information of the same type? To wit, an inability to tell a story, to build up the story of her own biography. Step out of the self and picture yourself in fragmentary representations. Factualness versus inwardness.

Whereas the girl does not internalize the event, her father seems to be physically immersed in the pain of his loss. Shots of his tear-drenched shirt and long painful cries punctuate the girl's story. A physical internalization of pain intensified by mental pictures of the grandfather: on a road, at night, in the middle of the forest, an old man walks toward us. When he reaches the camera (the surface of consciousness), his features become clear. It's the grandfather… For a few seconds, he stares at the camera (etching an impression on the surface of consciousness), then walks away and lies down across the road. To wit, a sequence of mental pictures that initiate the son's monologue, and stand in for a lack of words. In fact, if the son feels the pain of his loss, he is unable to formulate it in words. The mental picture of the grandfather meeting his death, and the lack of verbalization as signs of his incapacity to translate this death into experience. Is this incapacity due to the nature of the event (the unnamable)? To the father's personality? To a defect in language that Ahtila's montage would remunerate? Does the focus on the exclusively visible signs of pain and behavior (deprivatized interiorization) that characterizes the teenager's monologue also stem from an incapacity to translate time and events into experience? Can my subjectivity be reduced to the fact that I'm in an armchair, that I have a boyfriend and that there is something on my lap?

Giorgio Agamben:

> For modern man's average day contains virtually nothing that can still be translated into experience. Neither […] sitting for minutes on end at the wheel of his car in a traffic jam [nor] the journey through the nether world of the subway […] nor queuing up at a business counter, nor visiting […] the supermarket […] Modern man makes his way home in the evening wearied by a jumble of events, but however entertaining or tedious, unusual or commonplace, harrowing or pleasurable they are, none of them will have become experience. It is this non-translatability into experience that now makes everyday existence intolerable.[1]

If the living conditions and everyday surroundings of the family pictured in *Today* potentially contain fewer events than those encountered in big cities, the question of the impossibility of translating one's day into experience comes up in the same terms. On the everyday surroundings: a few shots of the family home and garden, some pictures of a forest and a lake in the vicinity. A peaceful family environment (a chair in the shade of a tree, an empty plate on a branch, a green lawn… a close-up of three insects…): events are rare, activities repetitive (doing the dishes, resting in an armchair, bouncing a ball off a wall, sitting in front of the television, etc.)… A modest living environment hardly affected by the consumer imaginary—hardly penetrated by the market (shots of the garden tools against the wall of the house, a few flowers, old furniture at the back of the garden, some clothes drying on the line). If the identities depicted in *Today* seem reduced to the functional dimensions of the rooms or places they occupy (washing up in the kitchen, sitting in the living room, playing in the garden…), they do not seem to have integrated the imaginary of the planetary technologically advanced country's petty bourgeoisie—an imaginary founded on the turnover of consumer goods and services. In the event, *Today* displays the signs of a permanence (a ritual) and durability situated at the periphery of the supply turnover and the desires it elicits (the novelty). The girl about her father: "If he starts doing something that he likes, his back starts aching so much that he has to stop everything. Then he can't do anything else than sit and watch TV […] Granddad lived to be old. He had retired from working life long ago. My dad retired from life." Here, the absence of activities (the possibility of building up the self through an activity); elsewhere, in Vera's monologue, the absence of desire: "The streets are swarming with people who look alike, and boast about having done precisely what's undone […] People make love at least twice a week only because nobody wants to feel shame." A verbal inflation that hides a deficit of experience. A good average that stands in for feeling. To conform to arbitrary and consensually fixed norms ("twice a week") or not to ("to feel shame"). The good average as the *sine qua non* condition less of belonging to a homogenous community ("people who look alike") than of being presentable to this same community. A social determinism that stands in for desire. Cease being the subject of your desires and let norms organize our timetable and govern our affects (the becoming-statistic of man). Vera's monologue as evidencing a process of expropriating desire.

If the girl seems able to see herself and the people around her only from an external, factual point of view, maybe it is because the models of being in the world and in relation to others available to her have annihilated any possibility of having experiences of her own (deprivatized interiorization). Vera's soliloquy (the isolation) as an example (the paradigm): "I preserved the fear inside my body and made myself it." The internalization of feeling as self-negation. Can self-compliance with standards (the disabling of the self) be translated into experience? If this compliance with standards entails a loss of desire, then existences cannot strive toward any goal. Existences exclusively moved by the necessities of keeping the household going and losing awareness of time passing by… The permanence of this same necessity as the rhythm of life. Inertia as the mode. The norm as the setting. The negation of one's *owness* as the model… Being there as the condition.

If the teenager cannot internalize the events she is describing, if the father's lived time is characterized by an absence of activity (the passive form), and if Vera's existence comes down to keeping the household spick-and-span (the active form) while denying anything that could be her own (self-compliance with standards), then *Today* shows different forms of one and the same dispossession: that of the possibility of building up a biography. The protagonists give us a biography of their relatives ("My dad normally doesn't cry, he normally don't do nothin'. Except he used to work"; "At home in the morning he made coffee and held a newspaper so that he couldn't touch anybody") and neighbors ("In this city adults have become failed teenagers"), but they tell us nothing of themselves and repress anything intimate ("I preserved the fear inside my body and made myself it"). The ability to say *I*—and to talk about yourself—disappears to the profit of the third-person singular ("My dad," "he") or plural ("people," "they"). An inability to speak of oneself that stands out against the mediatization and the culture of me, myself, and I that constitutes the middle-class imaginary in the world's most technologically advanced countries. Could the family unit represented in *Today* be impervious to all the psychological dramas aired on the major television networks? To all the shrink advice columns in popular magazines? To all the talk shows? What does the father watch when he's not working? Where do Vera's thoughts about sexual behavior come from? Why doesn't she appropriate the information that she gives us to build her own way of life on the margins of the standards she rejects?

Vera's monologue swings from general considerations about the local petty bourgeoisie to recounting a dream ("I see a two-storied animal eating walls from the house. A rattling tram pronounces my dad's name"). To wit, two types of discourse that she cannot seem to connect in a conscious way to her own experience (describing without conscientizing). While she's talking, the camera lingers on a bottle of alcohol, a glass, a toaster, a thermos, a pile of newspapers (signs of lived time), and moves through a train corridor and a forest (places with a strong symbolic thrust). Two image registers that reflect an incompatibility between the contexts of experience—of lived time and oneiric time—and those of discourse. A sequence of images that do not derive from Vera's discourse and that develop independently from the sequence of domestic gestures on which the camera lingers. The slow motion shot of Vera washing up as emphasizing the domestic work that she does not talk about and in which she seems to engage no value—no engagement in constructing a subjectivity through her work. An absence of experience of the self here and now. The abundance of comments on questions foreign to this same work (extrinsic to her condition) as a promise of emancipation. An emancipation that comes up against her incapacity to appropriate time for herself. As if the fact that she is not the conscious subject of the thoughts, images, and discourses that run through her deprived her of a sense of self in the present. By removing herself from her activity (here, washing dishes) to focus her attention on what she is not living (I am thinking not about what I am experiencing, but about what others are experiencing), Vera not only denies her own lived time, she also precludes any possibility of translating it into experience and thereby freeing herself from it. Consequence: Vera lives the house more than she lives in the house. Question: How is it possible not to live to the rhythm of the chores to be done?

The Family Unit of the Spectacle (The Separation of Affects and the Need to Talk)

Has the possibility of experiencing *ownness* and proximity to the self been definitively annihilated by the society of the spectacle (life deported behind the screen) and the normalization of behaviors (conformity)? Vera's disillusioned reply: "Newspapers glorify pain and horror. Pleasure is pornography or petty bourgeoisie. Exactly the ideas which start to clot are merchandise" (the spectacle)… "The streets are swarming with people who look alike, and boast about having done precisely what's undone" (the standard of presentability). If pleasure has become a product, if it only takes shape in a representation codified by the law of supply and demand and if, in the case of pornography, this same representation is built out of an exclusively male point of view (the camera as duplicating the male gaze—the subject of desire—fixed on a female body fragmented into objects of desire), then the *I* in the feminine gender cannot agree with pleasure (deported outside her body), nor can it be the subject of its own desire. Experience the spectacularized body (make use of pornographic images) or relinquish pleasure. Accept the absence of exchange with the people around you and articulate your emotional potential with its representations, or sink into isolation. Giorgio Agamben rereading Guy Debord:

> The spectacle does not simply coincide, however, with the sphere of images or with what we call today the *media*: it is "a social relation among people, mediated by images," the expropriation and the alienation of human sociality itself.[2]

Yet the culture of the spectacle and its standards do not constitute the sole causes of self-dispossession here. Between two sobs, the father recalls his father ("At home, in the morning he made coffee and held a newspaper so that he couldn't touch anybody") and what he used to say ("Your life is just drifting from one accident to another. You can't even decide, you can't even decide.") But hasn't the father inherited his isolation and his passive acceptance of physical weakness from the grandfather (atavism)? An atavism that shows through in a few verbal tics picked up from his father, particularly in the way he also has of ending statements of general truths—here about his incapacity to make decisions when it comes to the main direction of his life—by repeating the last phrase. To wit, an inadvertent revelation of hereditary determinism that stands out against the social determinism that Vera talks about. Two forms of determinism coupled with an incapacity to speak for oneself. A difficulty in speaking one's own language that is paradoxical in a mise-en-scène that gives pride of place to speech. Indeed, in most of Eija-Liisa Ahtila's video works, in *If 6 Was 9* and *Today* as in her "commercials" *Me/We*, *Okay* and *Gray*, moments of silence are rare. The mise-en-scène gives priority to speaking and telling stories over action and experience (the need to fill the void with a flood of words)… For want of experiencing a lived moment (being here and now), give it a verbal representation. Moreover, Ahtila's filmic construction gives priority to monologues over dialogues. *Today*: three people who seem to be living (in) separate realities. Realities (monologues and shots—the daughter looking at the father, a quick shot of the girl in the garden in the middle of Vera's soliloquy…) that may intersect but that share no feelings, no activities, no desires, no common history. The story of a family with no history, and of its members with no biography. In addition, whereas the relationship between the father and daughter is clearly stated, what makes us think that the third person is part of the family unit? Whereas the man asserts that he has a daughter who "throws a ball," and asks her to "look," and the teenager describes her father's state of despondency, Vera gives us no information whatsoever about her relationship to the teenager or the father. Who is she? A mother, a companion, a wife, an aunt, a friend? All we know for sure is that the three people live in the same space and one of the last shots accompanying the father's story shows them together in a car speeding through the forest. A car that seems to bear down on a man lying in the middle of the road… A man who barely has the time to jump up and turn to face the headlights… The screeching of tires, a harsh white light over the entire screen, and the sound of an impact in the form of a question (Who ran over the grandfather?)… Cut. The choice of the monologue form and of splitting the stories over three separate screens projected alternately in the exhibition space as if formulating the split between the members of the family (the separation of affects). A separation of affects that is found again in the description of the grandfather who, according to his son, avoided physical contact with the people around him. Behaviors that freeze the circulation of meaning inside the family unit, and monologues that do not participate in the construction of a single story. A nondescript family with no events to speak of.

To whom, then, are the protagonists speaking? When Vera, her arms plunged into the washing up, talks to the camera, what type of picture are we looking at? A documentary on the condition of middle-class women in Finland? A talk show? A commercial that hasn't yet shown us the product being hyped? A fiction film? How do these general considerations on the society of the spectacle relate to the different points of view on the accident that inaugurates the three narratives? The blurring—or rather the mixing— of different types of discourse, different aesthetics, and different contents—fictive, documentary, and commercial—as a proposition for representations in step with the tools offered by contemporary middle-class culture. A culture in which our existences are built up after a delay, after the fact (the shrink's, the TV or radio talk shows, advice from experts, etc.). Work from the contexts and narrative structures of media aesthetics to try to translate into experience a time that we seem to be having a hard time living.

Practical Living (Is there Life Beyond Use?)

1998. A cell phone commercial informs us that "calling has become a sixth sense"… Based on what we read in magazines, hear on the radio, and see on certain TV shows, it seems that our lives boil down to our sole use of products and services available in the world's most technologically advanced countries. One look at the number of hours spent shopping each week confirms the becoming-user of man. A life of demands in a world of supplies.

1993. *Me/We* (Eija-Liisa Ahtila): While hanging the laundry out to dry, a man turns to the camera to communicate the state of his relations with various members of his family. Consider a 90-second film in which Eija-Liisa Ahtila diverts the function of commercials. If the aesthetics, the narrative structure, the framing, and the directing that characterize the advertising form are maintained (the position of the protagonists around the white sheets, the dazzling brightness of the laundry, close-ups of a typical spot of dirt, ultra-bright smiles of satisfaction, etc.), the words commenting the supposed action of the advertised product—here, a detergent—soon give way to words of intimacy. The man approaches the clothesline… His wife is already busy hanging a sheet on the line: "Sometimes I feel that I do not know what my wife really wants." To wit, a statement introducing the need to select a new detergent… Ultra-bright smile from the wife. "My daughter, however, has always got on well with her mother." If the pictures are still embedded in a process of exhibiting the product's qualities (an ultra-bright smile from the daughter), the father's monologue builds up a narrative that, instead of attracting the viewer's attention to the dazzling whiteness of the laundry—or the teeth—refers to the difficulties in communicating and living together that seem to afflict more and more families: "But she does not have very close relationships with others." Psychological communication is substituted for product communication. Cut. Camera moves to the center of the garden. At a table, before entering the discussion, a young man is sorting socks… At this stage in the commercial, a question: What accounts for the smile addressed to the camera? The presence of the father/husband or the effectiveness of the detergent?

If over the past few decades our aspirations and desires have often been materialized by the acquisition and use of products, if a good part of our emotional capital has been invested in their management, are we to conclude that being in the world boils down to using it (the becoming-user of man)? Guy Debord:

> The spectacle is the moment when the commodity has attained the *total occupation* of social life. Not only is the relation to the commodity visible, but it is all one sees: the world one sees is its world.[3]

Can we be something other than a man or woman vacuuming the carpet or hanging the clothes out to dry? Are there any reasons for smiling other than those hyped by businesses in their attempt to increase their shares in the market? Could the whiteness of the clothes in *Me/We* be a last ditch effort to get the people in *Today* to smile? Has the laundry penetrated my subjectivity to such an extent? And does the refusal to live to the rhythm of the supply and the desires it implies condemn me to depression? Has the practical dimension become the sole dimension of our lives? When we hang out the laundry, what are we thinking about? The laundry, or something else? Is our consciousness totally occupied by use? Has the intensification of the dynamics linking supply and demand brought with it a total absorption of the self in the product? If telephoning has become a sixth sense, if the radiance of the person I'm living with depends less on our way of being together than on her relationship to the products she uses, are we to conclude that our capacity of being and our imaginary are necessarily linked to the way in which we integrate the supply?

Ways of Being a User (How to Mix Utility with Interiority)

How can utility be mixed with interiority without reducing the latter to a way of being a user? In the event, *Me/We* connects two incompatible dimensions—the advertising dimension and the psychological dimension. A connection that conflates a mode of representation aimed at a population seen in generic, statistical terms (potential customers in target categories) with a mode of identification aimed at a specific psychological, family situation close to the mode of confessions that can be heard on TV and radio talk shows. The media show us pictures of ourselves on the job in documentaries, as consumers in commercials, involved in love affairs in fictions, or as citizens in television debates, so that we are fragmented into several dimensions. Dimensions separated for the needs of specialized genres. The advertising representation will not recognize our dimension as citizens, the fictive representation will not address our emotional dimension, our involvement in work will find a form of representation only in documentary films (fiction being interested only in our ability to love or hate others), and so on. As if it were impossible to grasp the complexity of the contemporary individual. As if the latter were unidimensional. Ahtila's commercials may act, in this respect, as models of reappropriating the separate spaces and forms of representation that speak to us (and for us), that shape, fragment, and isolate us. If the spaces and forms of representation of our media culture founded on the specialization of these same representations—a specialization that ineluctably conveys unidimensional representations of ourselves—reduce us to the single dimension needed to satisfy sponsor interests (the consumer dimension for ad men, the citizen for politicians, etc.), then relating separate forms of representation may indeed constitute an aesthetic issue.

On a table covered with a tablecloth, four cups of coffee. In slow motion, a hand deliberately knocks one over. Why was the coffee spilled on the tablecloth? To make a coffee stain that only one particular brand of detergent can get rid of? Or because the father was upset?

The father: "We had more or less an ethical crisis [...] I can see the reason... probably love had faded away." The image: a stain that needs to be cleaned. A fusion of advertising and psychological reasons. In the event, *Me/We* conflates documentary (the confession and addressing the viewer), fiction (a family story), and advertising (the commercial showing the whiteness and brightness of the laundry being hung out to dry) into a synthetic form. Reappropriate situations in life (here, a moment of family life and a household activity) and an interiority of which we have been dispossessed by fiction and ad narratives. Jürgen Habermas:

> The literary patterns that once had been stamped out of [privacy's] material circulate today as the explicit production secrets of a patented culture industry whose products, spread publicly by the mass media, for their part bring forth in their consumers' consciousness the illusion of bourgeois privacy.[4]

Re-become an actor in your own story. Retrieve our place as subjects in a media and film culture that has turned us into targets (advertising), objects of scrutiny (documentary), or spectators in search of experiences (fictional events

representing what we are unable to live). Deepen our
practical lives (the moment of using a product) with an
existential dimension. A question for Eija-Liisa Ahtila to end
with: Is there an equivalent in Finish for "washing your
dirty laundry in public"?

[1]   Giorgio Agamben, *Infancy & History, Essays on the Destruction
      of Experience*, trans. Liz Heron, Verso, New York 1993, p. 13–14.
[2]   Giorgio Agamben, *Id, The Coming Community*, trans. Michael
      Hardt, University of Minnesota Press, Minneapolis 1993,
      p. 79.
[3]   Guy Debord, *The Society of the Spectacle* (HTML version
      of Black & Red 1977 edition) http://www.marxists.org/
      reference/archive/debord/society.htm (last accessed
      May 2014).
[4]   Jürgen Habermas, *The Structural Transformation of the
      Public Sphere: An Inquiry into a Category of Bourgeois Society*,
      trans. Thomas Burger, Frederick Lawrence, MIT Press,
      Massachusetts 1989, p. 161.

Sight(s) and/or Sound(s). On Three Works by James Coleman
Jacinto Lageira

Parachute, no. 95, Summer 1999
Translated from the French by Harvey L. Mendelsohn

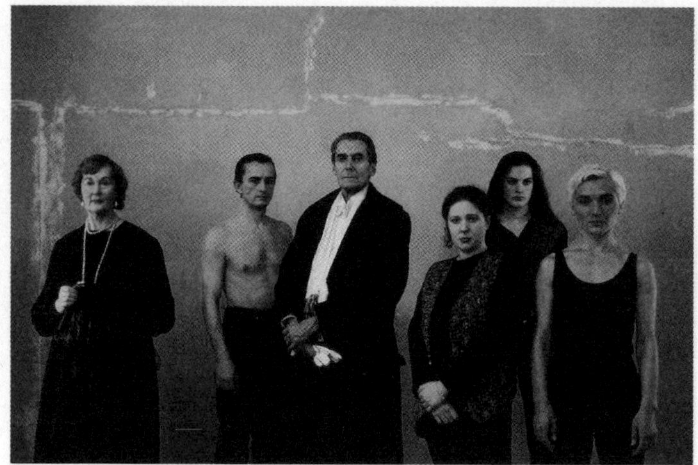

James Coleman, *INITIALS*, 1993–1994
Projected slide images with synchronized audio narration, duration: 18'

His first works of the 1970s already display the concern with image and perception that would become the basic problematic of Coleman's oeuvre. Thus *Slide Piece* (1972) is a repeated wall projection of a single slide, accompanied by descriptive commentaries on its content. And in the film *Playback for a Daydream* (1974)—in which one sees a drawing representing either a rabbit's or a duck's head, depending on what aspect of it one pays attention to—the perceptual act and the modes of recognition it brings into play are the work's main subject. Little by little, Coleman began to construct more complex narrative and representational systems, mixing photographic or filmic elements, video, slide projection, literature, theater, and the manipulation of voice and sound, a key work in this regard being the installation *Box* (1977). The montage of slides called *Seeing for Oneself* (1987–1988), which draws on the codes and archetypes of the story, of the tale, and of the theater, and which intersects these with the English gothic novel, the detective story, and the melodrama, is very revealing in terms of the role accorded to the viewer in the process of perceiving the work. In the installations the viewer is an essential link in the construction of the story's logic and perception. Their point of view, calculations, hypotheses, and even errors turn the viewer into a central actor of the story James Coleman is staging for them, but also with them. Continuity and discontinuity, synchronism and diachronism, constancy and rupture, unity and plurality—these are the terms that may be used to characterize the artist's sound and visual mise-en-scènes, which have perhaps been analyzed too often from a formalist perspective, although that is one of the necessary steps in understanding them.[1] In the three works to be studied here, I will specifically treat their sound and visual dimensions in terms of how these veil or make explicit the aspects of emptiness or lack in them. For, in spite of their spectacular presentation, the main impetus in them is almost always incompleteness, an inability to have "clear and distinct ideas," the nagging feeling that something is missing. But what?

Box (Abareturnabout), 1977

Box (Abareturnabout) is a rather primitive installation: a room plunged into darkness, a screen on which a black and white film is projected—silent at the beginning, then with sound added by the artist; the footage is drawn from a documentary about the fight between Gene Tunney and Jack Dempsey during the world boxing championship of 1927— and an old-fashioned projector. The latter produces a continuous noise, and one can see the film threading through it. *Box* is a "primitive" production in the sense that the apparatus and the images coincide in their relative mechanical brutality. Whatever one might say about the "noble art" of boxing, the blows that the adversaries give each other have no other goal than to knock down or "lay out" the other one, to vanquish him by physical force. And although one may indeed invoke the beauty of the movements, the skill involved in dodging the blows, the craft, and the tactical intelligence required to establish the pacing of the rounds, we are nevertheless confronted by a very violent fight whose end result, scarcely veiled, is none other than symbolic death. One boxer must make the other one physically disappear from the ring in order to win. Coleman's work thus highlights, too obviously of course, the coincidence of a mechanism that has become inhuman (the boxer) as a result of training and fighting, and the cinematographic mechanism that records and then coldly projects the actual details of a destructive battle. The fusion of the mechanical aspect of the boxers and of the film is immediately visible in the pulsations established between the image and the soundtrack, since the images are not projected continuously, but rather appear in stroboscopic fashion as space-time flashes at intervals of several seconds. Now, curiously, but with Coleman no doubt not fortuitously, under "stroboscope" *Le Petit Robert* offers at least three definitions that could apply in part to *Box*: "1) Rotary apparatus that gives the illusion of motion by means of a sequence of images. 2) *Phys.* Instrument designed to make objects animated by a rapid periodic movement appear to be either immobile or animated by a slow movement. 3) *Med.* Apparatus that emits luminous flashes of adjustable frequency, used to study the convulsive fits of epileptics." Watching the sudden appearances of the images of the boxers brings the three definitions to mind, since one in fact does have the impression of seeing them sometimes slowed down and at other times speeded up (in both cases, however, they are always in motion), and the conjunction of the sound and visual elements is such that the boxers' bodies take on a convulsive, uncontrolled, and disordered appearance.

Nevertheless, the effect produced by pausing or accelerating the visual elements does not fit with the tempi of the film's sounds, which repeat regularly and at the same volume, nor with the perfectly constant and uniform humming of the projector. In addition, once the socio-political and personal references have been exhausted—knowing that Tunney, who had beaten Dempsey the year before and was risking his title, was Irish, like Coleman—one can surely see in the work a metaphor for the struggle of a people, or of an artist with respect to his own work, as if the boxing match were the setting of an interior struggle. One can see that, at a very different level, the struggle takes place between the sound and the visual dimensions. A struggle of this kind in the work can then be transferred to the viewer, who is physically grabbed, even attacked, by this installation, which we could term "optophonic," since it causes a beating sound, which is no doubt cardio-vascular, to coincide in a regular fashion with a visual perception. The coincidence, moreover, is not only that of the installation's sound and image; it is above all the coincidence with the perceptual system of the viewer, who of course is constrained to follow the optophonic syncopation, but whose natural bodily rhythms, such as breathing, heartbeat, and spatial displacements and rotations, etc., have been incorporated in the work, although at an accelerated pace. In a sense it is the human physiological rhythm that served as the model of the machinery of *Box*. More than in any other work, Coleman here takes into account the viewer's entire body, intensifying the normal cadences and pulsations into which he integrates it, as if the latter occupied the place of the boxer. But the boxer's body—and the same is true of the body of the installation in its entirety—is no longer the idealized body into which the crowd projects itself and likes to recognize itself in a sublimated form. Here we have a solitary body. A body experienced from the interior. The spectators who attended this historic encounter actually don't appear very often, as if the power of the crowd, present in a certain fashion through the cinematographic gaze—boxing and cinema being popular spectacles that assemble large audiences—were momentarily rendered incapable of doing harm. The isolation of the bodies in *Box* is all the greater inasmuch as they are determined by the gaze of others (those who attended the fight or the installation's viewers), but in an inverse ratio, since the sound and visual split and/or duality isolates the bodies of the viewers confronted with the work. In reality, even if this sensation or perception is partially correct, the physical and psychic force of the installation lies not so much in what is perceived, as in *what is not seen* or felt when the image disappears and one returns to darkness and to the silence of the room. Thus, in a repetitive fashion, an image is associated with a pulsation, a breath, a voice, and the darkness is associated with silence. On the one hand, sight and sounds, and on the other, momentary blindness and absence of sounds. The slight uneasiness that one can experience with *Box* stems from this kind of passage into emptiness. A continuity of images could have preserved a visual link when the sound was lacking; and, inversely, the sound could have continued during the absence of images. This is not at all the case, and the installation produces the strange sensation of clinging to certain corporal realities and, simultaneously, dissociating itself from the eye and the body, but also from language.

Let us recall that in this same year, 1927, movies started to talk, and that the film used by Coleman is, to begin with, a silent film to which he added sound. The words one hears, spoken by a single boxer or, alternatively, by both of them— *the bout, the bout, the b-o-u-t, again, a-g-a-i-n, ah, ah, push, push, the left, stand, s-t-a-n-d*, for example—also establish a rhythm that is inseparable from the action in the images and from the viewer's perceptual activity. This tripartite division, if one conceives the work from the perspective of dissociation, or this trinity, if one conceives it from the perspective of unification is, above all, a filmic image that brings together what Marshall McLuhan, in his book *Understanding Media*, called the "verbi-voco-visual."[2] Now, one of the constants of Coleman's works is the refusal to opt for the dissociation or for the unification of the "verbi-voco-visual," thus calling upon the viewer to choose a possible route, though, contrary to the work itself, it will be a possibility which, inevitably, will exclude the other. Either one or the other, or one after the other, but not both at the same time; dissociation and unification thus split, through diminution of the "verbi-voco-visual" structure in the first case, or augmentation of it in the second. The stronger the dissociation and the more fragmented the information, the stronger the unification will be and the better organized the information; such structural possibilities fundamentally determine the meaning(s) of the works. In other words, the viewer must choose the form to give not only to what is being said at that moment, but also to what will occur when a cycle of the projection is completed. And to the degree that the choice made at the beginning determines the point of arrival, the viewer is summoned, no more and no less, to choose between two conceptions of the world—but that is something he/she does not yet know when the story begins.

For the documentary film footage that Coleman selected is
not used only as a purely visual image, but also as a sequence
of images that tell a story, presenting themselves as the
pulsations of the start of a logical narrative. The use that
the artist generally makes of media that have been diverted
from their usual function—cinema, photography, slides,
theater—should be understood precisely as the diversion
or, better, subversion of traditional narrative forms with
respect to images or actors perceived in time and space. It
should be emphasized that Coleman's works are spatialized
in time, but in a way that contradicts the systems of representation and narration that constituted a considerable
portion of modernity. Accordingly, in *Box*, the ways in which
the images function display several distortions and changes
in classification of a potential narrativity. First of all, the
match is presented in the form of an endless loop, and the
boxers never stop to rest, whereas a real match is punctuated
by pauses, consists of a certain number of rounds, and
always has a beginning, a middle, and an end; and this, one
notes, is the dominant narrative paradigm of a tale, of a
short story, of a novel. In *Box*, the narrativity is broken by
the pulsation of the images that endlessly repeat, but it is
reintroduced through the words spoken by one or both of
the boxers, which are presented without repetition (within
any one complete cycle) and thus possess a beginning,
a middle, and an end. The verbal, optical, and phonic
pulsation is, it is true, produced in a uniform fashion, but
the sequences diverge more and more as the pulsations
begin to overlap. One could say that there is a coincidence
in the divergences through the intermediary of the pulsation,
but that, at the same time, the pulsations, in succeeding
each other, produce these same divergences. Coleman has
clearly chosen to concentrate on the ambivalence of
an optical and sonic process that is sometimes unitary and
sometimes ruptured, but he does so by basing himself on
a reality that is often overlooked as a result of too formal a
reading of *Box*, namely the struggle for recognition. What
is the point of a boxing match if it is not to hit a human
being in order to obtain recognition, be it personal, financial,
social, or political? We thus encounter again, at another
level, the optophonic paradox of the installation's apparatus,
since in order to attain, in the case where one wins, a

positive state or status—recognition—the boxer must pass through contrary states—the negation of the other. In a similar fashion, in order to reconstitute the "story," or at the very least the process that unfolds in *Box*, the viewer has to accept certain lacunae in the apparatus. The source of recognition here is precisely the lacuna that one must fill to be recognized by the other.

Living and Presumed Dead, 1983–1985

This work begins with the projection of a scene unlikely to occur in the theater: 20 characters are lined up side by side as if taking a bow at the end of a performance. And, in fact, what will take place before us is the story of the end of a show or, more precisely, of the brutal end of the acrobat Capax, a sword-swallower who has cut his tongue and disappeared. Is he dead? We are left in doubt. Several actors/narrators, corresponding to the image of certain characters projected onto the wall—including Capax's son, Chris, two women—Abbas and Borras—a mysterious person named Mr., who might be the murderer, and another, or others, who are perhaps Capax himself—take part in this strange story that mixes carnival, painting, the circus, puppet theater, tableau vivant, the detective story, and Shakespearian drama. Moreover, the narrator beings his tale with a melody (*Greensleeves*) that is often counted among the "songs" of Shakespeare's theater, and his voice brings to mind that of the actors who have portrayed this author on the screen. The viewer thus attends a theatrical presentation that functions like a primitive movie projection and that, at the same time, makes reference to pictorial representation. The mélange of genres and of periods is further enriched by the off-stage voices of the protagonists—played successively by the same actor—who are trying to determine if the one presumed dead (Capax) is alive or not. To show and to tell, to screen from view and to keep quiet, to hide and to reveal—these are the main structural elements of a story in which the repeated permutations and the appearances and disappearances of the characters are presented as a kind of giant puzzle that one must complete in order to learn the logic of the story, but also as another way of hiding the truth and making it disappear, just as the body of the presumed victim has been made to disappear. Thus, as in most of the murders in detective stories, the truth here is that of the body, for to find it is to know the truth. Knowledge is therefore not linked to the work's discursive system, nor to the actors' speeches, but rather to the presence or non-presence of a body. Even though *Living and Presumed Dead* is constructed entirely of visual perceptions and discursive modalities, what is missing is neither visual nor discursive but corporal, literally the "body of the crime," which in fact is absent, or presumed to be, from the start of the projection. And it is precisely because the body is missing in the play that the play takes place. In this respect, *Living and Presumed Dead* calls to mind the film *L'Hypothese du tableau vole* (*The Hypothesis of the Missing Picture*, 1978) by Raúl Ruiz, in which the mystery is centered around a missing picture belonging to a series of paintings by the painter Tonnerre, a picture that is central to the meaning of the ensemble, and which neither the protagonists nor the viewers will ever see (unless the "picture" is the film itself). Another striking aspect is that many of the scenes in Ruiz's film consist of "tableaux vivants" in which the characters reproduce at full scale the existing pictures of the series, thus playing with a mise en abyme encompassing the pictorial, the theatrical, the photographic, and the cinematographic realms. The action in these two works by Coleman and Ruiz is thus based on *an object that is meant to be seen*—the acrobatics of Capax and the missing picture—but that is not visible, and which derives its force from its very disappearance inasmuch as it sets into motion a whole other machinery of replacement and reconstitution. And since what is missing in *Living and Presumed Dead* is by definition physically beyond reach, three characters (Abbas, Borras, and Chris) seek to restore the thread of the story and of the events through various modes of replacement.

The drama, deliberately ambiguous and complex, and as such worthy of the fictions of Borges, assumes, it could be said, the enigmatic figure of the double. Among the multiple inversions, substitutions, duplicities, and doublings among the characters, one may cite, for example, the little boy who is sometimes to the left of the character out of the Middle Ages and sometimes to his right; two women dressed in

19th-century clothes; a little magician and a little fairy, and the two mannequins. The most striking is that of Chris, the son, who wears his father's clothes, becomes his spirit, takes his place, and plays his role so that the play can continue. As in a mirror, to this natural replacement there corresponds a supernatural one, since a single character becomes transformed before our eyes. The character who was dressed all in white and resembled a dancer in the performances choreographed by Schlemmer becomes, thanks to the magic wand of the little fairy, like two other characters already present on stage, a third character wearing a mask and a red and yellow robe. He will end up by killing the faceless character who is wearing a white mask and is dressed in red. But these faces, are they two or do they belong to the same person? Have they finally killed Capax, or perhaps his murderer? Is this a new suicide or the same one repeated? Or indeed is it Chris, who, in a supreme piece of subterfuge or imposture, has arranged to have himself killed in place of his father?

Another form of substitution—less noticed, perhaps because it is too much in evidence, like the letter in Poe's short story—occurs in the names of the characters. One observes that there are two women and two men; that the names of Abbas and Borras (two women who have relationships with Capax) contain double letters and have the same ending. Now, the two letters at the beginning of these names are followed in the alphabet by C, which is none other than the first letter of Capax and of Chris; and these last two names contain the same number of letters, namely five, the number of protagonists named in the work, if one counts the presumed murderer, Mr. Since *Living and Presumed Dead* is in large part linked to the theater by its form, how can one not, continuing the play on words, think of the old word "mystery" (*Mister*), which in the 12th century was used to designate religious plays. And since we are talking about religious drama, one must not forget that Chris is simply the diminutive form of Christian (Christ, Christian …), and that, like the Savior, he is the son of an invisible father, whose place he has taken and for whom he has become flesh. It would no doubt be an exaggeration to speak here of "corpus Christi," but, in *Living and Presumed Dead* we are very definitely dealing with a body that has disappeared, like the body of Christ missing from the tomb after the Resurrection, and therefore living but presumed dead. Continuing in this vein, consider the strange things that the dictionary brings to light: the expression *habeas corpus* ("you have the body"—one could perhaps read into this Abbas corpus) is the name of an English law guaranteeing the freedom of the individual by ordering that the body of the detainee be produced before the court so that it can rule on the validity of the arrest. Now, in *Living and Presumed Dead* the body cannot be produced so as to make possible a ruling on the truth of the supposed murder. Again, in the dictionary (Larousse) one reads, just after the expression *habeas corpus*, the expression *hapax legomenon* ("something said once"), "Greek expression referring to a word or phrase of which only one example is known." Now, the Capax of *Living and Presumed Dead* knows at least a second example, his son Chris, dressed like him and playing the same role; in a certain manner, Capax is *said* a second time. Finally, following this same way of thinking, one may wonder— knowing that most of Coleman's works deal with the ability to memorize—whether names such as Abbas and Borras are not simple formulas, like those invented by the Scholastics, enabling one to retain more easily various forms of rhetorical reasoning, each letter being the beginning of a word. But in the case of Coleman, to what would they in fact correspond?

Whereas in *Box* and other works we are dealing with dissociation and/or unification, in *Living and Presumed Dead* we find something different: the optical and narrative structure likewise encompasses a lack, but this time one that operates in the mode of *transition*. At an initial level one may distinguish the transitions between the images and the narration, then within the narration itself, to the degree that the actor plays in alternation all the roles in the story, and then again among the images, as they appear and disappear in a sequence in which one dissolves into the next. Another form of substitution and replacement, this dissolving sequence may be considered a metaphor of how the whole installation works, in the sense that its transitions extend not only to the concrete material of the images and of the sounds but also, and above all, to the passages from the words to the images and from the images to the words. It is as if we were in the presence of a dissolving sequence that moved from the verbal to the visual and from the visual to the verbal by infinitesimal transitions, with the result that we were no longer exclusively the recipients of messages indefectibly joined as signifier/signified even though they are distinct, but rather recipients of verbal-visual entities that slowly transit through states in which, at certain moments, the verbal dissolves into the visual and the visual dissolves into the verbal. No doubt this is more an effect than an optical or linguistic reality, and here Coleman is no longer seeking this effect primarily to draw attention to clear and perfectly defined separations or unifications with respect to the problematic of lack; rather, he wants to draw attention to the fact that this lack is nothing other than the result of what is visible and utterable, a lack that could be thought of as the residue of the various transitions. One of the most obvious of these transitions is, moreover, literally inscribed in the sound and visual aspects of the work when the narrator brings out the alliteration of "s" and "a" (Abbas, Borras, Capax, Chris) in naming the characters, who thus, as it were, visually slide over each other. At another level, Chris' taking of his father's role and putting on the latter's clothes, and the very fact that there is filiation between Chris and Capax is another way of establishing a more elaborated transition between the verbal and the visual, just like between one body and other body. In other words, even if Chris takes the place of his father, it is only a partial substitution, because he is the "son of"; there still survives and subsists in him a part of the body of Capax. Thus, we have a game in which the sounds "s" and "c" pass between Capax and Chris, as if the sounds had become their bodies, as if the sounds themselves took on a body that was visible and not merely audible; and, in contrast to substitution, where nothing is retained of what has been replaced, here, in this transition, what has been and is no longer is still preserved for a moment. *Living and Presumed Dead* shows another aspect of those verbi-voco-visual *double binds*, since it creates a new modality that the viewer must once again confront, this time consisting of the pair transition and/or substitution, neither element of which is to be confused with the other. This brings us back to the question of the presence or non-presence of Capax's body, of his real or presumed death. Is the body lying on the floor at the end of the story a simple transition, that is to say, is it still Capax, returned from some space-time or other, or is it rather his son who has killed himself; or is it in fact an entirely different character (substitution), since what is actually there is a mannequin? If we propose a psychoanalytic hypothesis, we could also imagine (an extreme and very rare case) that transition and substitution are both true, if we think that Chris has killed his father in order to take his place, a real and symbolic place. But this is to forget that both of them are actors and that they play at being someone else, that they do not do what they say and they do not say what they do: they are in a performance. A performance of which we are the dupes, since the supreme subterfuge undoubtedly consists in making us believe that a body has disappeared some time ago or has just disappeared, whereas perhaps it is right here, before our eyes, in one disguise or another. What is missing is perhaps not a body. Instead, it could be an omission in the story, at least as it is told to us. At the end of *Living and Presumed Dead* the woman who was holding a book open and seemed herself to be reading the story that we were observing now stands behind the body of the person that has just been killed and simply closes her book. *Finita la commedia.*

INITIALS, 1994

Despite its numerous combinations, the narrative form of *Living and Presumed Dead* is more linear than *INITIALS*, which is constructed by means of a marked temporal dilation of its visual and audio elements, as can be seen already in the spacing of the letters in the title. The word "initials" can mean the initials of a name, i.e. letters, but also the start, the beginning, or rather the beginnings, since it is in the plural. The voice of the child that one hears spelling letters, like the initials, is not, however, that of a beginner reader, since the words and phrases are pronounced easily. The sighs one sometimes hears are rather those of an actor who is in the process of learning a text word by word, letter by letter. Doesn't the voice say on several occasions "return to words"? Yet not all the letters spelled out are then pronounced as words; certain remain, as it were, in suspense, distended in sonic space, calling upon only the auditory memory of the viewer, who must themself recompose the words. It could certainly be a question here of words of beginnings, but which words and which beginnings? The different stories of the creation of the world, beginning with the Adamic story in *Genesis*, report on the naming of things and beings, but it is often forgotten that this naming concerns what already exists. Undoubtedly, the biblical text affirms that "In the beginning was the Word," but *then*, in order *to name*, there has to be something to name; it is necessary to show or to designate a perceptible physical entity. At this point we are already in the period after the beginning. From there to saying that one names what one sees, that one names the visible, and therefore that one names images, would, of course, be too rapid, but it would not contradict Western history with respect to what has occurred in the relationship between the verbal and visual. The purpose of *I N I T I A L S* is certainly not to retrace this vast history, but rather, taking it into account, to bring to light something namable to which something visible does not always correspond and some-thing visible that could remain unnamed. Is the enterprise even possible?

    At the start, the viewer is shown photographs taken during the shooting of a film, an episode of a story told in pictures [*roman photo*], or the staging of a play that is just at its *beginning*, with the actors rehearsing. The idea that the actors are possibly just rehearsing arises almost entirely from hearing a voice that repeats the same words several times, while the visual story seems, for its part, to be taking place in a linear fashion. We thus have an initial scission, generated by the linearity of the work's visual component, which follows its course without necessarily taking into account or corresponding to what is being said. Once the projection has come full cycle, the viewer, moreover, is left with the strange notion that what they have just *heard* doubtless had *no relation* to what they have just *seen*. Yet what was said and what was seen nevertheless occurred in the same place, and the two components appeared to form an ensemble, not to say a whole, a term that would be mislead-ing here. It is true that in certain parts of the work the verbal and the visible seem to correspond, but most of the time they are set forth in such a way that only a simple parallel appears to exist between their respective signification (the meaning of what the voice says/the meaning of what we see) and their signifiers (a strictly verbal utterance/ the images) without any overlapping or obvious intersections between them. Are we not victims here of a kind of cinematographic "Kuleshov effect," by means of which Coleman, in quite simply juxtaposing a text and completely independent images, pushes the viewer to project a meaning onto this optophonic story, to find an order, a logic, or a principle enabling them to legitimate and justify links between the images and the words pronounced… links that perhaps do not exist. This recalls the experiment designed by Kuleshov, who by showing the same image three times, each time accompanied by a completely different statement, led the viewer to believe they have seen three different scenes. The characters in *INITIALS*, moreover, have neutral expressions, and their bodies, empty of emotions or psychological states, are like receptacles ready to be filled with meanings supplied by the viewer. Like the statues in a wax museum with their rigid bodies and facial expressions, the actors, displaying no attitudes that would indicate movement, have only hieratic poses. They do not move and never open their mouths, whereas the off-stage voice emits sound continuously and in a varying dynamic range. This second set of ruptures between the visual and the sound components thus creates another possibility in terms of the idea of the "initial." Is the voice the beginning of the images, or, inversely, are the images primary with respect to sound, to the words? Is the voice a commentary on the images, or do the images illustrate the story? Even if this were the case, the image would not be able to exhaust the meaning of the words, nor would the words be able to exhaust the visuality of the images, inasmuch as everything that could be said is not everything that is seen. Everything that is perceived is doubly questioned, first as a fixed image and then as the process of fabricating that image, as if we were presented with an allegory of the photographic act, indeed an allegory of representation itself. The attitudes assumed by the actors invite the viewer to consider such images as photographic poses, but the ambivalent and dull staging draws their attention more toward what is taking place in the image as such than to the narrative thread that is given by the linking of these same images. What is occurring in the image seems to be an attempt to grasp the pure appearance of the photographic medium itself, not so much the technical and chemical aspects of the image as the revelation, the manifestation, the phenomenon of its corporal, one might even say its carnal appearance. But this concrete materiality of the image is like an epiphany in which the visible and visuality are excessive to the point of becoming a kind of blind spot that cannot be situated in the chain of appearances. We thus seem to have arrived at one lack due to an excess of visuality in the images and at another lack due to an insufficiency in certain parts of the discourse of the off-stage voice.

 Such a scission can nevertheless display some unexpected connections if one thinks of the dream process. As in a dream—and the subject does come up in one phrase, "dreams are bitter"—there can be either an interdependence of word and image or a very clear separation. If one recalls Freud's demonstration concerning the two main processes of dreaming, displacement and condensation,[3] the images and words of *I N I T I A L S* that seemed at the beginning to have nothing in common could easily be seen to possess meanings linking one to the other through the effects of condensation and displacement. Seen from this perspective, the deficiencies, the holes in the story, the separations between the letters and the words, as well as between the letters, the words, and the images, would thus possess a logic of their own, the meaning of which would have to be decoded. And the voice seems to want to overcome the separations by offering several beginnings, several "initials." For the voice can be by turns personal or impersonal, the expression of the inner thoughts of a character, the beginning of a dialogue, the commentary of one of the characters or possibly of a viewer concerning what they are in the process of seeing—"why do you gaze one at the other?"—or else the directions of an off-stage director— "say it" … "t h e r h y m e."

Since we are talking about rhymes, two further pieces of information may be noted here. First, the character in

19th-century costume appears to be rehearsing one or several
scenes from a play in verse, or reciting a poem (the words
have to be spelled out and the feet counted). Second, the
rhymes are generally the *final* sounds of the words and not
the initial ones. The voice would thus seem to be that of a
poet who, in order to write his/her text, has to spell out
each letter and pronounce the words in order to come up
with the right rhyme or the right verse, so that the poem
may become, in Valery's formulation, "a hesitation between
the sound and the meaning." Another reading of the work
would interpret the "initials" as actually being the letters
themselves, pronounced simply for the beauty of their
sounds, although the letters had to submit to a certain order
so that at least some meaning, however minimal, could be
produced. In this view, *I N I T I A L S* could thus be understood not as a plastic work, but rather as a poetic one, linked
to a whole tradition of the spatialization of the poem on
the page and in the space of its utterance when it is recited
out loud—a tradition extending from Mallarmé's *Coup de dés*
(1897), to the *parole in liberta* of the Italian Futurist writer
Marinetti, the *zaoum* poems of Krutchenykh and Khlebnikov
and their manifestoes on *The Word as Such* and *The Letter as
Such* (1913), the Dadaists (Huelsenbeck, Hausmann, Tzara),
the poems of Schwitters, Gertrude Stein, Charles Olson,
and e. e. cummings, and reaching our days with contemporary *Poesie sonore*,[4] which accords great importance to
silences, to sounds, to the tessitura of pronunciation, and
to rhythms, all factors that are equally fundamental in this
work by Coleman. Moreover, in a passage in *I N I T I A L
S*—"it's hard to make out the initials … growing still …
ex-communicating as we speak … "—the artist makes
reference to the "autograph tree" located in Coole Park, in
Galway County, on which the members of the Irish literary
Renaissance (W. B. Yeats, G. B. Shaw, J. M. Synge, and Sean
O'Casey, among others) carved their initials.[5] When one
carves one's initials on a tree trunk, one wants to make them
last, but at that very moment one destines them to an
inevitable disappearance. The beginnings of the statement
are already its termination; the initial may be called the
beginning of the end. And if the word, since the time of the
Greeks, is linked in the Western tradition to Being, since to
say is to say Being, it is doubtless not by chance that one

finds somewhere in a Platonic dialogue an allusion to a tree on the trunk which there appear signatures, a distant echo of another beginning, the scriptural *logos*, to which the Greeks preferred the *phone*, the voice.[6]

In according such importance to the phonic event in *INITIALS*, since the statement is also the actual stating of it, Coleman severely tests the viewers, who seek to recompose the letters in order to obtain words, and then, if possible, sentences, but whose often fallible auditory memory does not always store the information necessary to do this. Too dispersed and separated in time, or too numerous, the stated elements cannot be retained and joined together in order to create any meaning, something Köhler was able to observe in several experiments on the memorization of syllables designed to study the degree of association and organization involved in this process.[7] In *INITIALS* one cannot relax one's vigilance in memorizing if one does not want to lose the thread of the sounds and of the meaning, as well as the possible links that might join them to the images. One must maintain a sequence of letters, even if this is difficult—"it's hard to make out the initials growing still." And it is doubtless the search for an equilibrium, a harmony, or simply the composition of the drama unfolding before us that causes the narrator to play with the words and phrases, by manipulating and interchanging their letters. The actors themselves may thus also be thought of as having become the equivalent of letters— not verbal letters, but ones spatialized in the form of images—that are displaced, transformed, and directed. The alliterations and the resonances of the names in *Living and Presumed Dead* in relationship to the substitutions and/or transitions of bodies already bore an identification between what was said and the appearance/disappearance of the images. Similarly, in *INITIALS* the letters, spelled in isolation, are small individuals who can form a group of syllables and therefore also words, even a statement, producing a way of structuring the story to which the characters' bodies correspond as images, sometimes alone, sometimes in twos and threes, sometimes in a group. Even though they do not make any precise gestures, the way they are positioned might be thought of as a kind of spatial syntax in which bodies take on the function of minimal units of meaning. And throughout the whole projection one observes a constant ambivalence with respect to gender (short hair and long hair, masculinized feminine faces, feminized masculine faces), reflections in mirrors and doublings (dark colors and light colors, extending to even the slightest details, such as the pearl necklace or the gloves), all culminating in the final permutations, in which the three men and women adopt all the possible positions, as if they themselves were letters, the initial letters of a poem with a deliberately limited vocabulary that someone was trying to write in a space consisting of both sound and visual dimensions.

The paradox of the different modalities creating ruptures between the sound and visual elements should be inter-preted as arising from a lack. The latter does not occur incidentally in the story or in the images by a kind of internal logic, as when an author or film director leaves something out in order to compose the text in a certain precise way or obtain a specific visual effect; rather it is determined by what does not take place and by what does not occur between the sound and visual elements. Some-thing is lacking between these two elements that is not found a posteriori in the work—which would yield the type of narrative or plastic construction that is quite common at the moment in various media—but rather at the beginning of the vision of reality that Coleman offers us. All things considered—and this is another paradox—the only thing that unifies his older and more recent productions is lack. In his works we certainly find, at an initial, formal level, lacks such as those we have examined and which had to be analyzed in order to become apparent; but at a deeper level these lacks emerge from some primordial conception. What is it? It would be tempting to situate it somewhere between "being that is lacking" [*l'être qui manque*] and "lack of being" [*manque à être*], but that would be too dramatic. A literary comparison with certain significant characteristics of Beckett's stories would perhaps be more cogent—notably the noises, the silences, the actors' bodies that are at once present and absent, their improbable names, the loss of memory, the determination to recall something, the solitude, the strange relationships, etc.—but Coleman's oeuvre is much less catastrophist. All the same, an analogy, or rather a metaphorical comparison, with a passage from *Endgame* (1957) could perhaps provide a temporary explanation of this Colemanian lack, which is never located in some distant past or in an immediate present, but in what is going to take place without one's knowing when, where, or how. As Clov and Hamm put it, "It's going to end," but though it is in the process of ending, it never ends. And what is it, moreover, that should end? Of this continual dissatisfaction and this lack that is so hard to delineate in Coleman's works, over which the figure of Melancholy seems to preside, one could say the following: what is lacking is that one does not know what it is that is lacking.

[1] For other interpretations and fuller information on the works, see *James Coleman*, exh. cat., Musée national d'art moderne, Paris 1996; *James Coleman: Projected Images, 1972–1994*, exh. cat., Dia Center for the Arts, New York 1995; *James Coleman*, exh. cat., Art Gallery of York University, Toronto 1990; *James Coleman*, exh. cat., Musée d'art contemporain, Lyon 1990; *James Coleman*, exh. cat., Stedelijk Van Abbemuseum, Eindhoven 1989); *James Coleman*, exh. cat., Musée d'Art moderne de la Ville de Paris, Paris 1989; *James Coleman: Selected Works*, exh. cat., The Renaissance Society at the University of Chicago, Chicago 1985.

[2] Marshall McLuhan, *Understanding Media: The Extensions of Man*, McGraw Hill, London and New York 1964.

[3] Sigmund Freud, *The Interpretation of Dreams* (1900), trans. James Strachey, Basic Books, New York 1953.

[4] See the anthology of texts in *Poesure & Peintrie*, Musées de Marseille/Réunion des Musées Nationaux, 1993.

[5] Jean Fisher, "Sur les oeuvres recentes de James Coleman," *James Coleman*, exh. cat., Musée national d'art moderne, Paris 1996.

[6] On this subject see Jacques Derrida, *Of Grammatology* (1967), trans. Gayatri Chakravorty Spivak, Johns Hopkins University Press, Baltimore, Maryland 1998.

[7] Wolfgang Köhler, *Gestalt Psychology: An Introduction to New Concepts in Modern Psychology* (1929), Liverlight Publishing Corporation, New York 1992; in particular the chapter "Association," p. 248–278.

Another Day in Paradise: The Film and Video Work of Rodney Graham
Jack Liang

Parachute, no. 95, Summer 1999

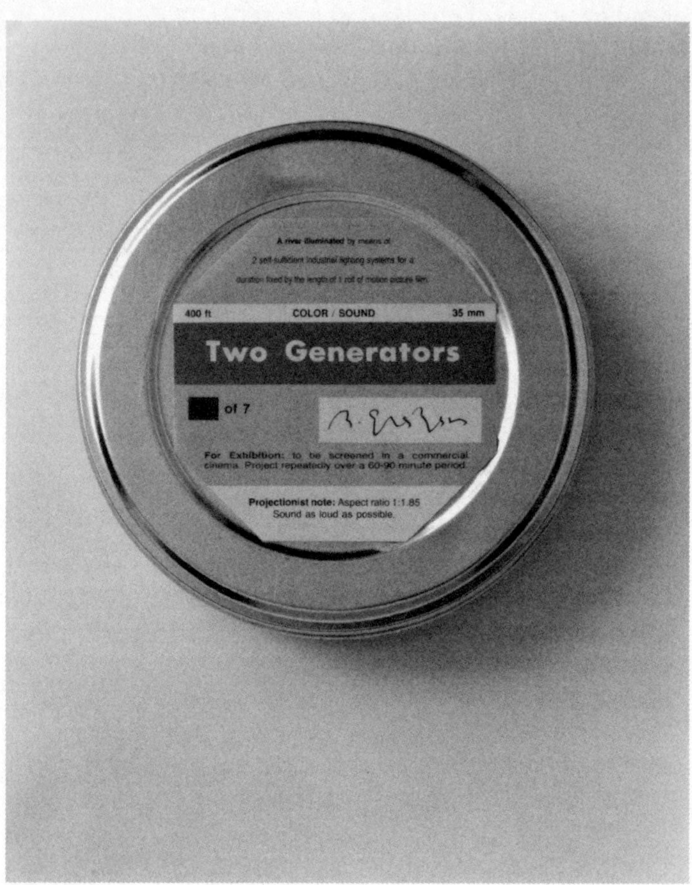

Rodney Graham, *Two Generators*, 1984
Film canister

In the summer of 1997, in a ramshackle hut on the eastern edge of Venice, Italy, Rodney Graham unveiled *Vexation Island*.[1] It was a fitting debut to be certain, highly appropriate for Venice. Outside of Las Vegas, is there a place in the world more quixotic, more fascinating and foreign than this city submerged in water, this highbrow Disneyland? Walk a mile in Venice—through its labyrinthine streets and alleyways—and every wrong corner that you take intimates *Vexation Island*. Every claustrophobic path seems familiar and strange. Because in this city, this insular city, whose stunning scenery is matched by an equally stunning sense of confusion, walking a mile means, more often than not, ending up exactly where you began.

Such is how it goes for the bleary-eyed traveler in this waterlogged town, where progress is measured in inches, if it is measured at all.

Slowly subsiding into the surrounding lagoon, slowly shrinking and decaying—its natives increasingly heading for the mainland—Venice is, more and more, a town of visitors. Mostly confused visitors. In this wondrous and perplexing environment it is almost conceivable that a man could awake from a long slumber to find himself stranded in some strange location. In Venice's tangled network of streets and sights and water all around, *Vexation Island* seems, somehow, almost rational.

Almost but not quite. Because Rodney Graham is, after all, a master at the logic of the absurd. And in the dynamics of Graham's world, simple concepts lead to complex systems that in turn generate implausible consequences all the while maintaining a semblance of logical progression. That is, in some odd way, it all makes sense. Graham's art dwells in that narrow space between absolute perfection and complete chaos—much as Venice does. A clever twist in a Grahamian narrative produces an endlessly repeating story, in the same way a wrong turn in Venice sends you trekking in circles. Rodney Graham's world is a world filled with Sisyphean acts and impossible scenarios, an absurd universe built upon the certainty that things— no matter how perfect—will always remain incomplete.

It has been said that artists only ever make one work of art in their lives; the rest of the time they make improvements. Everything produced becomes an extension of everything preceding, like a better mousetrap as it were. Which I think is an apt analogy for Graham's body of endeavors, where each successive work seems to find new and better ways to suspend its protagonist (or the viewer) in some kind of narrative loop. Themes recur here with a regularity that invokes the spirit of Sigmund Freud, who admittedly has played a prominent role in Graham's art. Ideas like the "unconscious," that musty buzzword developed by Freud a century ago—and unconsciousness in general—surface repeatedly. One finds in Graham's art a compulsion toward repetition that is much in the spirit of Freud's theories on the subject.[2] Both within specific works and across bodies of projects, the recurrence of themes is a near-constant component of Graham's endeavor. It is particularly manifest in the looped narratives and circular structures of works like *Vexation Island* and its cousins,

Two Generators (1984), *Coruscating Cinnamon Granules* (1996), and *Halcion Sleep* (1994). Together these works represent Graham's film and video output, and in their connectedness what you invariably stumble across is an accidental (read: unconscious) thematic triumvirate involving the institution of cinema, the realms of consciousness and sleep, and the willful use of repetition. With a good measure of absurdity to boot.

Consider first the tale of *Vexation Island*, which begins with a premise that is only too familiar: man wakes to find himself marooned on desert isle. Here is a shopworn idea that is replete with its own set of expectations, something more or less along these lines: (1) shipwrecked man comes to consciousness on beach, usually somewhere near the equator; (2) shipwrecked man makes attempts to leave island—likely involving but not limited to the building of a large signal fire; (3) shipwrecked man fails to escape, so turns attention to survival—again, likely to involve the building of a large fire. If these are the loose priorities of your typical island adventure, then *Vexation Island* falls short of expectation. Our castaway here neither seeks escape nor tries to cope, and in reality wakes with only the slimmest, fragile grasp of his hapless circumstance. Through his own foolish actions, our man short-circuits the possibility of further plot development, and repeatedly sends himself reeling back to the beginning of the story.

And that story begins (if there really is a beginning) with a bird's-eye view of a tiny tropical island. A roar of crashing waves resounds. A palm tree rises out of the ground, swaying so the high sun shimmers through its leaves. In the sand lies an unconscious figure, an 18th-century Englishman with a purple bruise on his forehead. Nearby sits a parrot, squawking for the man to wake up, and we too anticipate his coming round. A time span close to eternity passes while the Englishman lingers unconscious, and the world around him continues—waves keep crashing, the parrot keeps screeching, the palm keeps swaying. And we continue to wait. More time elapses, until at last, there is a barely perceptible flicker of the Englishman's eyelids.

The self-contained world continues its course and slowly the Englishman stirs. As the hazy cloud of sleep dissipates from his head, he comes to realize his misfortune (perhaps with a sense that he's been here before). He eyes the bird perched before him. He touches the bruise on his head. He notices the tree swaying nearby, and the coconuts resting high in its branches. In a fit of hunger or aggression (or even instinct maybe), the Englishman now approaches the palm and begins to shake it violently, with the predictable result: a coconut falls and strikes the man on the forehead, sending him cascading dramatically to the ground. As the coconut rolls to the shoreline, and the waves wash it down the beach, the narrative cycle repeats, returning us once again to a shot of the tropical island, the unconscious figure in the sand, the bird hovering nearby, the tree swaying in the breeze…

Vexation Island is, in Graham's words, "a costume picture, that is to say a travesty,"[3] the highly cinematic depiction of an absurd world, where long bouts of unconsciousness meet with brief awakenings, repeatedly, forever. It is a constant cycle of waking and sleep, gorgeously presented in Technicolor and CinemaScope. And therein, really, lies a fitting précis of Graham's entire body of film and video work, which in one form or another seems always to return to ideas of active and passive time, to the repetitive loop, and, above all, to cinema. So it is no coincidence, for example, that *Vexation Island* has the production values of a Hollywood movie. Graham has flirted with film memories for most of his life, recollections traced to a childhood spent in a British Columbia logging camp where his father, camp manager and sometime projectionist, would show films on Sundays in the cookhouse. This indelible relationship to the movies is evident in *Vexation Island*, where Graham mimics to perfection the style and feel of an epic film, going so far as to shoot the work in widescreen format, and including all the color and sounds and scenery that you would expect from such a production. And though the work takes the final form of a laserdisc video projection (which more easily facilitates the looping effect of the narrative), there is no question where the work's allegiance lies. And where the origins of video art were largely predicated upon an opposition to the hegemonic structures of cinema, here comes Graham, professional film crew in tow, shouting "More makeup!"

And yet *Vexation Island* is not a Hollywood movie, but a shrewd impostor that knows the rules and chooses not to play by them. Graham is aware of our cinematic expectations—those of narrative and pacing, of character and plot development—and uses them to his advantage. With dramatic camera angles and dolly shots, a rich soundtrack, and suitably costumed hero, Vexation Island looks, on the surface, much like cinema. But as the work unfolds and time supplants our cinematic prospects with doubt, you soon begin to realize that Vexation Island does not behave like cinema. It does not, to adopt movie lingo, cut to the chase, but rather opts for a slower, more deliberate pace. Which seems odd to say about a work that is little more than eight minutes long, but we are talking about that model of expectation which sees seven-minute pop songs labeled "not radio-friendly," and slow-moving films described as sleepy (and really slow-moving films described as art). Furthermore, *Vexation Island*'s cyclical story line means that the work never truly ends. A wayward coconut meets a witless head and the entire story repeats seamlessly from the beginning. In this way *Vexation Island*'s self-contained system functions much like a frame that encloses the work, likening Graham's island tale more to a painting than to a film proper. Unlike the linearity of a normal movie-viewing experience, here you engage the work at any point in time, staying for as long—or as briefly—as you feel necessary. And then you leave. All the while the work remains there on the wall, ready to be engaged again at all moments and at any point you wish to re-enter the story.

 Vexation Island's circular nature calls to mind that archetypal image of the serpent devouring its own tail, the Ouroboros, a near-universal symbol that has throughout history connoted various concepts of totality, renewal, or the inevitable return to the beginning. One often finds this circular snake portrayed with two distinct halves: one black, representing the Earth, the Night, or the dark, negative yin; the other white, signaling the Heavens, the Day, or the light and positive yang. Such are the antithetic forces at play in *Vexation Island*, where the story, according to Graham, oscillates between vegetable and animal poles, a concept he credits to Gilles Deleuze.[4] These oppositional poles—the former representing passive, vegetative action and the latter, active, aggressive movement—alternate throughout the course of the story, each realm, in time, overtaking the other in an endless cycle. Deleuze, writing about cinema, speaks of both poles possessing an equal potential for violence. That is, a film's passive moments or an actor's silence can be just as intense as any action sequence.[5] Thus, in the case of *Vexation Island*, the Englishman's long bouts of unconsciousness can seem as forceful as his brief, waking moments of aggression. During that vegetative time in which the Englishman lies passed out, the viewer, like the parrot, must wait—impatiently perhaps—for a sign of life from the unconscious man. And in that wait, in the seven-or-so minutes of recurring sleep, *Vexation Island* forces us to adjust to the slow, deliberate pace of the film, to linger in an oppressively long period of non-action.

This, I believe, is good strategy. For were the film reduced to a 60-second spot, as one reviewer casually suggested,[6] the effect of its crescendo would not nearly have been so potent. *Vexation Island* succeeds because it exploits our cinematic expectations. It offers us the look and feel of a full-blown Hollywood picture, the effective by-product of which is an expectation that the story should move along at a good clip. But instead of a quick pace, we are forced to downshift our expectations, to linger a while before proceeding. It is something Umberto Eco speaks of when he cites the example in literature of overly descriptive passages and an abundance of minute detail at times serving "less as a representational device than as a strategy for slowing down the reading time, until the reader drops into the rhythm that the author believes necessary to the enjoyment of the text."[7] Such is the mechanism at work in *Vexation Island*, where the slow build-up to the climax can be seen as a structuring device that gives a palpable presence to the Englishman's unconsciousness and, at the same time, makes the final active gesture that much more intense.

Lest we think such strategies are only confined to the realm of "high art," consider Eco's example of how the technique of lingering can appear in a work of popular film.[8] In John Sturges' 1955 movie *Bad Day at Black Rock*, Spencer Tracy plays a one-armed World War II veteran who arrives in an isolated desert town to search for the father of a dead Japanese-American soldier. From the moment he arrives in town, Tracy's character is looked upon with suspicion, and he becomes the object of daily persecution by racist

individuals. For the entire first hour of the film, Tracy
is forced to endure intolerable agony at the hands of the
town's inhabitants. We the audience thus are made to
identify with his anguish, and we sit on the edge of our seats
hoping for some kind of retribution. At last we arrive at the
moment in the film when Tracy is accosted in a luncheonette
by the town bully. Suddenly, unexpectedly, Tracy strikes
with his one good arm, launching the hateful man across the
room and out the door onto the street. It is a violent,
cathartic act that has been prepared for by the slow hour
of torment that Tracy and the viewers undergo.

Eco saw this film in Italy where, according to him,
custom permits one to enter a cinema at any point during a
film, and then stay to see the film again from the beginning.
This he believes is a favorable custom, for Eco holds that
film, like life, is a continual retracing of events that have
already occurred. That is, you come into this life at a point
where your parents are already born and Homer's *Odyssey*
written, and then you work your way backward until you
more or less understand everything that has happened in the
world before you arrived. It seems quite right then, according to Eco, that one should do the same with film:

The night I saw *Bad Day at Black Rock*, I noticed that
after Spencer Tracy's violent gesture (which doesn't occur
at the end of the film) half of the audience got up and left.
They were spectators who had come in at the start of that
delectatio morosa and had stayed on to enjoy the preparatory
phases of that moment of liberation all over again. From this
you can see that the trepidation time functions not only to
keep the attention of the naive first-level spectator, but also
to stimulate the aesthetic enjoyment of the second-level
spectator.[9]

In the case of Graham's *Vexation Island*, a second pass
of the narrative cycle brings advance knowledge of the
Englishman's fate. And so equipped, the privileged viewer
sits back and lets the perpetual story unfold, viewing the
unresolvedness as an end in itself, or like Eco's audience in
the Italian cinema, waiting again for the cathartic moment.
Either way, the viewer is rewarded for his or her investment.

That sort of reward never comes for the viewer of
Two Generators, a film that Graham made in 1984 and the first
of his works to use the structure of the loop. Where the

trepidation time in *Vexation Island* eventually leads to a cathartic moment, here trepidation time is all there is. Tough slogging for anyone with expectations otherwise. In this four-minute film where the camera sits trained on the rushing waters of a river at night, nothing really seems to happen. Which doesn't mean that nothing is happening, only that events perceived on the screen remain consistent. And that is only half the story, because *Two Generators* encompasses more than just the film. *Two Generators* entails a whole cyclical production wherein a projectionist would show a 35mm film in a real cinema house for as many times as possible within a duration determined by how much he or she was being paid. The work is a looped composition which involves the projectionist slowly dimming the house lights, running the film until it reaches the end of the reel, allowing a few seconds of light to flood the screen, turning up the house lights, rewinding the film, turning down the house lights, and projecting the film again. This cycle repeats for the duration of the event, normally 60 to 90 minutes.

And what's being projected on the screened turns out to be nothing more than a fixed location shot of the waters of Gold Creek, near Graham's hometown of Vancouver. Nothing here approaches the visual appeal of *Vexation Island*. But then, the essence of *Two Generators* lies not within the film itself, but rather in its presentation. That is, in the cyclical actions involved in dimming the house lights, turning on the projector, screening the film, rewinding the film, and so on. In this way the passive moments of the work—when the house lights are up and the film is rewinding—are as important as the actual time that the projection is on screen. *Two Generators*, then, is not a film per se. It is a film and the projector and the projectionist and the lights and the screen and the movie house. Viewers often miss this point when they sit down to watch what is, essentially, running water and the sound of loud motors. They are relying on the language of cinema, when Graham is giving them the cinema itself.

But this is not to dismiss what is actually on the screen, because those images are, after all, a fundamental component of the work. The trouble arises, however, when we expect the said images to do something, instead of permitting them to simply pass as part of the course of things. In the real world, rivers just run. But on the screen they need to run for a reason. Which is understandable since context is everything. When we are in Algonquin Park watching the river rush by, it is for the experience of watching that river. When we are in a cinema confronted by this scene, watching the river is not enough. The difference may be a function of the virtual experience in relation to the real, but it is also about being in a cinema and the expectations that come with that. So the four minutes of nature we experience in Graham's short film corresponds to four minutes of nature in the real world, but the real world and film are not the same thing. And the task before the viewer of *Two Generators* is to redefine the experience of seeing so that the two are, at least, similar. That is, you watch the four minutes of film as if it were four minutes in the real world. And sitting by the water for that amount of time hardly seems insufferable.

That being said, watching this film will always remain a trying endeavor, a fact attributable to the film's earsplitting soundtrack, which no amount of perceptual leaping can seem to overcome. The clamorous noise that accompanies the film (courtesy of diesel-powered generator lights used during filming to illuminate the water) would no doubt make sitting beside any river—anywhere—a less than pleasant experience. Moreover, our perception of this river scene is further disrupted by an incongruity that exists between the film's image and its soundtrack. That is, as Alexander Alberro notes, at no point in this film do we ever see and hear the water simultaneously.[10] During the film's opening sequence, the screen remains black while the viewer listens to the calm babble of the river's waters washing over rocks. Soothing stuff. But this tranquil auditory introduction is short-lived, as the sound of the water is quickly obliterated by the firing up of one diesel-powered generator, followed by a second. With the generators now on (to provide the film crew with a source of light), the scene then fades in (or becomes illuminated) to reveal a close-up shot of Gold Creek. For the next few minutes we watch this fixed scene, while the theater becomes engulfed by the sound of the two generators bellowing out of phase. Three minutes later the image again fades to black before one generator is turned off, and then the second, to again reveal the sound of the water. In *Two Generators*, image and sound can never coincide, owing to the simple fact that the film was shot in the darkness of night. Under such conditions, an exposure on film would not register without the aid of the diesel-powered lights. And the use of the diesel-powered lights, in turn, preclude the recording of any natural sounds. As a result, we can only see the river or hear the river, but not both at the same time.

For Rodney Graham, *Two Generators* was intended as "a burlesque travesty and a spectacle that would inspire negative thoughts about cinema, which [Graham] neurotically hated at that time."[11] It seems he has changed his tune since then (see *Vexation Island*). But intentional irritations aside, what we see on the screen is but one phase in a cyclical production that continuously alternates between periods of excitation and repose. It is not long after the image on screen fades to black and the blaring generators are turned off that you realize you have shifted phases—when relief from the harsh noise comes in a welcomed transition to silence. All of which is to say that were the film not so bleeding loud, watching this river scene might not have been at all unpleasant. But the purview of *Two Generators* never included the pleasingly-rendered experience of Nature. Rather, distanciation was Graham's intent, to isolate the viewer from both the realm of Nature and the vernacular of cinema.

In 1996, Graham turned again to the use of the cinema house for another film work, *Coruscating Cinnamon Granules*, in which the cinema itself took the form of a deliberately makeshift structure bearing the dimensions of Graham's own kitchen. Viewers would enter this temporary movie house to watch a film loop documenting the turning on and off of a spiral range element that had been dusted with cinnamon—a practice used by real estate agents to induce homey sensations in prospective buyers: you fill the air with the comforting smell of baking and you'll trigger unconscious memories. Coincidentally, a similar surfacing of recollections is behind Graham's desire to present his film in a kitchen-size, temporary cinema, an idea that unconsciously harks back to Graham's fuzzy logging-camp memories of his father's Sunday cookhouse screenings.

Viewed in the darkened cinema, the spectacle of burning cinnamon becomes akin to witnessing the birth and death of stars in a spiral galaxy. Graham filmed the work in his own kitchen, which becomes the galaxy's encapsulating universe, as the kitchen-size cinema contains its virtual counterpart. This four-minute film begins with darkness while the burner gathers energy and the cinnamon stars lie dormant as mere potential. Slowly, progressively, the heat increases and the cinnamon begins to burn, lighting up here and there like tiny celestial bodies, continuing to burn while the mini-galaxy charges to life, increasing until the nebula becomes one continuous spiraling coil of energy and light. At which point the element is turned off and gradually, inevitably, the galaxy again returns to darkness, leaving only the ember traces of dying cinnamon stars. Presented as a loop, *Coruscating Cinnamon Granules* is like the birth and death of countless mini-galaxies in an infinitely expanding universe.

Like *Two Generators* and *Vexation Island*, this film work slides through the phases of active and passive time, or consciousness and sleep as it were. In successive four-minute cycles, the work transforms gradually from a period of total blackness to a spectacular, glittering light show that Graham has described as consonant with the stars one sees after a mild blow to the head.[12] Like the stars, one presumes, our castaway observes when the falling coconut strikes his skull. In fact, with a small mental leap we might imagine *Coruscating Cinnamon Granules* as the film that runs inside the Englishman's head: projecting blackness at first as the Englishman lies unconscious; followed by a spark of light that signals the groggy man's awakening; leading to the coconut strike that sends nerves firing (like a thousand stars); and back to blackness as he collapses to the ground. Bringing us again to the beginning of the cycle. And so we revel in this cycle, in its unwavering repetition that lets us choose how long we stay committed to the story. The work itself never ends, but just moves from phase to phase— self-contained and always cyclical.

This is the beauty of the film loop, which, for all its temperamental mechanics, seems the ideal device for Rodney Graham's work. The structure of *Coruscating Cinnamon Granules* is that of a makeshift cinematic experience. And anyone who has worked with film loops knows that this is as makeshift as it gets. It isn't unusual to encounter technical problems with film-looping systems or to be replacing film stock every few weeks because of a rapidly degraded image. Yet there is a quality inherent to a looped film—the flickering light, the clack of the projector—that one cannot reproduce with a digital or electronic image. So you put up with the precariousness of the medium for the sake of the experience. And if the machine happens to break down, well, that's all part and parcel of understanding Graham's art. Things are never quite right in the Grahamian scheme of things, where the Modernist idea of progress is continually foiled by its compulsion to repeat.

The transient viewer who happens upon one of Graham's narrative loops, of course, always has the option to exit the story, unlike the heroes of these stories, who can never leave. But then they scarcely ever realize they are trapped. In Graham's text work *Lenz* (1983), for example, an obscure Romantic poet survives a harrowing journey through the mountains, enduring fits of madness and attempts at suicide, only to set out the next morning on the same trip as if for the first time. And in *Parsifal* (1882-38,969, 364,735) (1989), a Round Table knight attempts an interminable climb up a rocky slope, an ascent that theoretically outlasts the end of the world. These are the sorts of ill-starred voyagers who end up tossed into the waves of Fate. Graham, of course, plays Fate, a role he seems to relish—blithely arranging lives that spin in circles.

Herr Doktor Freud would suggest that Graham's recurring themes and looping narratives indicate a yearning to return to an earlier stage of development, that is, to childhood. And to some extent this may be true. Childhood memories do seem often to inspire Graham's work. In his 1994 video *Halcion Sleep* he attempted to evoke such a memory, a common memory that most of us share: that of sleeping in the back seat of your parents' car on the way home from a long family road trip, of waking ever so momentarily before falling back into a deep and peaceful slumber. *Halcion Sleep* is a 26-minute single-take video in which a pajama-clad Graham is recorded in real time, sleeping in the back seat of a minivan that carries him from the outskirts of Vancouver, through the streets and avenues of the city, to his home in the urban centre where he is then carried, still sleeping, to his own waiting bed. The work documents a planned performance in which Graham, prior to the recording, ingested a strong dose of the sedative Halcion, "chosen for the pleasant thoughts of the past evoked by its name—that of the bird of legend (halcyon) who builds her nest in the sea."[13] The video shows the limp body of an unconscious Graham sleeping in the back seat of the minivan, rainy views of the city hovering in the rear window above him, like a dream. Implicit in the work is a sense of longing, a desire for some impossible return to the blissful security of childhood, which now it seems can only appear as faint memories in a dream bubble—showing the past as points of light in constant retreat.

In this work where nothing much happens to the protagonist, where the most poignant action occurs outside the parameters of the video—that is, Graham's ingestion of Halcion which takes place prior to the recording—*Halcion Sleep* speaks less about what is going on than what you think might be going on. It is a reversal of imperatives, with events on the periphery—those activities outside the recorded time frame or beyond the vehicle's window frame—taking priority. The beginning and the end of the performance are not recorded, and so we do not see Graham being taken from the motel or ever reaching his destination. Instead, the video is presented as a loop and as a consequence the sleeping figure remains always on the move, in a perpetual dream state in the back seat of this van. But we, being creatures in need of stimuli, keep half-expecting that something else will happen. And when it doesn't, when all we get in return is more of Graham's dream, well, that dream by default becomes the happening. And so we take this flat-line narrative and we make our own stories. *Halcion Sleep*, after all, lends itself to a good story; it is an inversion of the film noir cliché of the victim that is drugged and taken somewhere out of town (here the drugged victim is driven into the heart of the city).[14] Fittingly, the work is presented in black and white, like in the movies. The lone pair of headlights trailing us down the road becomes a menacing tail, and the flashing lights of the parked fire truck signal foul play. The man crossing the rain-swept street has his own shady story.

Halcion Sleep lets us discover our own grand themes, but, more importantly, leaves us room to find pleasure in the minute details, in the restoration of experience to smaller units of measure. In this oddly comic work, with its "actor" who literally sleeps through his performance, you only get what you're willing to take. And to get anything of significance, you must by necessity slow down your perceptions, so that a momentary stimulant can give cause to stir. Like the golden arches we occasionally see flying past the rear window, intermittent events invite us to pay attention to the tiny increments of life. Watching *Halcion Sleep* is like watching small, isolated moments pass, like single frames of a running film.

Thus we turn again to the lingua franca of cinema, which is unavoidable in these works by Graham. In *Vexation Island* and *Two Generators*, in *Coruscating Cinnamon Granules* and *Halcion Sleep*, screen memories appear from everywhere. Maybe Umberto Eco is onto something when he says that film is much like life, and that we are all working our way backward until we more or less get it.

Some people, like Graham, work backward more than others. Always searching for the lost past, for the comfort that comes from the back seat of your parents' car, from the serenity of a warm sleep that lasts till dawn. And in the end maybe that's what Graham's art is all about: floating dreams of divided consciousness. Simply put, there is waking and there is sleep, and the two keep swapping places. An endless round of waking and sleep, waking and sleep, waking and sleep. Absurd? Maybe. And maybe Graham's work is a little like that. But as a friend once told me when we were trapped in a freak snowstorm on Highway 401 somewhere between Toronto and Windsor: "Absurdity is the beautiful resting ground at the end of a fruitless journey."

[1] Rodney Graham's *Vexation Island* premiered in the Canadian Pavilion at the 1997 Venice Biennale. While on a reconnaissance trip to Venice prior to the exhibition, Graham noted how most of the buildings in the Biennale Gardens had been boarded up for the winter, and in particular how the hoarding around the humble Canadian Pavilion had transformed that building into a "rustic hut." He immediately recognized that this provided a perfect context for his island film, and thus retained the wooden boards for the duration of the exhibition.

[2] According to Freud, "the compulsion to repeat" is an innate tendency to restore an earlier state of things that has since been abandoned because of external forces. It involves a constant cycle of excitation and the subsequent return to calm. The cycles of waking and sleeping —a theme of particular interest to Graham—is a common example of "repetition-compulsion" in everyday life. See Sigmund Freud, *Beyond the Pleasure Principle*, trans. James Strachey, Liveright Publishing Corporation, New York 1961.

[3] Rodney Graham, "Siting *Vexation Island*," *Island Thought*, Art Gallery of York University, Toronto 1997, p. 15.

[4] Ibid., p. 16.

[5] Gilles Deleuze, *Cinema 1: The Movement Image*, trans. Hugh Tomlinson and Barbara Habberjam, Athlone Press, London 1986, p. 155–159.

[6] Marcia E. Vetrocq, "The 1997 Venice Biennale: A Space Odyssey," *Art in America*, September 1997, p. 76.

[7] Umberto Eco, *Six Walks in the Fictional Woods*, Harvard University Press, Cambridge 1994, p. 59.

[8] Ibid., p. 64–65.

[9] Ibid.

[10] Alexander Alberro, public lecture delivered at York University, October 8, 1998.

[11] Graham, "Siting Vexation Island," p. 11.

[12] Ibid., p. 12.

[13] Ibid., p. 13.

[14] Rodney Graham, *Rodney Graham: Selected Artist's Notes*, Morris and Helen Belkin Art Gallery, Vancouver 1996, p. 7.

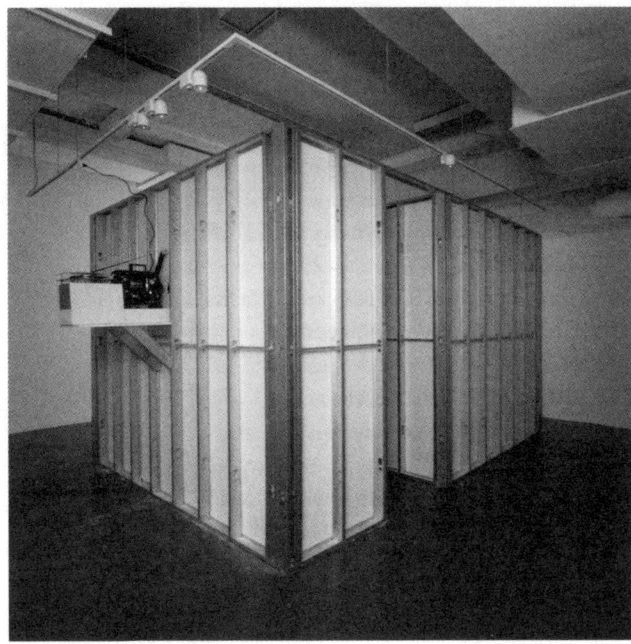

Rodney Graham, *Coruscating Cinnamon Granules*, 1996
Installation view

Imprint

Edited by Chantal Pontbriand

EDITORIAL COORDINATION
Clément Dirié

COPY EDITING
Clare Manchester

DESIGN CONCEPT
Gavillet & Rust, Geneva

DESIGN
Nicolas Leuba

TYPEFACE
Genath (www.optimo.ch)

PRINT AND BINDING
Présence Graphique, Monts (Indre-et-Loire)

PHOTO CREDITS
p. 32, 61: Courtesy of Vito Acconci; p. 96: Courtesy of Karen Knorr; p. 111: Courtesy of Mark Lewis; p. 112, 129: Courtesy of Bill Viola, photos: Kira Perov; p. 130: Courtesy of Tadashi Kawamata/Collection Centre Canadien d'Architecture–Canadian Centre for Architecture, Montreal; p. 144, 157: Courtesy of Stan Douglas & David Zwirner Gallery, New York; p. 158: Courtesy of Women Make Movies; p. 170, 182–183: Courtesy of David Tomas; p. 188, 207: Courtesy of Nan Goldin & Matthew Marks Gallery, New York; p. 222: Courtesy of James Coleman & Marian Goodman Gallery, New York/Paris; p. 242, 257: Courtesy of Rodney Graham & Art Gallery of York University, Toronto

ACKNOWLEDGMENTS

Parachute: The Anthology is a project initiated in 2000, on the occasion of the 25th anniversary of the publication.
A selection of texts was elaborated with the contribution of the editorial team at the time: Chantal Pontbriand (editor), Colette Tougas (managing editor), Jim Drobnick, and Thérèse Saint-Gelais (both assistant editors).
Sarah-Jane Lewis coordinated the project for *Parachute* in the years 2003 and 2004. A book in French entitled *Parachute, Essais choisis 1975-2000* was published in 2004 by La Lettre volée, Brussels. The current table of contents was established following the initial selection, with the input of the editors at JRP|Ringier.

Parachute wishes to thank the authors for giving their permission for the reproduction of their texts, as well as the artists and other lenders who have supplied images. We are also most grateful to our readership, to the governmental agencies in Canada and Quebec for their continuous support, and to the galleries and museums that also supported the publication through publicity throughout the years. This particular project has been realized through the support of the Canada Council for the Arts and the Conseil des Arts et Lettres du Québec.

Canada Council Conseil des arts
for the Arts du Canada

Conseil des arts
et des lettres
Québec

Every effort has been made to contact copyright holders and to obtain their permission for the use of copyright material. The publisher apologizes for any inaccurate acknowledgments or omissions and would be grateful if notified of any corrections that should be incorporated in future reprints or editions of this book.

© 2014, the authors, the photographers, the editors, and JRP | Ringier Kunstverlag AG

All rights reserved. No part of this publication may be reproduced, stored in a retrieval system, or transmitted, in any form, or by any means, electronic, mechanical, or otherwise, without prior permission in writing from the publisher.

PUBLISHED BY
JRP | Ringier
Limmatstrasse 270
CH−8005 Zurich
T +41 43 311 27 50
E info@jrp-ringier.com
www.jrp-ringier.com

IN CO-EDITION WITH
Les presses du réel
35, rue Colson
F−21000 Dijon
T +33 3 80 30 75 23
E info@lespressesdureel.com
www.lespressesdureel.com

ISBN 978-3-03764-382-2 (JRP | Ringier)
ISBN 978-2-84066-758-2 (Les presses du réel)

Distribution

JRP | Ringier publications are available internationally
at selected bookstores and from the following distribution
partners:

GERMANY AND AUSTRIA
Vice Versa Distribution
www.vice-versa-distribution.de

FRANCE
Les presses du réel
www.lespressesdureel.com

SWITZERLAND
AVA Verlagsauslieferung AG
www.ava.ch

UK AND OTHER EUROPEAN COUNTRIES
Cornerhouse Publications
www.cornerhouse.org/books

USA, CANADA, ASIA, AND AUSTRALIA
ARTBOOK | D.A.P.
www.artbook.com

For a list of our partner bookshops or for any general
questions, please contact JRP | Ringier directly at
info@jrp-ringier.com, or visit our homepage
www.jrp-ringier.com for further information about
our program.

Documents Series 17:
Parachute: The Anthology [Vol. III]

This book is the seventeenth volume
in the "Documents" series,
dedicated to critics' writings.

The series is directed by
Lionel Bovier and Xavier Douroux.

Parachute: The Anthology

Already available:

Museums, Art History, and Theory
[Vol. I]

Performance & Performativity
[Vol. II]

Forthcoming:

*Painting, Sculpture, Installation,
and Architecture*
[Vol. IV]

Also available

DOCUMENTS SERIES (IN ENGLISH)

Saul Anton, *Warhol's Dream*
ISBN 978-3-905770-35-3 (JRP | Ringier)
ISBN 978-2-84066-200-6 (Les presses du réel)

John Baldessari, *More Than You Wanted to Know
About John Baldessari*
ISBN 978-3-03764-192-7 (JRP | Ringier) [Vol. 1]
ISBN 978-3-03764-256-6 (JRP | Ringier) [Vol. 2]

Raymond Bellour, *Between-the-Images*
ISBN 978-3-03764-144-6 (JRP | Ringier)
ISBN 978-2-84066-513-7 (Les presses du réel)

Joshua Decter, *Art Is a Problem*
ISBN 978-3-03764-195-8 (JRP | Ringier)
ISBN 978-2-84066-621-9 (Les presses du réel)

Gabriele Detterer & Maurizio Nannucci, *Artist-Run Spaces*
ISBN 978-3-03764-191-0 (JRP | Ringier)
ISBN 978-2-84066-512-0 (Les presses du réel)

Christian Höller, *Time Action Vision*
ISBN 978-3-03764-124-8 (JRP | Ringier)
ISBN 978-2-84066-396-6 (Les presses du réel)

Hans Ulrich Obrist, *A Brief History of Curating*
ISBN 978-3-905829-55-6 (JRP | Ringier)
ISBN 978-2-84066-287-7 (Les presses du réel)

Hans Ulrich Obrist, *A Brief History of New Music*
ISBN 978-3-03764-190-3 (JRP | Ringier)
ISBN 978-2-84066-619-6 (Les presses du réel)

Igor Zabel, *Contemporary Art Theory*
ISBN 978-3-03764-238-2 (JRP | Ringier)
ISBN 978-2-84066-573-1 (Les presses du réel)